Economics of
PUBLIC AND
MACRO ISSUES

CUSTOM EDITION

Taken from:

The Economics of Macro Issues, Fourth Edition
by Roger LeRoy Miller and Daniel K. Benjamin

The Economics of Public Issues, Sixteenth Edition
by Roger LeRoy Miller, Daniel K. Benjamin,
and Douglass C. North

Learning Solutions

New York   Boston   San Francisco
London   Toronto   Sydney   Tokyo   Singapore   Madrid
Mexico City   Munich   Paris   Cape Town   Hong Kong   Montreal

Cover Art: Courtesy of PhotoDisc/Getty Images

Taken from:

The Economics of Macro Issues, Fourth Edition
by Roger LeRoy Miller and Daniel K. Benjamin
Copyright © 2010, 2008, 2006, 2004 by Pearson Education
Published by Addison-Wesley
Boston, Massachusetts 02116

The Economics of Public Issues, Sixteenth Edition
by Roger LeRoy Miller, Daniel K. Benjamin, and Douglass C. North
Copyright © 2006 by Pearson Education, Inc.
Published by Addison-Wesley
Boston, Massachusetts 02116

This special edition published in cooperation with
Pearson Learning Solutions.

All trademarks, service marks, registered trademarks, and registered
service marks are the property of their respective owners and are used
herein for identification purposes only.

Pearson Learning Solutions, 501 Boylston Street, Suite 900, Boston, MA 02116
A Pearson Education Company
www.pearsoned.com

Printed in the United States of America

1 2 3 4 5 6 7 8 9 10 XXXX 14 13 12 11 10 09

2009400169

DE

ISBN 10: 0-558-54881-4
ISBN 13: 978-0-558-54881-0

CONTENTS

PART SIX
Fiscal Policy 159

PART SEVEN
Monetary Policy 195

PART ONE
Foundations

Chapters 1–7 taken from *The Economics of Public Issues,* Sixteenth Edition, by Roger LeRoy Miller, Daniel K. Benjamin, and Douglass C. North

C h a p t e r   1

DEATH BY BUREAUCRAT

How would you rather die? From a lethal reaction to a drug prescribed by your doctor? Or because your doctor failed to prescribe a drug that would have saved your life? If this choice sounds like one you would rather not make, consider this: Employees of the Food and Drug Administration (FDA) make that decision on behalf of millions of Americans many times each year. More precisely, FDA bureaucrats decide whether or not new medicines (prescription drugs) should be allowed to go on sale in the United States. If the FDA rules against a drug, physicians in America may not legally prescribe it, even if thousands of lives are being saved by the drug each year in other countries.

The FDA's authority to make such decisions dates back to the passage of the Food and Drug Safety Act of 1906. That law required that medicines be correctly labeled as to their contents and that they not contain any substances harmful to the health of consumers. Due to this legislation, Dr. Hostatter's Stomach Bitters and Kickapoo Indian Sagwa, along with numerous rum-laden concoctions, cocaine-based potions, and supposed anticancer remedies, disappeared from druggists' shelves. The law was expanded in 1938 with the passage of the Food, Drug, and Cosmetic Act, which forced manufacturers to demonstrate the safety of new drugs before being allowed to offer them for sale. (This law was prompted by the deaths of 107 people who had taken Elixir Sulfanilamide, an antibiotic that contained poisonous diethylene glycol, a chemical cousin of antifreeze.)

The next step in U.S. drug regulation came after a rash of severe birth defects among infants whose mothers during pregnancy had taken a sleep aid known as thalidomide. When these birth defects first became apparent, the drug was already widely used in Europe and Canada, and the FDA was nearing approval for its use in America. In fact, about 2.5 million

3

thalidomide tablets were already in the hands of U.S. physicians as samples. The FDA ordered all of the samples destroyed and prohibited the sale of the drug here. This incident led to the 1962 Kefauver-Harris Amendments to the 1938 Food, Drug, and Cosmetic Act, radically altering the drug-approval process in the United States.

Prior to the 1962 amendments, the FDA was expected to approve a new drug application within 180 days unless the application failed to show that the drug was safe. The 1962 amendments added a "proof of efficacy" requirement and also removed the time constraint on the FDA. The FDA has free rein to determine how much and what type of evidence it will demand before approving a drug for sale and thus may take as long as it pleases before either granting or refusing approval.

The 1962 amendments drastically increased the costs of introducing a new drug and markedly slowed the approval process. Prior to 1962, for example, the average time between filing and approval of a new drug application was seven months; by 1967, it was thirty months; and by the late 1970s, it had risen to eight to ten *years*. The protracted approval process involves costly testing by the drug companies—$800 million or more for each new drug—and delays the receipt of any potential revenue from new drugs. Because this reduced the expected profitability of new drugs, fewer of them have been brought onto the market.

Debate continues over how much FDA regulation is needed to ensure that drugs are both safe and efficacious, but there is little doubt that the 1962 amendments have resulted in a U.S. "drug lag." On average, drugs take far longer to reach the market in the United States than they do in Europe. Admittedly, it takes time to ensure that patients benefit from, rather than are harmed by, new drugs, but regulation-induced drug lag can itself be life-threatening. Dr. George Hitchings, a winner of the Nobel Prize in Medicine, has estimated that the five-year lag in introducing Septra (an antibiotic) to the United States killed 80,000 people in this country. Similarly, the introduction of a class of drugs called beta blockers (used to treat heart attack victims and people with high blood pressure) was delayed nearly a decade in America relative to Europe. According to several researchers, the lag in the FDA approval of these drugs cost the lives of at least 250,000 Americans.

In effect, the law requires FDA bureaucrats to make what is truly a terrible trade-off. Lives are saved because unsafe or ineffective drugs are kept off the market, but the regulatory process delays (or even prevents) the introduction of some safe and efficacious drugs, thereby costing lives. Let us now take a more systematic look at this trade-off.

Every time a new drug is introduced, there is a chance that it should not have been—either because it has adverse side effects that outweigh the therapeutic benefits (it is not safe) or because it really does little to help the individuals who take it (it is not effective). When such a drug is introduced, we say that a **Type I error** has been committed. Since 1962, the incidence of Type I error—the thalidomide possibility—has been reduced by the added testing required by the FDA. But other people have been the victims of what is called **Type II error.** Their cost is the pain, suffering, and death that occur because the 1962 amendments have prevented or delayed the introduction of safe, efficacious drugs. Type II error—as with Septra or beta blockers—occurs when a drug *should* be introduced but is held back by FDA regulation.

Over the past twenty or thirty years, outcries over the harm caused by the drug lag have in some cases induced the agency to shorten the testing period when the costs of Type I error are small relative to the damages due to Type II error—as in the case of terminally ill patients. One famous example involved azidothymidine (AZT), which emerged as a possible treatment for AIDS. Gay men, among whom AIDS was most prevalent at the time, took the lead in pressuring the FDA to approve the drug quickly, and the FDA responded accordingly, giving it the OK after only eighteen months of testing. Similarly, Taxol, an important new drug used to treat breast cancer, received expedited review by the FDA, in this case because of pressure applied by women in whose families there was a history of breast cancer. The FDA now has a formal program in which it seeks to expedite testing for drugs that seem to offer great promise for alleviating death or suffering. Nevertheless, although the average approval time for new drugs has shortened considerably, it still takes more than ten times as long for a new drug to be approved as it did before the 1962 amendments.

What can we learn from the FDA regulation of new drugs that will guide us in thinking about other public issues of our time? There are several key principles:

1. *There is no free lunch.* Every choice, and thus every policy, entails a **cost**—something must be given up. In a world of **scarcity,** we cannot have more of everything, so to get more of some things, we must give up other things. Although FDA review of drugs saves lives by preventing the introduction of unsafe or ineffective drugs, the cost is billions of dollars of added expenses, plus delayed availability of safe and efficacious drugs, resulting in the deaths of hundreds of thousands of people.

2. *The cost of an action is the alternative that is sacrificed.* Economists often express costs (and benefits) in terms of dollars because this is a simple means of accounting for and measuring them. But that doesn't

mean that costs have to be monetary, nor does it mean that economics is incapable of analyzing costs and benefits that are quite human. The costs that led to the 1938 and 1962 amendments were the very visible deaths caused by sulfanilamide and the terrible birth defects due to thalidomide. Subsequent revisions to the FDA process for reviewing drugs, as with AZT and Taxol, have been in response to the adverse effects caused by the regulation-induced drug lag.

3. *The relevant costs and benefits are the marginal (incremental) ones.* The relevant question is not whether safety is good or bad; it is instead how much safety we want—which can only be answered by looking at the added (marginal) benefits of more safety compared to the added (marginal) costs. One possible response to the sulfanilamide poisonings or thalidomide was to have outlawed new drugs altogether. That would guarantee that no more people would be harmed by new drugs. But surely this "solution" would not be sensible, because the marginal cost (due to higher Type II errors) would exceed the marginal benefit (caused by reduced Type I errors).

4. *People respond to incentives.* And this is true whether we are talking about consumers, suppliers, or government bureaucrats. Here the incentive to amend the law in 1938 and 1962 was the very visible death and disfigurement of individuals. The eventual FDA decision to speed up the review process was prompted by intense lobbying by individuals who believed (correctly, as it turned out) that they might be benefited by drugs not yet approved.

5. *Things aren't always as they seem.* Many analyses of the effects of government policies take an approach that doesn't fully recognize the actions that people would otherwise have taken. Thus official pronouncements about the effects of policies routinely misrepresent their impact—not because there is necessarily any attempt to deceive but because it is often difficult to know what would have happened otherwise. Pharmaceutical manufacturers, for example, have strong incentives to avoid introducing drugs that are unsafe or ineffective because the companies are subject to loss of reputation and to lawsuits. For similar reasons, physicians have strong incentives to avoid prescribing such drugs for their patients. Even without FDA regulation, there would thus be extensive testing of new drugs before their introduction. Hence it is incorrect to ascribe the generally safe and effective nature of modern drugs entirely to FDA protection. The flip side, however, is that the drug development process is inherently long, complicated, and costly. Even without FDA oversight, some people would die waiting for new drugs because self-interested

manufacturers would insist on some testing and cautious physicians would proceed slowly in prescribing new drugs.

The people who work at the FDA (and members of Congress) are publicly castigated when they "allow" a Type I error to occur—especially when it is a drug that kills people. Thus FDA bureaucrats have a strong incentive to avoid such errors. But when testing delays cause a Type II error, as with Septra, it is almost impossible to point to specific people who died because the drug was delayed. As a result, officials at the FDA are rarely attacked directly for such delays. Because the costs of Type II errors are much more difficult to discern than the costs of Type I errors, many observers believe that there is an inherent bias at the FDA in favor of being "safe rather than sorry"—in other words, excessive testing.

6. *Policies always have unintended consequences, and as a result, their net benefits are almost always less than anticipated.* In the case of government regulations, balancing incremental costs and benefits (see principle 3) fails to make good headlines. Instead, what gets politicians reelected and regulators promoted are *absolute* notions such as safety (and motherhood and apple pie). Thus if a little safety is good, more must be better, so why not simply mandate that drug testing "guarantee" that everyone is free of risk from dangerous drugs? Eventually, the reality of principle 3 sinks in, but in this case not before the drug lag had killed many people.

As is often true with important public issues, our story has one more interesting twist. Thalidomide is back on the market. In 1998, it was approved by the FDA for use in treating Hansen's disease (leprosy), and in 2006, the FDA gave physicians the OK to use it in treating bone marrow cancer. In each instance, there are strong protections to prevent pregnant women from taking the drug. And so perhaps the very drug that brought us the deadly drug lag will turn out to be a lifesaver for a new generation of patients.

DISCUSSION QUESTIONS

1. Does the structure of the drug industry have any bearing on the types of errors that drug firms are likely to make? That is, would a drug industry made up of numerous highly competitive firms be more or less likely to introduce unsafe drugs than an industry consisting of a few large firms?

2. How could the incentives facing the people at the FDA be changed to reduce the incidence of Type II errors? (*Hint:* Is it possible to compare the FDA approval process with the drug-approval process in other nations?)

3. What would be the advantages and disadvantages of a regulatory system in which, rather than having the FDA permit or prohibit new drugs, the FDA merely published its opinions about the safety and efficacy of drugs and then allowed physicians to make their own decisions about whether or not to prescribe the drugs for their patients?

4. Suppose, for simplicity, that Type I and Type II errors resulted in deaths only. Keeping in mind that too little caution produces Type I errors and too much caution produces Type II errors, what would be the best mix of Type I and Type II errors?

Chapter 2

ETHANOL
MADNESS

Henry Ford built his first automobile in 1896 to run on pure ethanol. If Congress has its way, the cars of the future will be built the same way. But what made good economic sense in the late nineteenth century doesn't necessarily make economic sense in the early twenty-first century—although it does make for good politics. Indeed, the ethanol story is a classic illustration of how good politics routinely trumps good economics to yield bad policies.

Ethanol is made in the Midwest just like moonshine whiskey is made in Appalachia: Corn and water are mixed into a mash, enzymes turn starch to sugar, yeast is added, and heat ferments the brew. Once this is distilled, the liquid portion is ethanol and the solids are used as a high-protein animal food. The high-proof ethanol is combustible but yields far less energy per gallon than gasoline does. Despite this inefficiency, federal law requires that ethanol be added to gasoline, in increasing amounts through 2022. This requirement is supposed to conserve resources and improve the environment. It does neither. Instead, it lines the pockets of American corn farmers and ethanol makers and incidentally enriches some Brazilian sugarcane farmers along the way.

Federal law has both encouraged and subsidized ethanol as a so-called alternative fuel for more than thirty years. But it was not until 2005 that ethanol really achieved national prominence. The use mandates of the Energy Policy Act, combined with surging gas prices and an existing 51-cent-per-gallon federal ethanol subsidy, created a boom in ethanol production. Soon ethanol refineries were springing up all over the Midwest, and imports of ethanol from Brazil reached record-high levels.

Three factors are typically used to justify federal use mandates and subsidies for ethanol. First, it is claimed that adding ethanol to gasoline reduces air pollution and so yields environmental benefits. That may have been true fifteen or twenty years ago, but even the Environmental

Protection Agency acknowledges that ethanol offers no environmental advantages over other modern methods of making reformulated gasoline. Hence neither the congressional mandate to add ethanol nor the 51-cent-per-gallon subsidy for its use as a fuel additive can be justified on environmental grounds.

A second argument advanced on behalf of ethanol is that it is "renewable," in that fields on which corn is grown to produce ethanol this year can be replanted with more corn next year. This is true enough, but we are in little danger of running out of "nonrenewable" crude oil any time in the next century. Indeed, proven reserves of oil are at record-high levels. Perhaps more to the point, the production of ethanol uses so much fossil fuel and other resources that under most circumstances, its production actually *wastes* resources overall compared to gasoline. In part, this is because ethanol is about 25 percent less efficient than gasoline as a source of energy. But it is also because the corn used to make ethanol in the United States has a high **opportunity cost:** If it were not being used to make fuel, it would be used to feed humans and livestock. Moreover, because ethanol production is most efficiently conducted on a relatively small scale, it must be transported by truck or rail, which is far more costly than the pipelines used for gasoline.

The third supposed advantage of ethanol is that its use reduces our dependence on imports of oil. In principle, this argument is correct, but its impact is tiny, and the likely consequences are not what you might expect. Total consumption of all **biofuels** in the United States amounts to less than 3 percent of gasoline usage. To replace the oil we import from the Persian Gulf with corn-based ethanol, at least *50 percent* of the nation's total farmland would have to be devoted to corn for fuel. Moreover, any cuts in oil imports will likely *not* come from Persian Gulf sources. Canada and Mexico are two of the three biggest suppliers of crude oil to the United States, and both countries send almost 100 percent of their exports to the U.S. market.

All of this raises an interesting question: If ethanol doesn't protect the environment, conserve resources, or have any compelling foreign policy advantages, why do we mandate its use and subsidize its production? The answer lies at the heart of **political economy,** the use of economics to study the causes and consequences of political decision making. It is true that a critical component of what the government does (such as providing for national defense and law enforcement) provides an institutional structure necessary for the creation and retention of our total wealth. Nevertheless, the essence of much government policymaking has nothing to do with making the size of the economic pie larger than it otherwise would be. Instead, many government policies are directed at dividing up the pie in new ways so that one group gets more resources at the expense of some other group. To do this successfully, politicians must be adept at concentrating the benefits of policies among a few favored recipients while dispersing the costs of those policies across a large number of disfavored individuals.

At first blush, such an approach sounds completely at odds with the essence of democracy. After all, under the principle of "one person, one vote," it seems that benefits should be widely spread (to gain votes from many grateful beneficiaries) and costs should be concentrated (so that only the votes of a few disfavored constituents are lost). The concept of **rational ignorance** explains what is really going on. It is costly for individuals to keep track of exactly how the decisions of their elected representatives affect them. When the consequences of political decisions are large enough to outweigh the **monitoring costs,** voters swiftly and surely express their pleasure or displeasure, both in the voting booth and in their campaign contributions. But when the consequences to each of them individually are small relative to the monitoring costs, people don't bother to keep track of them—they remain "rationally ignorant."

In the case of ethanol, about one-fifth of all ethanol for fuel is made by one company, Archer Daniels Midland (ADM). Clearly, even small changes in the price of ethanol are important to ADM. Because federal use mandates and the federal ethanol subsidy both increase the profitability of making ethanol, ADM has strong incentives to ensure that members of Congress are aware of the benefits (to ADM) of such policies. Similarly, corn farmers derive most of their income from sales of corn. Federal ethanol policies increase the demand for corn and thus increase its price; again, because the resulting benefits are highly concentrated on corn farmers, each has a strong incentive to ensure that his or her members of Congress understand the benefits (to the farmer) of such policies.

Contrast this with the typical taxpayer or consumer of gasoline. It is true that the $3 billion or so spent on ethanol subsidies each year must come out of taxpayers' pockets. Nevertheless, this amount is spread thinly across tens of millions of federal taxpayers. Similarly, although the mandated use of ethanol in gasoline is estimated to raise the cost of gas by about 8 cents per gallon, this amounts to no more than $50 per year for the typical driver. Neither taxpayer nor motorist is likely to spend much time complaining to his or her senator.

Thus it is that farmers and ethanol producers are willing to lobby hard for use mandates and subsidies at the same time that taxpayers and drivers put up little effective resistance to having their pockets picked. It may make for bad economics, but it is classic politics.

DISCUSSION QUESTIONS

1. Brazilian ethanol producers (who make ethanol from sugarcane) have lower production costs than U.S. producers. Indeed, even though it costs 16 cents per gallon to transport ethanol from Brazil to the United States, which also imposes an **import tariff** of nearly 60 cents per gallon on Brazilian ethanol, the United States still imports millions of gallons of ethanol per year from Brazil. If Congress really cares about protecting the environment and reducing our reliance on foreign crude oil, why do you suppose we have a large import tariff on ethanol?

2. If imports of Brazilian ethanol begin to rise sharply in the future, what do you predict will happen to the size of the import tariff levied on this good?

3. Why do you suppose the federal government gives special treatment to owners of fertile farmland rather than, say, automobile mechanics?

4. Use the theory of rational ignorance to explain why the ethanol subsidy is only 51 cents per gallon rather than, say, $5 per gallon.

Chapter 3

FLYING THE FRIENDLY SKIES?

Most of us hop into our car with little thought for our personal safety, beyond perhaps the act of putting on seat belts. Yet even though travel on scheduled, commercial airlines is safer than driving to work or to the grocery store, many people approach air travel with a sense of foreboding, if not downright fear.

If we were to think carefully about the wisdom of traveling 600 miles per hour in an aluminum tube 7 miles above the earth, several questions might come to mind: How safe is this? How safe should it be? Because the people who operate airlines are not in it for fun, does their interest in making a buck ignore our interest in making it home in one piece? Is some form of government regulation the only way to ensure safety in the skies?

The science of economics begins with one simple principle: We live in a world of **scarcity,** which implies that to get more of any good, we must sacrifice some of other goods. This is just as true of safety as it is of pizzas or haircuts or works of art. Safety confers benefits (we live longer and more enjoyably), but achieving it also entails **costs** (we must give up something to obtain that safety).

As the degree of safety rises, the total benefits of safety rise, but the marginal (or incremental) benefits of additional safety decline. Consider a simple example: Adding exit doors to an airplane increases the number of people who can escape in the event of an emergency evacuation. Nevertheless, each *additional* door adds less in safety benefits than the previous one; if the fourth door enables, say, an extra ten people to escape, the fifth may enable only an extra six to escape. (If this sounds implausible, imagine having a door for each person; the last door added will enable at most one more person to escape.) So we say that the marginal (or incremental) benefit of safety declines as the amount of safety increases.

Let's look now at the other side of the equation: As the amount of safety increases, both the total and the marginal (incremental) costs of providing safety rise. Having a fuel gauge on the plane's instrument panel clearly enhances safety, because it reduces the chance that the plane will run out of fuel while in flight.[1] It is always possible that a fuel gauge will malfunction, so having a backup fuel gauge also adds to safety. Because having two gauges is more costly than having just one, the total costs of safety rise as safety increases. It is also clear, however, that while the cost of the second gauge is (at least) as great as the cost of the first, the second gauge has a smaller positive impact on safety. Thus the cost per unit of additional (incremental) safety is higher for the second fuel gauge than for the first.

How much safety should we have? For an economist, the answer to such a question is generally expressed in terms of **marginal benefits** and **marginal costs.** The economically *efficient* level of safety occurs when the marginal cost of increasing safety just equals the marginal benefit of that increased safety. Put somewhat differently, if the marginal benefits of adding (or keeping) a safety feature exceed the marginal costs of doing so, the feature is worthwhile. But if the added benefits of a safety device do *not* exceed the added costs, we should refrain from installing the device. Note there are two related issues here: How safe should we *be,* and how should we *achieve* that level of safety?

Both of these issues took on added urgency on the morning of September 11, 2001, when terrorists hijacked and crashed four U.S. commercial jetliners. This episode revealed that air travel was far less safe than previously believed. Immediately, it was clear that we should devote additional resources to airline safety; what was not clear was how *much* additional resources should be thus devoted and precisely *what* changes should be made. For example, almost everyone agreed that more careful screening of passengers and baggage at airports would produce important safety benefits. But how should we achieve this? Should carry-on bags be prohibited or just examined more carefully? How thoroughly should checked luggage be screened for bombs? Even now, our answers to these questions are evolving as we learn more about the extent of the threat and the costs of alternative responses to it. Nevertheless, throughout the process, economic principles can help us make the most sensible decisions.

---

1. Notice that we say "reduces" rather than "eliminates." In 1978, a United Air Lines pilot preoccupied with a malfunctioning landing gear evidently failed to pay sufficient attention to his cockpit gauges. When the plane was forced to crash-land after running out of fuel, eight people died.

In general, the efficient level of safety will not be perfect safety, because perfection is simply too costly to achieve. For example, to be absolutely certain that no one is ever killed or injured in an airplane crash, we would have to prevent all travel in airplanes—an unrealistic and impracticable prospect. This means that if we wish to enjoy the advantages of flying, we must be willing to accept *some* risk—a conclusion that each of us implicitly accepts every time we step aboard an airplane. Changes in circumstances can alter the efficient level of safety. For example, if a technological change reduces the costs of bomb-scanning equipment, the marginal costs of preventing terrorist bomb attacks will be lower. It will be efficient to have more airports install the machines and to have extra machines at large airports to speed the screening process. Air travel will become safer because of the technological change. Similarly, if the marginal benefits of safety rise for some reason—perhaps because the president of the United States is on board—it could be efficient to take more precautions, resulting in safer air travel. Given the factors that determine the benefits and costs of safety, the result of a change in circumstances will be some determinate level of safety that generally will be associated with some risk of death or injury.

Airplanes are complex systems, and an amazing number of components can fail. Over the century that humans have been flying, airplane manufacturers and airlines have studied every one of the malfunctions thus far and have put into place design changes and operating procedures aimed at preventing recurring error. Of course, consumers have the greatest incentive to ensure that air travel is safe, and if information were free, we could assert with some confidence that the actual level of safety supplied by firms was the efficient level of safety. Consumers would simply observe the safety offered by different airlines, the prices they charge, and select the degrees of safety that best suited their preferences and budgets, just as with other goods. But information is not free; it is a **scarce good,** costly to obtain. As a result, passengers may be unaware of the safety record of various airlines or the competence of the pilots and the maintenance procedures of an airline's mechanics. Indeed, even the airlines themselves may be uncertain about the efficient level of safety, perhaps because they have no way of estimating the true threat of terrorist attacks, for example. Such possibilities have been used to argue that the federal government should mandate certain minimum levels of safety, as it does today through the operation of the Federal Aviation Administration (FAA). Let's look at this issue in some detail.

One argument in favor of government safety standards rests on the presumption that, left to their own devices, airlines would provide less safety than passengers want. This might happen, for example, if customers could not tell (at a reasonable cost) whether the equipment, training, and procedures employed by an airline are safe. If passengers cannot cheaply gauge the level of safety, they will not be willing to reward airlines for being safe or punish them for being unsafe. If safety is costly to provide and consumers are unwilling to pay for it because they cannot accurately measure it, airlines will provide too little of it. The conclusion is that government experts, such as the FAA, should set safety standards for the industry.

This conclusion seems plausible, but it ignores two simple points. First, how is the government to know the efficient level of safety? Even if the FAA knows the costs of all possible safety measures, it still does not have enough information to set efficient safety standards because it does not know the value that people place on safety. Without such information, the FAA has no way to assess the benefits of additional safety and hence no means of knowing whether those benefits are greater or less than the added costs.

The second point is that people want to reach their destinations safely. Even if they cannot observe whether an airline hires good pilots or bad pilots, they can see whether that airline's planes land safely or crash. If it is *safety* that is important to consumers—and not the obscure, costly-to-measure *reasons* for that safety—the fact that consumers cannot easily measure metal fatigue in jet engines may be totally irrelevant to the process of achieving the efficient level of safety.

Interestingly, evidence shows that consumers are indeed cognizant of the safety performance of airlines and that they "punish" airlines that perform in an unsafe manner. Researchers have found that when an airline is at fault in a fatal plane crash, consumers appear to downgrade their safety rating of the airline (that is, they revise upward their estimates of the likelihood of future fatal crashes). As a result, the offending airline suffers substantial adverse financial consequences over and above the costs of losing the plane and being sued on behalf of the victims. These findings suggest a striking degree of safety awareness on the part of supposedly ignorant consumers.

Of course, this discussion leaves open the issue of how to handle safety threats posed by terrorists and other miscreants. For example, much of the information that goes into assessing terrorist threats is classified as secret, and its revelation to airlines or consumers might compromise key sources of the data. Hence there could be an advantage to having the government try to approximate the efficient safety outcome by mandating certain screening provisions without revealing exactly why they are being chosen. Similarly, because airlines are connected in networks (so that people and baggage move from one airline to another in the course of a trip), achieving the efficient level of safety might require a common set of screening rules for all airlines. Even so, this does not inform us whether the government should impose those rules or the airlines should come to a voluntary joint agreement on them.

We began this chapter with the commonplace observation that airlines are safer than cars. Yet many people still worry for their safety every time they get on an airplane. Are they being irrational? Well, the answer, it seems, is in the eye of the beholder. Measured in terms of fatalities per mile traveled, airplanes are some 15 times safer than cars (and 176 times safer than walking, we might add). But this number masks the fact that 68 percent of aircraft accidents happen on takeoff and landing, and these operations occupy only 6 percent of flight time. It is presumably this fact that quite sensibly makes people nervous whenever they find themselves approaching an airport.

DISCUSSION QUESTIONS

1. Is it possible to be too safe? Explain what you mean by "too safe."

2. Many automobile manufacturers routinely advertise the safety of their cars, yet airlines generally do not mention safety in their advertising. Can you suggest an explanation for this difference?

3. Many economists would argue that private companies are likely to be more efficient than the government at operating airlines. Yet many economists would also argue that there is a valid reason for government to regulate the safety of those same airlines. Can you explain why the government might be good at ensuring safety, even though it might not be good at operating the airlines?

4. Professional football teams sometimes charter airplanes to take them to their away games. Would you feel safer on a United Air Lines plane that had been chartered by the Washington Redskins than on a regularly scheduled United Air Lines flight?

Chapter 4

THE MYSTERY OF WEALTH

Why are the citizens of some nations rich while the inhabitants of others are poor? Your initial answer might be "because of differences in the **natural-resource endowments** of the nations." It is true that ample endowments of energy, timber, and fertile land all help raise wealth. But natural resources can be only a very small part of the answer, as witnessed by many counterexamples. Switzerland and Luxembourg, for example, are nearly devoid of key natural resources, yet the real incomes of citizens of those lands are among the world's highest. Similarly, Hong Kong, which consists of a few square miles of rock and hillside, is one of the economic miracles of modern times, while in Russia, a land amply endowed with vast quantities of virtually every important resource, most people remain mired in economic misery.

A number of studies have begun to unravel the mystery of **economic growth.** Repeatedly, they have found that it is the fundamental political and legal **institutions** of society that are conducive to growth. Of these, political stability, secure private property rights, and legal systems based on the **rule of law** are among the most important. Such institutions encourage people to make long-term investments in improving land and in all forms of **physical capital** and **human capital.** These investments raise the **capital stock,** which in turn provides for more growth long into the future. And the cumulative effects of this growth over time eventually yield much higher standards of living.

Consider first the contrasting effects of different legal systems on economic growth. Many legal systems around the world today are based on one of two models: the English **common law system** and the French **civil law system.** Common law systems reflect a conscious decision in favor of a limited role for government and emphasize the importance of the judiciary in constraining the power of the executive and legislative branches of government. In contrast, civil law systems favor the creation

TABLE 4-1 Differing Legal Systems

Common Law Nations	Civil Law Nations
Australia	Brazil
Canada	Egypt
India	France
Israel	Greece
New Zealand	Italy
United Kingdom	Mexico
United States	Sweden

of a strong centralized government in which the legislature and the executive branches have the power to grant preferential treatment to special interests. Table 4–1 shows a sampling of common law and civil law countries.

Research reveals that the security of **property rights** is much stronger in common law systems, such as observed in Britain and its former colonies, including the United States. In nations such as France and its former colonies, the civil law systems are much more likely to yield unpredictable changes in the rules of the game—the structure of **property and contract rights.** This unpredictability makes people reluctant to make long-term fixed investments, a fact that ultimately slows the economic growth of these nations and lowers the standard of living for their citizens.

The reasoning here is simple. If you know that the police will not help you protect your rights to a home or a car, you are less likely to acquire those assets. Similarly, if you cannot easily enforce business or employment contracts that you make, you are less likely to make those contracts—and hence less likely to produce as many goods or services. And if you cannot plan for the future because you don't know what the rules of the game will be in ten years or perhaps even one year from now, you are less likely to make the kinds of productive long-term investments that take years to pay off. Common law systems seem to do a better job at enforcing contracts and securing property rights and so would be expected to promote economic activity now and economic growth over time.

Research into the economic performance of nations around the world from 1960 until the 1990s found that economic growth was one-third higher in the common law nations, with their strong property rights, than in civil law nations. Over the more than three decades covered, the standard of living—measured by real **per capita income**—increased more than 20 percent in common law nations compared to civil law nations. If such a pattern persisted over the span of a century, it would produce a staggering 80 percent real per capita income differential in favor of nations with secure property rights.

Other research has taken a much broader view, both across time and across institutions, in assessing economic growth. Institutions such as political stability, protection against violence or theft, security of contracts, and freedom from regulatory burdens all contribute to sustained economic growth. Indeed, it is key institutions such as these, rather than natural-resource endowments, that explain long-term differences in economic growth and thus present-day differences in levels of real income. To illustrate the powerful effect of institutions, consider the contrast between Mexico, with per capita real income of about $12,000 today, and the United States, with per capita real income of about $48,000. Had Mexico developed with the same political and legal institutions that the United States has enjoyed, per capita income in Mexico would today be equal to that in the United States.

Given the great importance of such institutions in determining long-term growth, one might ask another important question: How have countries gotten the political and legal institutions they have today? The answer has to do with disease, of all things. An examination of more than seventy former European colonies reveals that a variety of strategies were pursued. In Australia, New Zealand, and North America, the colonists found geography and climates that were conducive to good health. Permanent settlement was attractive, so colonists created institutions to protect private property and curb the power of the state. But when Europeans arrived in Africa and South America, they encountered tropical diseases, such as malaria and yellow fever, that produced high mortality rates. This discouraged permanent settlement and encouraged a mentality focused on extracting metals, cash crops, and other resources. As a result, there were few **incentives** to promote democratic institutions or stable long-term property rights systems. The differing initial institutions helped shape economic growth over the years and, because of the broad persistence of those institutions, continue to shape the political and legal character and the standard of living in these nations today.

Recent events also illustrate that the effects of political and legal institutions can be drastically accelerated—in either direction. Consider China, which in 1979 began to change its institutions in two key ways. First, as we discuss more fully in Chapter 32, China began to experiment with private property rights for a few of its citizens, under narrow circumstances. Second, the Chinese government began to clear away obstacles to foreign investment, making China a more secure place for

Western companies to do business. Although the institutional changes have been modest, their combined effects have been substantial. Over the years since, economic growth in China has accelerated, averaging almost 7 percent per year. And if that doesn't sound like much, keep in mind that it has been enough over that period to raise real per capita income in China by a factor of 6.

For an example of the potential *destructive* impact of institutional change, we need look no further than Zimbabwe. When that country won its independence from Britain in 1980, it was one of the most prosperous nations in Africa. Soon after taking power as Zimbabwe's first (and so far only) president, Robert Mugabe began disassembling that nation's rule of law, tearing apart the institutions that had helped it grow rich. He reduced the security of property rights in land and eventually confiscated those rights altogether. Mugabe has also gradually taken control of the prices of most goods and services in his nation and even controls the price of its national currency, at least the price at which Zimbabweans are allowed to trade it. Moreover, the Mugabe government has confiscated large stocks of food and much of anything of value that might be exported out of or imported into Zimbabwe. In short, anything that is produced or saved has become subject to confiscation, so the incentives to do either are—to put it mildly—reduced.

As a result, between 1980 and 1996, real per capita income in Zimbabwe fell by one-third, and since 1996, it has fallen by an additional third. Eighty percent of the workforce is unemployed, investment is nonexistent, and the annual inflation rate reached an astonishing 231 million percent in recent years. (At that rate, the price level *doubles* every thirteen days.) The fruit of decades of labor and capital investment has been destroyed because the institutions that made that progress possible have been eliminated. It is a lesson we ignore at our peril.

DISCUSSION QUESTIONS

1. Consider two countries, A and B, that have identical *physical* endowments of a key natural resource. In country A, any profits that are made from extracting that resource are subject to confiscation by the government, while in country B, there is no such risk. How does the risk of expropriation affect the *economic* endowment of the two nations? In which nation are people richer?

2. In light of your answer to question 1, how do you explain the fact that in some countries there is widespread political support for government

policies that expropriate resources from some groups for the purpose of handing them out to other groups?

3. If the crucial factor determining a country's low standard of living is the adverse set of legal and cultural institutions it possesses, can you offer suggestions for how the other nations of the world might help in permanently raising that country's standard of living?

PART TWO
Globalization and Free Trade

Chapter 5

GLOBALIZATION
AND THE WEALTH
OF AMERICA

The past two decades have been a time of great change for international trade and **globalization**. The North American Free Trade Agreement (NAFTA), for example, substantially reduced the **trade barriers** among citizens of Canada, the United States, and Mexico. On a global scale, the Uruguay round of the General Agreement on Tariffs and Trade (GATT) was ratified by 117 nations, including the United States. Under the terms of this agreement, GATT was replaced by the **World Trade Organization (WTO),** whose membership now numbers about 150, and **tariffs** were cut worldwide. Agricultural **subsidies** were reduced, patent protections were extended, and the WTO established a set of arbitration boards to settle international disputes over trade issues.

Many economists believe that both NAFTA and the agreements reached during the Uruguay round were victories not only for free trade and globalization but also for the citizens of the participating nations. Nevertheless, many noneconomists, particularly politicians, opposed these agreements, so it is important that we understand what is beneficial about NAFTA, the Uruguay round, and free trade in general.

Voluntary trade creates new wealth. In voluntary trade, both parties in an exchange gain. They give up something of lesser value in return for something of greater value. In this sense, exchanges are always unequal. But it is this unequal nature of exchange that is the source of the increased **productivity** and higher wealth that occurs whenever trade takes place. When we engage in exchange, what we give up is worth less than what we get—for if this were not true, we would not have traded. And what is true for us is also true for our trading partner, meaning that both partners end up better off.

Free trade encourages individuals to use their talents and abilities in the most productive manner possible and to exchange the fruits of their efforts. The **gains from trade** lie in one of the most fundamental ideas in economics: A nation gains from doing what it can do best *relative to other nations*, that is, by specializing in endeavors in which it has a **comparative advantage.** Trade encourages individuals and nations to discover ways to specialize so that they can become more productive and enjoy higher incomes. Increased productivity and the subsequent increase in economic growth are exactly what the signatories of the Uruguay round and NAFTA sought—and are obtaining—by reducing trade barriers.

Globalization differs from free trade chiefly in the degree of integration across nations. For example, although there is free trade in wine, the wines produced in Australia, California, and France are each created wholly within the geopolitical borders indicated by their labels. Moreover, each remains a distinct economic entity, in that significant relative price changes between, say, French and California wines are observed. In contrast, the market for automobiles has become truly "global": If you purchase a "Japanese" automobile in the United States, assembly of the vehicle may have taken place in Japan, the United States, or even Mexico, and the components of the car may have come from a half-dozen or more different nations. And if you call for customer support for your car, the person answering the phone may be at a call center located in any of a variety of English-speaking nations. Globalization thus means that trade between nations becomes as seamless as trade between states, provinces, or cities within a given nation.

Despite the enormous gains from exchange, globalization is routinely opposed by some people. Many excuses are offered for this opposition, but they all basically come down to one issue: When our borders are fully open to trade with other nations, some individuals and businesses in our nation face more competition. As you saw in Chapter 19, most firms and workers hate competition, and who can blame them? After all, if a firm can keep the competition out, **profits** are sure to rise. And if workers can prevent competition from other sources, they can enjoy higher wages and greater selection among jobs. So the real source of most opposition to globalization is that the opponents to trade dislike the competition that comes with it. There is nothing immoral or unethical about this—but there is nothing altruistic or noble about it, either. It is self-interest, pure and simple.

One aspect of globalization that looms large in the minds of its opponents is the unremitting competitive vigilance that it requires. When world markets are completely integrated, one's competitors may emerge at any time from any place—often from corners of the world that one may least expect. And because competitors may only need to create a Web site to get started and can have their products delivered the next day by air freight, that competition can emerge devastatingly quickly. Thus when operating in a global economy, firms and their employees must contend with a level of uncertainty that is simply not present when trade patterns are less integrated. Note that this highly competitive atmosphere ultimately benefits all of us, but that doesn't make it any less unnerving for those who must endure its pressures, day after day. Competition is tough, and global competition is toughest of all. Because of this, opposition to globalization is nothing new. One of the most famous examples of such opposition led to passage of the Smoot-Hawley Tariff of 1930. This major federal statute was a classic example of **protectionism**—an effort to protect a subset of American producers at the expense of consumers and other producers. It included tariff schedules for more than twenty thousand products, raising taxes on affected imports by an average of 52 percent.

The Smoot-Hawley Tariff encouraged beggar-thy-neighbor policies by the rest of the world. Such policies represent an attempt to improve (a portion of) one's domestic economy at the expense of foreign countries' economies. In this case, tariffs were imposed to discourage **imports** so that domestic import-competing industries would benefit. The beggar-thy-neighbor policy at the heart of Smoot-Hawley was soon adopted by the United Kingdom, France, the Netherlands, and Switzerland. The result was a halt to globalization and a massive reduction in international trade that almost certainly exacerbated the worldwide depression of the 1930s.

Opponents of globalization sometimes claim that beggar-thy-neighbor policies benefit the United States by protecting import-competing industries. In general, this claim is not correct. It is true that some Americans benefit from such policies, but two large groups of Americans lose. First, there are the purchasers of imports and import-competing goods. They suffer from higher prices and reduced selection of goods and suppliers caused by tariffs and import **quotas.** Second, the decline in imports caused by protectionism also causes a decline in **exports,** thereby harming firms and employees in these industries. This follows directly from one of the most fundamental propositions in international trade: *In the long run, imports are paid for by exports.* This proposition simply states that when one country buys goods and services from the rest of the world (imports), the rest of the world eventually wants goods from that country (exports) in exchange. Given this fundamental proposition, a corollary becomes obvious: *Any restriction on imports leads to a reduction in exports.* Thus any business for import-competing industries gained as a result of tariffs or quotas means at least as much business lost for exporting industries.

Opponents of globalization raise a variety of objections in their efforts to restrict international trade. For example, it is sometimes said that foreign companies engage in dumping, that is, selling their goods in America below cost. The first question to ask is, below *whose* cost? Clearly, if the foreign firm is selling in America, it must be offering the good for sale at a price that is at or below the cost of American firms, or else it could not induce Americans to buy it. But the ability of individuals or firms to get goods at lower cost is one of the *benefits* of free trade, not one of its negatives.

What about claims that import sales are taking place at prices below the foreign company's costs? This amounts to arguing that the owners of the foreign company are voluntarily giving some of their wealth to us, namely, the difference between their costs and the lower price they charge us. It is possible, though unlikely, that they might wish to do this as a way of getting us to try a product that we would not otherwise purchase. But if so, why would we want to refuse this gift? As a nation, we are richer if we accept it. Moreover, it is a gift that will be offered for only a short while, for there is no point in selling below one's cost unless one hopes soon to raise price profitably above cost!

Another argument sometimes raised against globalization is that the goods are produced abroad using unfair labor practices (such as the use of child labor) or using production processes that do not meet American environmental standards. Such charges are sometimes correct. But we must remember two things. First, although we may find the use of child labor (or perhaps sixty-hour work weeks with no overtime pay) objectionable, such practices were once common in the United States. They used to be prevalent in America for the same reason they are now practiced abroad: The people involved were (or are) too poor to do otherwise. Some families in developing nations cannot survive unless all members of the family contribute. As unfortunate as this is, if we insist on imposing our attitudes—shaped in part by our great wealth—on peoples whose wealth is far lower than ours, we run the risk of making them worse off even as we think we are helping them.

Similar considerations apply to environmental standards[1] It is well established that individuals' and nations' willingness to pay for environmental quality is very much shaped by their wealth: Environmental quality is a **luxury good;** that is, people who are rich (such as Americans)

---

1. There is one important exception to this argument. In the case of foreign air or water pollution generated near enough to our borders (for example, with Mexico or Canada) to cause harm to Americans, good public policy presumably dictates that we seek to treat such pollution as though it were being generated inside our borders.

want to consume much more of it per capita than people who are poor. Insisting that other nations meet environmental standards that we find acceptable is much like insisting that they wear the clothes we wear, use the modes of transportation we prefer, and consume the foods we like. The few people who manage to comply will indeed be living in the style to which we are accustomed, but most people will simply be impoverished by the attempt.

Our point is not that foreign labor or environmental standards are, or should be, irrelevant to Americans. Our point is that achieving high standards of either is costly, and trade restrictions are unlikely to be the most efficient or most effective way to achieve them. Just as important, labor standards and environmental standards are all too often raised as smoke screens to hide the real motive: keeping the competition out.

If it is true that globalization is beneficial and that restrictions on trade are generally harmful, we must surely raise the question, how does legislation like the Smoot-Hawley Tariff (or any other such restriction) ever get passed? As Mark Twain noted many years ago, the reason the free traders win the arguments and the protectionists win the votes is this: Foreign competition often clearly affects a narrow and specific import-competing industry such as textiles, shoes, or automobiles, and thus trade restrictions benefit a narrow, well-defined group of economic agents. For example, restrictions on imports of Japanese automobiles in the 1980s chiefly benefited the Big Three automakers in this country: General Motors, Ford, and Chrysler. Similarly, long-standing quotas on the imports of sugar benefit a handful of large American sugar producers. And when tariffs of up to 30 percent were slapped on many steel imports in 2002, an even smaller number of American steelmakers and their employees benefited. Because of the concentrated benefits that accrue when Congress votes in favor of trade restrictions, sufficient funds can be raised in those industries to convince members of Congress to impose those restrictions.

The eventual reduction in exports that must follow is normally spread in small doses throughout all export industries. Thus no specific group of workers, managers, or shareholders in export industries will feel that it should contribute money to convince Congress to reduce barriers to globalization. Furthermore, although consumers of imports and import-competing goods lose due to trade restrictions, they too are typically a diffuse group of individuals, none of whom will be individually affected a great deal because of any single import restriction. It is the simultaneous existence of concentrated benefits and diffuse costs that led to Mark Twain's conclusion that the protectionists would often win the votes. (Concentrated benefits and dispersed costs are at the heart of Chapter 2, "Ethanol Madness," and in explaining some U.S. domestic policies.)

Of course, the protectionists don't win all the votes—after all, almost one-sixth of the U.S. economy is based on international trade. Despite the opposition to globalization that comes from many quarters, its benefits to the economy as a whole are so great that it is unthinkable that we might do away with international trade altogether. Thus when we think about developments such as NAFTA and the WTO, it is clear that both economic theory and empirical evidence indicate that Americans will be better off after—and because of—globalization.

DISCUSSION QUESTIONS

1. During the late 1980s and early 1990s, American automobile manufacturers greatly increased the quality of the cars they produced relative to the quality of the cars produced in other nations. What effect do you think this had on American imports of Japanese cars, on Japanese imports of American cars, and on American exports of goods and services other than automobiles?

2. Over the past twenty years, some Japanese automakers have opened plants in the United States so that they could produce (and sell) "Japanese" cars here. What effect do you think this had on American imports of Japanese cars, on Japanese imports of American cars, and on American exports of goods and services other than automobiles?

3. For a number of years, Japanese carmakers voluntarily limited the number of cars they exported to the United States. What effect do you think this had on Japanese imports of American cars and on American exports of goods and services other than automobiles?

4. Until recently, American cars exported to Japan had driver controls on the left side (as in the United States), even though the Japanese drive on the left side of the road and Japanese cars sold in Japan have driver controls on the right side. Suppose the Japanese tried to sell their cars in the United States with the driver controls on the right side. What impact would this likely have on their sales in this country? Do you think the unwillingness of American carmakers to put the driver controls on the correct side for exports to Japan had any effect on their sales of cars in that country?

Chapter 6

THE $750,000 STEELWORKER

In even-numbered years, particularly years evenly divisible by 4, politicians are apt to give speeches about the need to protect U.S. jobs from the evils of **globalization.** We are thus encouraged to buy American. If further encouragement is needed, we are told that if we do not voluntarily reduce the amount of imported goods we purchase, the government will impose (or make more onerous) either **tariffs** (taxes) on imported goods or **quotas** (quantity restrictions) that physically limit **imports.** The objective is to save U.S. jobs.

Unlike black rhinos or blue whales, U.S. jobs are in no danger of becoming extinct. There are an infinite number of potential jobs in the American economy, and there always will be. Some of these jobs are not very pleasant, and many others do not pay very well, but there will always be employment of some sort as long as there is **scarcity.** Thus when a steelworker making $72,000 per year says that imports of foreign steel should be reduced to save his job, what he really means is this: He wants to be protected from **competition** so he can continue his present employment at the same or higher salary rather than move to a different employment that has less desirable working conditions or pays a lower salary. There is nothing wrong with the steelworker's goal (better working conditions and higher pay), but it has nothing to do with saving jobs.

In any discussion of the consequences of restrictions on international trade, it is essential to remember two facts. First, *we pay for imports with exports.* It is true that in the short run, we can sell off assets or borrow from abroad if we happen to import more goods and services than we export. But we have only a finite amount of assets to sell, and foreigners do not want to wait forever before we pay our bills. Ultimately, our accounts can be settled only if we provide (export) goods and services to the trading partners from whom we purchase (import) goods and services.

Trade, after all, involves *quid pro quo* (literally, something for something). The second point to remember is that *voluntary trade is mutually beneficial to the trading partners.* If we restrict international trade, we reduce those benefits, both for our trading partners and for ourselves. One way these reduced benefits are manifested is in the form of curtailed employment opportunities for workers. In a nutshell, even though tariffs and quotas enhance job opportunities in import-competing industries, they also cost us jobs in export industries; the net effect seems to be *reduced* employment overall.

What is true for the United States is also true for other countries: They will buy our goods only if they can market theirs, because they too have to export goods to pay for their imports. Thus any U.S. restrictions on imports—via tariffs, quotas, or other means—ultimately cause a reduction in our exports, because other countries will be unable to pay for our goods. Hence import restrictions must inevitably decrease the size of our export sector. So imposing trade restrictions to save jobs in import-competing industries has the effect of costing jobs in export industries.

Import restrictions also impose costs on U.S. consumers. By reducing competition from abroad, quotas, tariffs, and other trade restraints push up the prices of foreign goods and enable U.S. producers to hike their own prices. Perhaps the best-documented example of this is the automobile industry.

Due in part to the enhanced quality of imported cars, sales of domestically produced automobiles fell from 9 million units in 1978 to an average of 6 million units per year between 1980 and 1982. **Profits** for U.S. automobile manufacturers plummeted as well, turning into substantial losses for some of them. U.S. automakers and autoworkers' unions demanded protection from import competition. They were joined in their cries by politicians from automobile-producing states. The result was a voluntary agreement by Japanese car companies (the most important competitors of U.S. firms) that restricted U.S. sales of Japanese cars to 1.68 million units per year. This agreement—which amounted to a quota even though it never officially bore that name—began in April 1981 and continued into the 1990s in various forms.

Robert W. Crandall, an economist with the Brookings Institution, has estimated how much this voluntary trade restriction has cost U.S. consumers in terms of higher car prices. According to his estimates, the reduced supply of Japanese cars pushed their prices up by $2,000 apiece, measured in 2009 dollars. The higher price of Japanese imports in turn enabled domestic producers to hike their prices an average of $800 per car. The total tab in the first full year of the program was over $8 billion. Crandall also estimated the number of jobs in automobile-related industries that were saved by the voluntary import restrictions at about 26,000. Dividing $8 billion by 26,000 jobs yields a cost to consumers of about $300,000 *per year* for every job saved in the automobile industry. U.S. consumers could have saved over $5 billion on their car purchases each year if instead of implicitly agreeing to import restrictions, they had simply given $100,000 to every autoworker whose job was preserved by the voluntary import restraints.

The same types of calculations have been made for other industries. Tariffs in the apparel industry were increased between 1977 and 1981, saving the jobs of about 116,000 U.S. apparel workers at a cost of $50,000 per job each year. At about the same time, the producers of citizens band radios also managed to get tariffs raised. Approximately six hundred workers in the industry kept their jobs as a result, at an annual cost to consumers of over $90,000 per job.

The cost of **protectionism** has been even higher in other industries. Jobs preserved in the glassware industry due to trade restrictions cost $200,000 apiece each year. In the maritime industry, the yearly cost of trade protection is $290,000 per job. In the steel industry, the cost of preserving a job has been estimated at an astounding $750,000 per year. If free trade were permitted, each worker losing a job could be given a cash payment of half that amount each year, and consumers would still save a lot of money.

Even so, this is not the full story. None of these studies estimating the cost to consumers of saving jobs in import-competing industries have attempted to estimate the ultimate impact of import restrictions on the flow of exports, the number of jobs lost in the export sector, and thus the total number of jobs gained or lost.

When imports to the United States are restricted, our trading partners will necessarily buy less of what we produce. The resulting decline in export sales means fewer jobs in exporting industries. And the total reduction in trade leads to fewer jobs for workers such as stevedores (who unload ships) and truck drivers (who carry goods to and from ports). On both counts—the overall cut in trade and the accompanying decline in exports—protectionism leads to job losses that might not be immediately obvious.

Several years ago, Congress tried to pass a domestic-content bill for automobiles. In effect, the legislation would have required that cars sold in the United States have a minimum percentage of their components manufactured and assembled in this country. Proponents of the legislation argued that it would have protected 300,000 jobs in the U.S. automobile manufacturing and auto parts supply industries. Yet the legislation's supporters failed to recognize the negative impact of the bill on trade in general and its ultimate impact on U.S. export industries. A U.S. Department of Labor study did recognize these impacts, estimating that the domestic-content legislation would actually cost more jobs in trade-related and export industries than it protected in import-competing businesses. Congress ultimately decided not to impose a domestic-content requirement for cars sold in the United States.

More recently, when President Bush decided in 2002 to impose tariffs of up to 30 percent on steel imports, the adverse effects on the economy were substantial and soon apparent. To take but one example, prior to the tariffs, the Port of New Orleans relied on steel imports for more than 40 percent of its revenues, in part because once steel coming into the port is offloaded, the ships are cleaned and refilled with U.S. grain for export. By reducing imports, the tariffs slashed economic activity at the port and also reduced U.S. grain exports. Businesses and farms all up and down the Mississippi River were adversely affected. More broadly, the higher costs of imported steel produced a decline in employment in U.S. industries that use steel as an input. Indeed, one study estimated that due to the tariffs, some 200,000 people lost their jobs in 2002 in these industries alone—a number that exceeded the total number of people actually employed by the steel manufacturing firms protected by the tariff.

In principle, trade restrictions are imposed to provide economic help to specific industries and to increase employment in those industries. Ironically, the long-term effects may be just the opposite. Researchers at the **World Trade Organization (WTO)** examined employment in three industries that have been heavily protected throughout the world: textiles, clothing, and iron and steel. Despite stringent trade protection for these industries, employment *declined* during the period of protection, in some cases dramatically. In textiles, employment fell 22 percent in the United States and 46 percent in the European Union. The clothing industry had employment losses ranging from 18 percent in the United States to 56 percent in Sweden. Declines in employment in the iron and steel industry ranged anywhere from 10 percent in Canada to 54 percent in the United States. In short, restrictions on free trade are no guarantee against job losses, even in the industries supposedly being protected.

The evidence seems clear: The cost of protecting jobs in the short run is huge. And in the long run, it appears that jobs cannot be protected, especially if one considers all aspects of protectionism. Free trade is a tough platform on which to run for office. But it is the one that yields the most general benefits if implemented. Of course, this does not mean that politicians will embrace it, and so we end up "saving" jobs at a cost of up to $750,000 each.

DISCUSSION QUESTIONS

1. Who gains and who loses from import restrictions?

2. What motivates politicians to impose trade restrictions?

3. If it would be cheaper to give each steelworker $375,000 per year in cash than impose restrictions on imports of steel, why do we have the import restrictions rather than the cash payments?

4. Most U.S. imports and exports travel through our seaports at some point. How do you predict that members of Congress from coastal states would vote on proposals to restrict international trade? What other information would you want to know when making such a prediction?

Chapter 7

THE LION, THE DRAGON, AND THE FUTURE

For decades after the Communists' rise to power in 1949, China was best known for poverty and repression, and its aggression came mostly on the military front. But in recent years, *economic* aggression has become the byword. Although both poverty and repression are still the norm, both are changing for the better. China, it seems, is trying to learn from capitalism, even if not converting to it.

China's economic offensive began thirty years ago in its southeastern province of Guangdong. The Chinese leadership decided to use this province as a test case, to see if capitalist **direct foreign investment** could stimulate **economic growth** in a way that could be politically controlled. The experience was deemed a success—economic growth soared amid political stability. What the government learned from the experience helped it smooth the 1997 transition of Hong Kong from British to Chinese control. Most important in terms of China's long-term economic aspirations, many foreign investors came to view the Guangdong experiment as solid evidence that they could invest in China without fear that the Communist government would confiscate their capital. The result: foreign investment in China soared.

There are two powerful forces that are attracting economic investment to China: **demand** and **supply.** On the demand side, 1.3 billion people live there, some 20 percent of the world's population. Although **per capita income** is still low by world standards, it has been increasing by more than 6 percent per year, after adjusting for inflation. At that rate, the standard of living for the Chinese people—and hence their **purchasing power** in world markets—is doubling every decade or so. China is already the world's largest cell-phone market, and within a few years, it is estimated, China will account for 25 percent of the world's purchases of personal computers. Indeed, China now spends over $100 billion per year on information technology and services. By 2030, the Chinese economy will likely have eclipsed the United States' and become the world's largest. With its huge population, China also offers attractions on the supply side. Highly skilled workers have been plentiful in the Chinese labor market with hundreds of thousands of engineering graduates each year. In many cities, the fact that the Chinese workforce is generally well educated and often English-speaking has helped make the country attractive to foreign employers. Collaborative scientific ventures between Chinese researchers and U.S. firms are becoming increasingly common. A research team at Beijing University played a role in deciphering the genetic makeup of rice, for example. American computer hardware and software firms Intel, IBM, Oracle, and Microsoft have shifted some key components of their research to China in recent years. Indeed, American firms of all types are setting up operations in China. Chinese firms, meanwhile, are proving to be formidable competitors both at home and abroad.

The situation has become critical in Japan, where wages are much higher than in China but whose technological lead over China is gradually eroding. "Are we to become a vassal of the Chinese dynasty again?" asked one Japanese official, clearly concerned that his nation's manufacturing firms were having trouble competing with Chinese firms. Eventually, Japanese firms will adjust to the growing economic presence of China, but the transition may be unpleasant.

Americans are more concerned about the likely impact on the U.S. economy of China's capitalist ambitions. Will the dragon consume American firms and jobs as it grows? The short answer is no. The long answer has two elements. To this point, a key element of China's competitiveness has been the low wages there. Even though American and European firms operating in China choose to pay their workers more than state-owned enterprises pay, this has still yielded considerable savings. As recently as five years ago, unskilled and semiskilled labor in China cost only 25 percent as much as in Europe. Moreover, in the past, foreign firms have been able to hire engineers for salaries that are only 10 to 20 percent of the cost of hiring engineers in the West.

Labor markets in China are changing rapidly, however. Between 2000 and 2008, average wages rose 50 percent, with bigger increases among higher-skilled workers. Many firms were unable to hire as many workers as they would have liked, and most firms had to upgrade their fringe benefits and other on-the-job amenities just to retain existing workers. Wages are still well below American and European levels, but the gap has closed, thereby cutting the competitive advantage of many Chinese firms. The recent worldwide recession has altered labor market conditions as significantly in China as anywhere. But it is unlikely to impede China's march to economic superpower status.

Higher wages in China will also translate into higher demand for goods produced by American and European firms. China, like all nations, must in the long run import goods equal in value to those it exports (unless China intends to give its exports away, which so far no one is claiming). This means that just as China has become a potent supplier of many goods and services, it is at the same time becoming a potent demander of still other goods and services.

Thus far, the Chinese demand for goods has not been as visible in American markets because American firms tend to produce goods and services designed for higher-income consumers, and China has relatively few of those. In the meantime, the demand-side influence of the Chinese economy is already showing up, albeit in odd places. To take one example, right now China's most important import from the United States is trash. Ranging from used newspapers to scrap steel, Chinese companies buy billions of dollars' worth of the stuff every year to use as raw materials in the goods they produce. In addition to yielding profits (and employment) in these U.S. export industries, this exportation of U.S. trash reduces the burden on U.S. landfills and, by pushing up the prices of recyclable scrap, encourages more recycling in the United States.

Eventually, of course, we'd like to be sending China more than our rubbish, and that time is coming. As China's economy grows, so will the number of affluent Chinese, and with 1.3 billion potential candidates, that ultimately means *plenty* of consumers for America's high-end goods. Thus the long-run effects of China's growth will mean a different American economy—we'll be producing and consuming different mixes of goods and services—but America will also be a richer nation. Voluntary exchange creates wealth, and the Chinese dragon is big enough to create a lot of wealth.

To China's southwest, another giant is stirring. Around 1990, the lion of India began to throw off the self-imposed shackles of nearly a half-century of markets largely closed to international **competition.** The central government, for example, began opening state-owned companies to competition from private-sector rivals. FedEx and United Parcel Service (UPS) have made huge inroads on the Indian postal service, and numerous foreign firms are now competing with the state-owned telephone service, which had long been a complete **monopoly.**

Entry into the Indian market brought familiarity with its workforce, many of whose members are fluent in English. The technical capabilities of graduates of top Indian universities, combined with their English skills and low wages, made them perfect staffers for a proliferation of call centers that have opened throughout India. Tens of thousands of technical and customer-relations jobs that used to go to Middle America are now held by the growing middle class in India. It was in many respects this very movement that brought **outsourcing** to the forefront of the American consciousness.

But India, too, is struggling with growth. The talent pool at the top is thin: Only a dozen or so of India's seventeen thousand universities and colleges can compete with America's best, and the wages of graduates of these top schools are soaring. Moreover, India suffers from overwhelming infrastructure problems: Much of its road system is either overcrowded or in disrepair, and its port facilities are in desperate need of modernization. For the time being, such transportation problems are likely to keep India from becoming a major manufacturing powerhouse. India has also been hampered by its huge and seemingly permanent government bureaucracy. For example, despite the fact that the postal service there has lost more than half of its business to newcomers such as FedEx and UPS, none of the 550,000 postal service employees can be fired.

At least India is a democracy, and its legal system, inherited from the British, who ruled there for so long, is in close conformity with the legal systems of most developed nations. Matters are rather different in China. As noted in Chapter 4, "The Mystery of Wealth," political and legal **institutions** are crucial foundations for sustained economic growth. Despite the advances China has made over the past thirty years, its wealth-creating future may be clouded unless it can successfully deal with two crucial institutional issues.

First, there is the matter of resolving the tension inherent when a Communist dictatorship tries to use capitalism as the engine of economic growth. Capitalism thrives best in an environment of freedom and itself creates an awareness of and appreciation for the benefits of that freedom. Yet freedom is antithetical to the ideological and political tenets of the Communist government of China. Will the government be tempted to confiscate the fruits of capitalist success to support itself? Or will growing pressure for more political freedom force the government to repress the capitalist system to protect itself? Either route would likely bring economic growth in China to a swift halt.

The second potential long-run problem faced by China lies in that nation's cultural attitude toward **intellectual property.** In a land in which imitation is viewed as the sincerest form of flattery, it is routine to use the ideas of others in one's own pursuits. As a result, patent and copyright laws in China are far weaker than in Western nations. Moreover, actions elsewhere considered to be commercial theft (such as software piracy) are largely tolerated in China. If foreign firms find that they cannot protect their economic **assets** in the Chinese market, foreign investment will suffer accordingly, and so will the growing dragon that depends on it so heavily.

DISCUSSION QUESTIONS

1. Currently, AIDS is spreading rapidly in China and India. If the governments of these nations fail to stop the spread of AIDS, what are the likely consequences for future economic growth in China and India?

2. In 1989, a massive protest against political repression in China was halted by the government's massacre of more than 150 individuals at Tiananmen Square in Beijing. What impact do you think that episode had on foreign investment and growth in China during the years immediately thereafter?

3. Most of the advances in institutions in China have come in the cities rather than in the countryside. Indeed, local officials in farming villages actively redistribute wealth among villagers to keep the distribution of income among local farmers roughly equal. Thus a farmer's success or failure with his crops has little impact on his family's standard of living. Given these facts, where do you think the economic growth in China has occurred over the past thirty years, in the cities or on the farms? Explain.

4. Explain how the following factors will influence India's ability to succeed in a highly competitive, rapidly changing global marketplace: (a) an educational system that is largely state-operated and that emphasizes job security for teachers and professors; (b) a transportation infrastructure that is largely antiquated and in disrepair; and (c) a political system that is adept at protecting favored constituents from competition and handing out favors that have concentrated benefits and widely dispersed costs.

Taken from *The Economics of Macro Issues,* Fourth Edition
by Roger LeRoy Miller and Daniel K. Benjamin

CHAPTER 8

The Opposition to Globalization

The period since the early 1990s has been a time of great change on the international trade front. The North American Free Trade Agreement (NAFTA), for example, substantially reduced **trade barriers** among citizens of Canada, the United States, and Mexico. On a global scale, the Uruguay Round of the General Agreement on Tariffs and Trade (GATT) was ratified by 117 nations including the United States. Under the terms of this agreement, the **World Trade Organization (WTO),** whose membership now numbers more than 150, replaced GATT, and **tariffs** were cut worldwide. Agricultural **subsidies** were also reduced, and patent protections were extended. The WTO has also established arbitration boards to settle international disputes over trade issues.

THE GAINS FROM TRADE

Many economists believe that both NAFTA and the agreements reached during the Uruguay Round were victories not only for free trade and **globalization** (the integration of national economies into an international economy) but also for the citizens of the participating nations. Nevertheless, many noneconomists, particularly politicians, opposed these agreements, so it is important to understand what is beneficial about NAFTA, the Uruguay Round, the WTO, and free trade and globalization.

Voluntary trade creates new **wealth.** In voluntary trade, both parties in an exchange gain. They give up something of lesser value to them in return for something of greater value to them. In this sense, exchanges are always unequal. But it is this unequal nature of exchange that is the source of the increased **productivity** and higher wealth that occur whenever trade takes place. When we engage in exchange, what we give up is worth less than what we get—if this were not true, we would not have traded. What is true for us is also true for our trading partner, meaning that the partner is better off, too. (Of course, sometimes after an exchange, you may believe that you were mistaken about the value of what you just received—this is called *buyer's remorse,* but it does not affect our discussion.)

Free trade encourages individuals to employ their talents and abilities in the most productive manner possible and to exchange the fruits of their efforts. The **gains from trade** arise from one of the fundamental ideas in economics: A nation gains from doing what it can do best *relative to other nations,* that is, by specializing in those endeavors in which it has a **comparative advantage.** Trade encourages individuals and nations to discover ways to specialize so that they can become more productive and enjoy higher incomes. Increased productivity and the subsequent increase in the rate of **economic growth** are exactly what the signatories of the Uruguay Round and NAFTA sought—and are obtaining—by reducing trade barriers and thus increasing globalization.

KEEPING THE COMPETITION OUT

Despite the enormous gains from exchange, some people (sometimes a great many of them) routinely oppose free trade, particularly in the case of international trade. This opposition comes in many guises, but they all basically come down to one: When our borders are open to trade with other nations, this exposes some individuals and businesses in our nation to more **competition.** Most firms and workers hate competition, and who can blame them? After all, if a firm can keep competitors out, its **profits** are sure to stay the same or even rise. Also, if workers can prevent competition from other sources, they can enjoy higher wages and perhaps a larger selection of jobs. So the real source of most opposition to globalization is that the opponents of trade dislike the competition that comes with it. This position is not immoral or unethical, but it is not altruistic or noble, either. It is based on self-interest, pure and simple.

Opposition to globalization is nothing new, by the way. In the twentieth century, it culminated most famously in the Smoot-Hawley Tariff Act of 1930. This federal statute was a classic example of **protectionism**—an effort to protect a subset of U.S. producers at the expense of consumers and other producers. It included tariff schedules for over twenty thousand products, raising taxes on affected imports by an average of 52 percent.

The Smoot-Hawley Tariff Act encouraged so-called *beggar-thy-neighbor* policies by the rest of the world. Such policies are an attempt to improve (a portion of) one's domestic economy at the expense of foreign countries' economies. In this case, tariffs were imposed to discourage imports in the hope that domestic import-competing industries would benefit. France, the Netherlands, Switzerland and the United Kingdom, soon adopted beggar-thy-neighbor policies to counter the American ones. The result was a massive reduction in international trade. According to many economists, this caused a worldwide worsening of the Great Depression.

Opponents of globalization sometimes claim that beggar-thy-neighbor policies really do benefit the United States by protecting import-competing industries. In general, this claim is not correct. It is true that *some* Americans benefit from such policies, but two large groups of Americans lose. First, the purchasers of imports and import-competing goods suffer from the higher prices and reduced selection of goods and suppliers caused by tariffs and import **quotas**. Second, the decline in imports caused by protectionism also causes a decline in *exports,* thereby harming firms and workers in these industries. This result follows directly from one of the fundamental propositions in international trade: *In the long run, imports are paid for by exports.* This proposition simply states that when one country buys goods and services from the rest of the world (imports), the rest of the world eventually wants goods from that country (exports) in exchange. Given this fundamental proposition, a corollary becomes obvious: *Any restriction on imports leads to a reduction in exports.* Thus any extra business for import-competing industries gained as a result of tariffs or quotas means at least as much business *lost* for exporting industries.

THE ARGUMENTS AGAINST GLOBALIZATION

Opponents of globalization often raise a variety of objections in their efforts to reduce it. For example, it is sometimes claimed that foreign companies engage in **dumping,** which is selling their goods in the United States "below cost." The first question to ask when such charges are made is, below *whose* cost? Clearly, if the foreign firm is selling in the United States, it must be offering the good for sale at a price that is at or below the costs of U.S. firms; otherwise it could not induce Americans to buy it. But the ability of individuals or firms to obtain goods at lower cost is one of the *benefits* of free trade, not one of its harmful aspects.

What about claims that import sales are taking place at prices below the foreign company's costs? This amounts to arguing that the owners of the foreign company are voluntarily giving some of their wealth to us, namely, the difference between their costs and the (lower) price they charge us. It is possible, though unlikely, that they might wish to do this, perhaps because this could be the cheapest way of getting us to try a product that we would not otherwise purchase. But even supposing it is true, why would we want to refuse this gift? As a nation, we are richer if we accept it. Moreover, it is a gift that will be offered for only a short time: There is no point in selling at prices below cost unless the seller hopes to soon raise the price profitably above cost!

Another argument sometimes raised against globalization is that the goods are produced abroad using "unfair" labor practices (such as the use of child labor) or production processes that do not meet U.S. environmental standards. Such charges are sometimes true. But we must remember two things here. First, although we may find the use of child labor (or perhaps sixty-hour workweeks with no overtime pay) objectionable, such practices were at one time commonplace in the United States. They were common here for the same reason they are currently practiced abroad: The people involved were (or are) too poor to do otherwise. Some families in developing nations cannot survive unless all family members contribute. As unfortunate as this situation is, if we insist on imposing our values and attitudes—shaped in part by our extraordinarily high wealth—on peoples whose wealth is far lower than ours, we run the risk of making them worse off even as we think we are helping them.

Similar considerations apply to environmental standards. Individuals' and nations' willingness to pay for environmental quality is very much shaped by their wealth. Environmental quality is a **normal good;** this means that people who are rich (such as Americans) want to consume more of it per capita than people who are poor. Insisting that other nations meet environmental standards that we find acceptable is much like insisting that they wear the clothes we wear, use the modes of transportation we prefer, and consume the foods we like. The few people who can afford it will indeed be living in the style to which we are accustomed, but most people in developing countries will not be able to afford anything like that style.

There is one important exception to this argument. When foreign air or water pollution is generated near enough to our borders (for example, in Mexico or Canada) to cause harm to Americans, good public policy presumably dictates that we seek to treat that pollution as though it were being generated inside our borders.

Our point is not that foreign labor or environmental standards are, or should be, irrelevant to Americans. Instead, our point is that achieving high standards of either is costly, and trade restrictions are unlikely to be the most efficient or effective way to achieve them. Just as important, labor standards and environmental standards are all too often raised as smokescreens to hide the real motive: keeping the competition out.

WHY ARE ANTITRADE MEASURES PASSED?

If globalization is beneficial and restrictions on trade are generally harmful, how does legislation such as the Smoot-Hawley Tariff Act and other restrictions on international trade ever get passed? The explanation is that because foreign competition often affects a narrow and specific import-competing industry, such as textiles, shoes, or automobiles, trade restrictions are crafted to benefit a narrow, well-defined group of economic agents. For example, limits on imports of Japanese automobiles in the 1980s chiefly benefited the Big Three automakers in this country: General Motors, Ford, and Chrysler. Similarly, long-standing quotas that limit imports of sugar benefit a handful of large U.S. sugar producers. Because of the concentrated benefits that accrue when Congress votes in favor of trade restrictions, sufficient funds can be raised in those industries to aggressively lobby members of Congress to impose those restrictions.

The eventual reduction in exports that must follow is normally spread throughout all export industries. Consequently, no specific group of workers, managers, or shareholders in export industries will be motivated to contribute funds to lobby Congress to reduce international trade restrictions. Furthermore, although consumers of imports and import-competing goods lose due to trade restrictions, they, too, are typically a diffuse group of individuals, none of whom will be greatly affected individually by any particular import restriction. This simultaneous existence of concentrated benefits and diffuse costs led Mark Twain to observe long ago that the free traders win the arguments but the **protectionists** win the votes.

Of course, the protectionists don't win *all* the votes—after all, about one-seventh of the U.S. economy is based on international trade. Despite the opposition to free trade that comes from many quarters, its benefits to the economy as a whole are so great that it is unthinkable that we might do away with international trade altogether. Both economic theory and empirical evidence clearly indicate that on balance, Americans will be better off with freer trade achieved through such developments as NAFTA and the WTO.

FOR CRITICAL ANALYSIS

1. For a number of years, Japanese automakers voluntarily limited the number of cars they exported to the United States. What effect do you think this had on Japanese imports of U.S. cars and U.S. exports of goods and services *other than* automobiles?

2. Until a few years ago, U.S. cars exported to Japan had the driver controls on the left side (as in the United States). The Japanese, however, drive on the left side of the road, so Japanese cars sold in Japan have the driver controls on the right side. Suppose the Japanese tried to sell their cars in the United States with the driver controls on the right side. What impact would this likely have on their sales in this country? Do you think the unwillingness of U.S. carmakers to put the driver controls on the "correct" side for exports to Japan had any effect on their sales of cars in that country?

3. Keeping in mind the key propositions of globalization outlined in this chapter, what is the likely impact of international trade restrictions on the following variables in the United States: employment, the **unemployment rate, real GDP,** and the **price level?** Explain your responses.

PART THREE
Supply and Demand

C h a p t e r 9

SEX, BOOZE, AND DRUGS

Before 1914, cocaine was legal in this country; today it is not. Alcoholic beverages are legal in the United States today; from 1920 to 1933, they were not. Prostitution is legal in Nevada today; in the other forty-nine states, it is not.[1] All these goods—sex, booze, and drugs—have at least one thing in common: The consumption of each brings together a willing seller with a willing buyer, creating an act of mutually beneficial exchange (at least in the opinion of the parties involved). Partly because of this property, attempts to proscribe the consumption of these goods have met with less than spectacular success and have yielded some peculiar patterns of production, distribution, and usage. Let's see why.

When the government seeks to prevent voluntary exchange, it must generally decide whether to go after the seller or the buyer. In most cases—and certainly where sex, booze, and drugs are concerned—the government targets sellers because this is where the authorities get the most benefit from their enforcement dollars. A cocaine dealer, even a small retail pusher, often supplies dozens or even hundreds of users each day, as did speakeasies (illegal saloons) during Prohibition; a hooker typically services three to ten "tricks" per day. By incarcerating the supplier, the police can prevent several, or even several hundred, transactions from taking place, which is usually much more cost-effective than going after the buyers one by one. It is not that the police ignore the consumers of illegal goods; indeed, sting operations, in which the police pose as illicit sellers, often make the headlines. Nevertheless, most enforcement efforts focus on the supply side, and so shall we.

---

1. These statements are not entirely correct. Even today, cocaine may be obtained legally by prescription from a physician. Prostitution in Nevada is legal only in counties that have chosen to permit it. Finally, some counties in the United States remain "dry," prohibiting the sale of beer, wine, and distilled spirits.

Law enforcement activities directed against the suppliers of illegal goods increase the suppliers' operating costs. The risks of fines, jail sentences, and possibly even violence become part of the costs of doing business and must be taken into account by existing and potential suppliers. Some entrepreneurs will leave the business, turning their talents to other activities; others will resort to clandestine (and costly) means to hide their operations from the police; still others will restrict the circle of buyers with whom they are willing to deal to minimize the chances that a customer is a cop. Across the board, the costs of operation are higher, and at any given price, less of the product will be available. There is a reduction in supply, and the result is a higher price for the good.

This increase in price is, in a sense, exactly what the enforcement officials are after, for the consumers of sex, booze, and drugs behave according to the **law of demand:** The higher the price of a good, the lower the amount consumed. So the immediate impact of the enforcement efforts against sellers is to reduce the consumption of the illegal good by buyers. There are, however, some other effects.

First, because the good in question is illegal, people who have a **comparative advantage** in conducting illegal activities will be attracted to the business of supplying (and perhaps demanding) the good. Some may have an existing criminal record and are relatively unconcerned about adding to it. Others may have developed skills in evading detection and prosecution while engaged in other criminal activities. Some may simply look at the illegal activity as another means of thumbing their noses at society. The general point is that when an activity is made illegal, people who are good at being criminals are attracted to that activity.

Illegal contracts are usually not enforceable through legal channels (and even if they were, few suppliers of illegal goods would be foolish enough to complain to the police about not being paid for their products). So buyers and sellers of illegal goods must frequently resort to private methods of contract enforcement, which often entails violence.[2] Hence people who are relatively good at violence are attracted to illegal activities and have greater **incentives** to employ their talents. This is one reason why the murder rate in America rose to record levels during Prohibition and then dropped sharply when liquor was again made legal. It also helps explain why the number of drug-related murders soared during the 1980s and why drive-by shootings became commonplace in many drug-infested cities. The Thompson submachine gun of the 1930s and

---

2. Fundamentally, violence—such as involuntary incarceration—also plays a key role in the government's enforcement of legal contracts. We often do not think of it as violence, of course, because it is usually cushioned by constitutional safeguards and procedural rules.

the MAC-10 machine gun of the 1980s were just low-cost means of contract enforcement.

The attempts of law enforcement officials to drive sellers of illegal goods out of business have another effect. Based on recent wholesale prices, $50,000 worth of pure heroin weighs about one pound; $50,000 worth of marijuana weighs about 100 pounds. As any drug smuggler can tell you, hiding a pound of contraband is a lot easier than hiding 100 pounds. Thus to avoid detection and prosecution, suppliers of the illegal good have an incentive to deal in the more valuable versions of their product, which for drugs and booze mean the more potent versions. Bootleggers during Prohibition concentrated on hard liquor rather than beer and wine; even today, moonshine typically has roughly twice the alcohol content of legal hard liquor such as bourbon, scotch, or vodka. After narcotics became illegal in this country in 1914, importers switched from the milder opium to its more valuable, more potent, and more addictive derivative, heroin.

The move to the more potent versions of illegal commodities is enhanced by enforcement activities directed against users. Not only do users, like suppliers, find it easier (cheaper) to hide the more potent versions, but there is also a change in relative prices due to user penalties. Typically, the law has lower penalties for using an illegal substance than for distributing it. Within each category (use or sale), however, there is commonly the same penalty regardless of value per unit. For example, during Prohibition, a bottle of wine and a bottle of more expensive, more potent hard liquor were equally illegal. Today, the possession of one gram of 90 percent pure cocaine brings the same penalty as the possession of one gram of 10 percent pure cocaine. Given the physical quantities, there is a fixed cost (the legal penalty) associated with being caught, regardless of value per unit (and thus potency) of the substance. Hence the structure of legal penalties raises the relative price of less potent versions, encouraging users to substitute more potent versions—heroin instead of opium, hashish instead of marijuana, hard liquor instead of beer.

Penalties against users also encourage a change in the nature of usage. Prior to 1914, cocaine was legal in this country and was used openly as a mild stimulant, much as people today use caffeine. (Cocaine was even an ingredient in the original formulation of Coca-Cola.) This type of usage—small, regular doses over long time intervals—becomes relatively more expensive when the substance is made illegal. Extensive usage (small doses spread over time) is more likely to be detected by the authorities than intensive usage (a large dose consumed at once), simply because possession time is longer and the drug must be accessed more frequently. Thus when a substance is made illegal, there is an incentive for consumers to switch toward usage that is more intensive. Rather than ingesting cocaine orally in the form of a highly diluted liquid solution, as was commonly done before 1914, people switched to snorting or injecting it. During Prohibition, people dispensed with cocktails before dinner each night; instead, on the less frequent occasions when they drank, they more often drank to get drunk. The same phenomenon is observed today. People under the age of twenty-one consume alcoholic beverages less frequently than people over the age of twenty-one. But when they do drink, they are more likely to drink to get drunk.

Not surprisingly, the suppliers of illegal commodities are reluctant to advertise their wares openly; the police are as capable of reading billboards and watching TV as potential customers are. Suppliers are also reluctant to establish easily recognized identities and regular places and hours of business because to do so raises the chance of being caught by the police. Information about the price and quality of products being sold goes underground, often with unfortunate effects for consumers.

With legal goods, consumers have several means of obtaining information. They can learn from friends, advertisements, and personal experience. When goods are legal, they can be trademarked for identification. The trademark cannot legally be copied, and the courts protect it. Given such easily identified brands, consumers can be made aware of the quality and price of each. If their experience does not meet expectations, they can assure themselves of no further contact with the unsatisfactory product by never buying that brand again.

When a general class of products becomes illegal, there are fewer ways to obtain information. Brand names are no longer protected by law, so falsification of well-known brands ensues. When products do not meet expectations, it is more difficult (costly) for consumers to punish suppliers. Frequently, the result is degradation of and uncertainty about product quality. The consequences for consumers of the illegal goods are often unpleasant and sometimes fatal.

Consider prostitution. In Nevada counties where prostitution is legal, the prostitutes are required to register with the local authorities, and they generally conduct their business in well-established bordellos. These establishments advertise openly and rely heavily on repeat business. Health officials test the prostitutes weekly for venereal disease and monthly for AIDS. Contrast this with other areas of the country, where prostitution is illegal. Suppliers are generally streetwalkers because a fixed, physical location is too easy for the police to detect and raid. Suppliers change locations frequently to reduce harassment by police. Repeat business is reported to be minimal; frequently, customers have never seen the prostitute before and never will again.

The difference in outcomes is striking. In Nevada, the spread of venereal disease by legal prostitutes is estimated to be almost nonexistent; to date, none of the registered prostitutes in Nevada has tested positive for AIDS. By contrast, in some major cities outside Nevada, the incidence of venereal disease among prostitutes is estimated to be near 100 percent. In Miami, one study found that 19 percent of all incarcerated prostitutes tested positive for AIDS; in Newark, New Jersey, 52 percent of the prostitutes tested were infected with the AIDS virus, and about half of the prostitutes in Washington, D.C., and New York City are also believed to be carrying the AIDS virus. Because of the lack of reliable information in markets for illegal goods, customers frequently do not know exactly what they are getting; as a result, they sometimes get more than they bargained for.

Consider alcohol and drugs. Today, alcoholic beverages are heavily advertised to establish their brand names and are carried by reputable dealers. Customers can readily punish suppliers for any deviation from the expected potency or quality by withdrawing their business, telling their friends, or even bringing a lawsuit. Similar circumstances prevailed before 1914 in this country for the hundreds of products containing opium or cocaine.

During Prohibition, consumers of alcohol often did not know exactly what they were buying or where to find the supplier the next day if they were dissatisfied. Fly-by-night operators sometimes adulterated liquor with far more lethal methyl alcohol. In tiny concentrations, this made watered-down booze taste like it had more kick, but in only slightly higher concentrations, the methyl alcohol blinded or even killed the unsuspecting consumer. Even in "reputable" speakeasies (those likely to be in business at the same location the next day), bottles bearing the labels of high-priced foreign whiskeys were refilled repeatedly with locally (and illegally) produced rotgut until their labels wore off.

In the 1970s, more than one purchaser of what was reputed to be high-potency Panama Red or Acapulco Gold marijuana ended up with low-potency pot heavily loaded with stems, seeds, and maybe even oregano. Buyers of cocaine must worry about not only how much the product has been cut along the distribution chain but also what has been used to cut it. In recent years, the purity of cocaine at the retail level has ranged between 10 percent and 95 percent; for heroin, the degree of purity has ranged from 5 percent to 50 percent. Cutting agents can turn out to be any of various sugars, local anesthetics, or amphetamines; on occasion, rat poison has been used.

We noted earlier that the legal penalties for the users of illegal goods encourage them to use more potent forms and to use them more intensively. These facts and the uncertain quality and potency of the illegal products yield a deadly combination. During Prohibition, the death rate from acute alcohol poisoning (due to overdose) was more than thirty times higher than today. In 1927 alone, twelve thousand people died from acute alcohol poisoning, and many thousands more were blinded or killed by contaminated booze. Today, about four thousand people a year die as a direct result of consuming either cocaine or heroin. Of that total, it is estimated, roughly 80 percent die from either an overdose caused by an unexpectedly potent product or an adverse reaction to the material used to cut the drug. Clearly, *caveat emptor* ("let the buyer beware") is a warning to be taken seriously if one is consuming an illegal product.

We noted at the beginning of this chapter that one of the effects of making a good illegal is to raise its price. One might well ask, by how much? During the early 1990s, the federal government was spending about $2 billion a year in its efforts to stop the importation of cocaine from Colombia. One study concluded that these efforts had hiked the price of cocaine by 4 percent relative to what it would have been had the federal government done nothing to interdict cocaine imports. The study estimated that the cost of raising the price of cocaine an additional 2 percent would be $1 billion per year. More recently, Nobel Laureate Gary Becker and his colleagues have estimated that America's war on drugs costs at least $100 billion per year. And the results? The prices of heroin and cocaine are at record-low levels.

The government's efforts to halt imports of marijuana have had some success, presumably because that product is easier to detect than cocaine. Nevertheless, suppliers have responded by cultivating marijuana domestically instead of importing it or by bringing it in across the relatively open U.S.-Canadian border rather than from elsewhere. The net effect has been an estimated tenfold increase in potency due to the superior farming techniques available in this country and Canada, as well as the use of genetic bioengineering to improve strains.

A few years ago, most states and the federal government began restricting sales of cold medicines containing pseudoephedrine because that ingredient was widely used for making the illegal stimulant methamphetamine in home laboratories. The restrictions succeeded in sharply curtailing home production of "meth." They also led to a huge increase in imports of a far more potent version of meth from Mexico. Overall, it is estimated that neither consumption of nor addiction to methamphetamine was reduced by the restrictions. But overdoses from the drug rose sharply because of the greater purity of the imports.

Consider also the government's efforts to eliminate the consumption of alcohol during the 1920s and 1930s. They failed so badly that the Eighteenth Amendment, which put Prohibition in place, was the first (and so far the only) constitutional amendment ever to be repealed. As for prostitution, it is reputed to be "the oldest profession" and by all accounts continues to flourish today, even in Newark and Miami.

The government's inability to halt the consumption of sex, booze, or drugs does not mean that those efforts have failed. Indeed, the impact of these efforts is manifested in their consequences, ranging from tainted drugs and alcohol to disease-ridden prostitutes. The message instead is that when the government attempts to prevent mutually beneficial exchange, even its best efforts are unlikely to meet with spectacular success.

DISCUSSION QUESTIONS

1. The federal government currently taxes alcohol on the basis of the 100-proof gallon. (Alcohol that is 100 proof is 50 percent pure ethyl alcohol; most hard liquor sold is 80 proof, or 40 percent ethyl alcohol, whereas wine is usually about 24 proof, and most beer is 6 to 10 proof.) How would alcohol consumption patterns change if the government taxed alcohol strictly on the basis of volume rather than also taking its potency into account?

2. During Prohibition, some speakeasy operators paid bribes to ensure that the police did not raid them. Would you expect the quality of the liquor served in such speakeasies to be higher or lower than in those that did not pay bribes? Would you expect to find differences (for example, with regard to income levels) among the customers patronizing the two types of speakeasies?

3. The markets for prostitution in Nevada and New Jersey have two important differences: (1) Prostitutes in New Jersey face higher costs because of government efforts to prosecute them, and (2) customers in New Jersey face higher risks of contracting diseases from prostitutes because the illegal nature of the business makes reliable information about product quality much more costly to obtain. Given these facts, in which state would you expect the price of prostitution services to be higher? Which state would have the higher amount of services consumed (adjusted for population differences)? Explain your answer.

4. According to the surgeon general of the United States, nicotine is the most addictive drug known to humanity, and cigarette smoking kills perhaps 300,000 to 400,000 people a year in the United States. Why isn't tobacco illegal in America?

Chapter 10

KIDNEYS FOR SALE

This year, more than seven thousand Americans will die waiting for an organ transplant. They will not die because physicians are unable to transplant organs or because their health insurance does not cover the cost of the transplant. They will die because since 1984, it has been against federal law to pay for human organs.[1] It is lawful to pay a man for his sperm, a woman for her eggs, and members of either gender for their blood. It is even lawful to donate an organ or to receive one as a gift. And it is certainly legal to pay the surgeons who perform the transplants. It is even lawful for hospitals to make a profit on organ transplants performed in their operating rooms. But it is against the law for you to sell a cornea or a kidney or a lobe of your liver; it is even unlawful for your loved ones to benefit from the harvesting of any of your organs after your death. And so seven thousand people die every year, waiting in vain for someone to donate an organ to them.

The transplantation of human body parts is not new. The first cornea was successfully transplanted in Austria in 1905. The first successful kidney transplant (between identical twins) was conducted in Boston in 1954. Since then, successful transplants of the pancreas, liver, heart, lung, hand, and even face have been performed. Indeed, there are now thirty-seven different organs and types of human tissues that can be transplanted. None of this is cheap. In the United States, a kidney transplant costs about $250,000 on average, a liver transplant runs $520,000, and a heart transplant costs an average of $650,000. But there are services that arrange for international transplants (performed, for example, in India or China) of any of these organs at less than half the price. None of these

---

1. This legislation was originally introduced by Rep. Al Gore (D., Tenn.), who went on to become vice president of the United States (1993–2001).

figures include payment for the organ itself because such payments are illegal in the United States and in most other countries. These astronomical sums are obviously out of the reach of most people. In fact, however, transplants done in the United States are generally not paid for directly by the recipients. For a person under the age of sixty-five with health insurance, private insurance pays for the transplant. For anyone sixty-five or older, the federal Medicare system pays for the transplant. And for people under sixty-five with neither private insurance nor the wealth to pay by themselves, transplants are paid for by the Medicaid system, which is financed jointly by the federal government and the states. (Neither private insurance plans nor Medicare or Medicaid will pay for international transplants, which are generally chosen only by relatively affluent people who are unwilling to wait—or to die waiting.)

Now, to begin our inquiry into the economics of organ transplants, let's consider the case of kidneys. We start here because the technical features of the transplant process have become relatively routine and because we each are born with two kidneys but can get by quite well with only one. In fact, thanks to the technique known as dialysis, humans can actually survive for years without functioning kidneys. In 2009, about eighty thousand people were awaiting kidney transplants in the United States. That same year, ten thousand Americans received transplants from deceased strangers. Another six thousand received a transplant from a living donor (recall that "extra" kidney we each have), usually a close friend or relative. Tragically, five thousand of the people waiting for a kidney either died or were dropped from the list because they had become too sick to qualify for a transplant. Another two thousand died that year waiting for a liver, heart, lung, or other critical organ. Could they be saved, if it were as lawful to pay for kidneys as it is to pay for the surgeons who transplant them? Or would a market for kidneys ultimately become a black market, relying on "donated" organs removed from unwilling victims by unscrupulous brokers motivated by cash rather than kindness? That is precisely the nexus of the debate over whether we should permit people (or the relatives of just-deceased donors) to be remunerated for lifesaving organ donations.

First things first: Surely we cannot object to a market for organs because the act of donating a kidney or the lobe of a liver is potentially hazardous to the donor. After all, we currently permit people to undergo such risks under the current system with *no* monetary compensation. If it is safe enough to allow friends or family to donate without payment, why is it too risky for someone to give up a kidney or part of his or her liver in return for money?

There are, of course, many other contentious issues. To start exploring them, let's look first at a nation where it *is* legal to pay people for human organs: Iran, which just happens to have the highest living-donor rate in the world, at twenty-three donations per million people. Monetary compensation for organs in Iran has been lawful there since 1988, and in the ensuing decade, Iran eliminated the *entire* backlog of kidney transplant patients, something no other nation has achieved.

Under the Iranian system, a person awaiting a kidney must first seek a suitable, willing donor in his or her family. If none is forthcoming, the person must wait up to six months for a suitable deceased donor. At that point, the potential recipient can apply to the national transplant association for a kidney from a willing donor who is paid for the kidney. The donor receives from the government $1,200 plus a year of fully paid health insurance and a payment of $2,300 to $4,500 from the recipient (or a charity, if the recipient is poor). Donor and recipient are also free to agree to an additional cash payment, although in most cases, the sums already mentioned are sufficient to get the job done. There are still purely altruistic donors in Iran, as well as cadaveric donations from the recently deceased. But it is the payment for organs that has permitted essentially all who seek kidney donations in Iran to get them, and the Iranian system has done so *without* leading to "back alley" donations or to people who are unable to afford a transplant because of the high cost of the organs themselves. Meanwhile, the system has saved the lives of thousands of Iranians.

Many people worry about a system of payment for human transplant because of the possibility that it would yield *involuntary* donors. That is, if there is a market for organs, some unscrupulous brokers might be tempted by profits to knock people over the head and harvest their organs for sale at the highest price. Yet it is generally agreed that the Iranian system has worked for more than twenty years without a hint of any such activities. Perhaps this should not be too surprising, given the medical techniques that have been developed to ensure that the tissue match between organ and recipient is close enough to make transplant feasible. These and other DNA tests can now quickly ascertain with substantial certainty that "organ A" came from voluntary "donor A" rather than from involuntary "donor B."

Indeed, apart from gruesome works of fiction, most of the horror stories about the hazards of allowing markets for human organs are stories about behavior caused by the *lack* of a market for organs. In China, for example, many "transplant tourists" in the past received organs taken from the bodies of the thousands of prisoners who are executed there every year. China insisted that the prisoners' organs were used only with their "consent," a claim that many human rights groups have disputed. But on one point all agree: There were no payments to the prisoners or their surviving relatives. The organs were simply taken (a practice now supposedly halted).

In both the United States and Britain, there have been highly publicized cases of what amount to "body snatching"—removal of organs and other body parts from the recently deceased. Some of these cases involved body parts used in research, while other body parts were intended for sale at a profit. In each of these cases, removal was done without the prior consent of the deceased or the postmortem consent of relatives. But this amounts to theft; it is singularly horrifying, but we must remember that it is theft. Consider another form of stealing: Every year many thousands of senior citizens are defrauded of their hard-earned retirement funds by unscrupulous individuals who masquerade as "financial advisers." Should we make it illegal for anyone to pay for investment advice— or should we devote our efforts to prosecuting and incarcerating the perpetrators of such crimes?

In Pakistan and the Philippines, there were small-scale markets for transplant organs until recently, although Pakistan has now banned the trade in human organs and transplants for non-Filipinos have now been outlawed in that nation. In both countries, there were anecdotes of donors who sold kidneys for $2,000 to $3,000 (about a year's worth of per capita income in either nation), but who later came to regret the transaction because of adverse long-term health effects. But this would be a potential issue even with unpaid donors, and in any nation such as the United States, donors in a market for organs would surely receive at least as much medical and psychological counseling as volunteer donors receive now.

Now, what about the added expense of allowing payments for donated organs? Would this break the budgets of Medicare or Medicaid or empty the coffers of the private insurance companies that pay for the bulk of transplants? In the case of kidneys, we have enough information from elsewhere to say the answer is probably not. In Iran, where per capita income is about $12,000 per year, payments to donors smaller than this amount have been sufficient to clear the market for kidneys. In Pakistan and the Philippines, payments equivalent to a year's worth of per capita income were enough to support a substantial transplant tourist market in both countries.

At almost $50,000 a year, average per capita income in the United States is clearly much higher than in any of these nations, suggesting that payments for kidneys would also have to be much larger to induce a substantial increase in the number of donations. But experts have estimated that even if the payment for a kidney were as much as $100,000, private and public insurance systems (which, as we have noted, pay for almost all of the transplants in the United States) could actually *save* money on many transplants because dialysis (at $70,000 per year) and the other treatments associated with chronic kidney disease are so expensive.

It is true that allowing payments for human organs would almost surely increase the number of transplants each year—indeed, this is the very point. Payments would bring forth more organs, and this would in turn reduce deaths among people waiting for transplants. A payment system would have added costs associated with it: There would be more transplant operations (at $250,000 each for kidneys, for example, plus another, say, $100,000 for each of the organs themselves). Suppose that the payments for kidneys enabled an additional five thousand transplants per year (assuming that the U.S. system would be as successful as the Iranian system in eliminating the excess demand for kidneys). That would yield added costs nationwide of about $1.75 billion (five thousand transplants estimated at $350,000 each).

And there is a second cost: Paying for organs would cause a reduction in the number of altruistic donations. How many fewer there would be we cannot know for sure, but let us make two assumptions to be on the safe side. First, we assume that there would be *no* altruistic donations from living donors under a payment system. Second, we assume that the relatives of all deceased donors would insist on payment. Together these assumptions imply there would be an added expense of $100,000 on each of the sixteen thousand kidney transplants performed under the current system. The added cost here would be $1.6 billion a year, which, when added to the $1.75 billion cost of the new transplants, yields a total added annual cost of $3.35 billion for the organ payment system.

In return for this sum, we would surely recoup some savings from the dialysis system, because at least five thousand people a year would no longer be on dialysis at $70,000 per year—they would instead have a kidney to do that work for them. Moreover, the current three- to four-year delay on kidney transplants would be sharply reduced, generating additional savings. But far more important, we would be saving the lives of five thousand people every year, at a cost per life saved of but $600,000— and this number does not count any of the savings from reduced dialysis treatments.

All these calculations seem a callous way to view a human life. But by the standards of medical care of today, allowing payments for human organs is almost surely a safe and remarkably cheap way to alleviate needless suffering and save thousands of lives every year. And once this is clear, aren't the truly callous people those who would deprive human beings of that opportunity?

DISCUSSION QUESTIONS

1. Why might the owners of the private insurance companies that pay for most organ transplants be in favor of a system that prohibits paying for a donated organ? Should the taxpayers of the United States, who ultimately cover the cost of Medicare and Medicaid transplants, similarly be opposed to paying for donated organs?

2. If payment for organs drives up the financial costs of transplants, is it possible that private insurance companies, and even Medicare and Medicaid, might tighten their standards for transplants so as to reduce the number of transplants each year? If they do, who would gain and who would lose compared to the current system?

3. The average waiting time on transplant lists is three to four years for kidneys (although this is expected to rise sharply, due to the rising incidence of diabetes, a major cause of kidney damage). Many of these people waiting must undergo dialysis, at a cost of $70,000 per year, paid for by private insurance, Medicare, or Medicaid. Suppose that if payment for organs were permitted, the transplant waiting time were shortened by three years, and that for the average patient, the result was eighteen months less on dialysis. At what price for a kidney would a system of paying for organs be a "break-even" proposition for insurers? Show all calculations, and explain your reasoning.

4. The United States currently has an "opt-in" system for organ donations from the deceased: People must explicitly choose postmortem donation ahead of time (as when they obtain their driver's licenses). Many other nations have "opt-out" systems: A desire to donate postmortem is presumed to exist unless an individual explicitly chooses ahead of time *not* to permit donation. How—if at all—would a shift to an opt-out system likely change the supply of cadaveric (postmortem) donations?

Chapter 11

WHEN HIGH PRICES
ARE LOW PRICES

Every few years, some important commodity, such as gasoline, electricity, or food, experiences a spike in prices. Reporters examine such price spikes and plaster newspapers, magazines, and Web sites with the appropriate headlines—sometimes day after day. Television commentators interview frustrated and worried Americans who proffer the expected negative reaction to the higher prices of essential items in their budgets. The world, it would seem, is coming to an end.

Let's just take one often-in-the-press example: gasoline prices. The authors of the book you are reading are old enough to remember the TV interviews that ensued when the price of gas first hit the unprecedented level of $1 per gallon, back in 1980. The same sorts of interviews occurred when the price of a gallon of gas broke the $2 barrier, early in 2005. Not surprisingly, virtually the same types of interviews occurred when the price of a gallon of gas rose to $3 in 2006 and then to $4 in the summer of 2008. At each point in time, everyone interviewed had the same response, even though years had passed between the price spikes: "I guess I'll just have to stop driving." "I'm going to get a bike." "I'm selling my big car and getting a small one." And of course, each time there was an accompanying story about how record numbers of people were (or soon would be) flocking to their neighborhood motor scooter dealerships.

If we wish to analyze sensibly the effects of higher prices on the quantity demanded and the quantity supplied of any good or service, we can rely neither on what journalists report nor on what Americans say when they are interviewed. After all, what is important is not what people say but what they do. As economists, we best understand consumers by their **revealed preferences.** Similarly, business owners are best understood by their actions, not their words. What people do is reflected in how much they actually buy of any good or service after its price changes—not by their complaints to a TV reporter or what they post on their blog or on Facebook or MySpace or Twitter.

For demand and supply analysis, the relevant price is the price *relative to* all other prices, because people's decisions are based on **relative prices,** not **nominal prices.** The latter simply tell us the number of pieces of paper (dollar bills) we must hand over for a good. Nominal prices tell us nothing about the real sacrifice (measured in terms of goods or our labor services) that we must make to obtain those goods. Relative prices, in contrast, tell us the real sacrifice involved in acquiring a good, because they tell us how much of other goods we must sacrifice.

Said another way, we have to separate the rise in the general price level, called **inflation,** from the rise in the nominal price of a particular good or service. If *all* nominal prices went up 3 percent in a given year, there would be no change in relative prices, but this inflation of 3 percent per year would not change the real sacrifice entailed in acquiring any particular good. In the real world, even during periods of inflation, some prices go up faster than others and some prices even go down— witness the price of computing power, of DVD players, and of MP3 players. Nevertheless, if we want to predict people's behavior, we must know what has happened to the *relative* price of a good, and to determine this, we must adjust for inflation.

Now let's get back to our example of gasoline prices. Your grandparents might be able to talk about buying gas for 30 cents a gallon (its typical nominal price most of the time between 1956 and 1964). Today, what you pay in dollars per gallon is many times that level. People still drive nonetheless; indeed, the use of gasoline for cars and trucks in the United States is roughly *triple* what it was when the nominal price of gas was only 30 cents. Something must have happened. The most important is a general rise in all nominal prices, including gasoline prices.

In the summer of 2008, the price of gasoline edged beyond $4 per gallon. Then-presidential candidate Barack Obama argued that the government should intervene on gas prices to "give families some relief." Two-thirds of American voters at that time said they thought that the price of gas was "an extremely important political issue." (Of course, when gas prices started tumbling in the fall of 2008, there were not many front-page articles or TV interviews with happy consumers. And the politicians simply became silent on this subject.) Consider, though, that at its nominal price at the end of 2008, the *relative* price of gas was lower than it had been in 1980, after correcting for overall inflation. For many people, this is a shocking revelation. But correcting for inflation is absolutely essential if you want to sensibly analyze the price of anything over time.

There is something else that we should mention here, particularly relevant when thinking about the real burden of gasoline. People are becoming more productive over time, because they are getting better educated and because ongoing technological change enables us to produce more with a given input of our time. As a result of this higher productivity, U.S. consumers' **disposable income** generally rises from one year to the next—and rises on average over longer periods of time. As Americans become richer on average, they are financially able to handle even higher relative prices of the items they wish to purchase, gasoline included.

To help us understand this point better, researchers Indur Goklany and Jerry Taylor came up with an "affordability index." They compared family income to the price of gas from 1949 to 2008. They arbitrarily set 1960 at an affordability index of 1; relative to this, a higher affordability index number means that something is more affordable. Even when gas was $4.15 per gallon, the affordability gas index was 1.35. In other words, the ratio of the average person's disposable income to the price of gasoline was higher by about 35 percent in 2008 than it was in 1960; gasoline was *more* affordable than it had been back in 1960, when your grandparents were filling up their tanks at 30 cents a gallon—hard to believe for some of us, but true nonetheless. And once gas prices started going down at the end of 2008, the gas affordability index rose even more, passing 2.0.

The quality of gasoline does not change over time. But the quality of many other products does change over time, usually for the better. Often we forget about this crucial aspect when we start comparing prices of a good or service over time. If you ask senior citizens today how much they paid for their first car, you might get prices in the range of $2,000 to $5,000. The average new car today costs around $24,000. By now, of course, you know that if you want to compare these numbers, you must first account for the inflation that has occurred over the time period you are examining. In this case, adjusting for inflation still means that the relative price of a car appears to be about 30 percent higher than it was, say, fifty years ago.

Does that necessarily mean that a car is really 30 percent more expensive than it was in 1960? Probably not. We must take into account improved quality features of cars today compared to those of half a century ago. Today, the average car has the following:

- Computer-controlled antilock power brakes
- Power steering
- Digital radio with CD or MP3 player
- Air conditioning
- Steel-belted radial tires

- Cruise control
- Power windows and locks
- Air bags
- Forty percent better fuel economy

The list of improved and new features is actually much longer. Today, the average car is safer, breaks down less often, needs fewer tune-ups, has a host of amenities that were not even dreamed of fifty years ago, and almost certainly lasts for at least twice as many miles. If you correct for not only inflation but also for these quality increases, the relative price of cars today has almost certainly *fallen* appreciably in the past fifty years, despite the "sticker shock" that you may experience when you go shopping for a new car. That is, appearances to the contrary, the inflation-corrected **constant-quality price** of automobiles is actually lower today than it was five decades ago.

The necessity of adjusting for inflation and quality changes continues to apply even when we are examining goods whose nominal prices have declined over time. A good example is computing power. The nominal price of the average personal computer has gone down in spite of general inflation over the past several decades. These days, a Windows-based desktop computer has an average price of about $550; for a laptop, the average price is around $700. A decade ago, the average machines in each category would have had nominal prices twice as high. You might be tempted to conclude, then, that the price of personal computing has fallen by 50 percent, but you'd be wrong. The price has actually fallen by more than 50 percent.

Why? There are two reasons. First, over the past ten years, the average dollar prices of all goods increased by 30 percent; that is how much overall inflation there has been. That means that the *relative* price of the average computer has fallen by two-thirds, which of course is greater than 50 percent. But even here we are missing something extremely important: The quality of what you are buying—computing power—has skyrocketed. The processor speed of the average computer today is at least ten times greater than it was ten years ago and is increasing exponentially. Moreover, hard drives are bigger; monitors are flat-screen LCDs instead of bulky old cathode ray tubes; laptops are lighter; RAM is larger—so the list of improvements grows. And despite people's frustrations with both the hardware and software of the personal computer today, longtime users can tell you that both are vastly more reliable than they were a decade ago. Thus if you look only at the inflation-corrected decrease in computer prices, you will be underestimating the true decrease in the *relative* price of computers.

The moral of our story is simple. At some point in your education, you learned that "what goes up must come down." Now you know that when it comes to prices, it is often the case that "what goes up has actually gone down." It is a lesson worth keeping in mind if you really want to understand the behavior of consumers and businesses alike.

DISCUSSION QUESTIONS

1. Try to explain why price increases for crude oil, gas, heating oil, electricity, and food are widely reported by the media, yet when these prices decline, there is almost no discussion in the media.

2. Make a list of goods (or services) whose qualities have improved over time to such an extent that the prices do not accurately reflect their real prices, even after adjusting for inflation. Now see if you can come up with a list of items whose quality has systematically *decreased* over time. Can you suggest why it is easier to find examples of the former than it is of the latter?

3. The demand for small-engine motor scooters jumped when the price of gasoline started moving up in the summer of 2008. Make a prediction about the demand for this form of transportation in, say, two years from today. Explain your answer.

4. Explain why you will make more accurate predictions if you focus on the changing incentives people face rather than listening to what they say they are going to do.

Chapter 12

ARE WE RUNNING OUT OF WATER?

If you believe the headlines, humans are about to die of thirst. A few samples should be enough to convince you:

"A World of Thirst" (*U.S. News & World Report*)
"Water Shortages May Lead to War" (*Financial Times*)
"Drying Up" (*The Economist*)
"Water Shortages Could Leave World in Dire Straits" (*USA Today*)

The world, it seems, is running out of water.

But how can this be true? After all, about 71 percent of the earth's surface is covered in water. Lake Michigan alone contains more water than the world's population uses in two years. Even more to the point, the earth is a closed system. Using water does not destroy water. Whether we drink it, flush it, irrigate with it, or even let it evaporate, it comes back to us eventually, just as clean and pure as the raindrops of a spring shower. In fact, every three weeks, enough rain falls to satisfy the water uses of the entire world's population for a year. So what, exactly, is the problem?

Water is the ultimate renewable resource: The act of using it begins the process that returns it to us. But—and this is the crux—water is also *scarce*. That is, having the amount of clean water we want, where we want it, when we want it there, is not free. We must sacrifice other resources to accomplish this. And as the level of economic activity grows, the demand for water grows, and so the costs of consuming water grow.

In this sense, water is no different from any other **scarce good**. If we want more of it, we must sacrifice more of other things to achieve that goal. But what makes water seem different is that unlike, say, broccoli, if we do entirely without it, disastrous things happen in a relatively short period of time. If water gets sufficiently scarce, people may start doing some pretty unpleasant things to each other to ensure that they, rather than their neighbors or enemies, are the ones who end up with it. But before we see if this is really something we should worry about, we had better start by learning a little more about water.

Of the enormous amount of water on the earth's surface, about 97.2 percent is ocean water, which is too saline under normal circumstances to drink or use for irrigation. Another 2.15 percent is polar ice, which is certainly not a very convenient source. Of the remaining 0.65 percent, about 0.62 percent is underground in aquifers and similar geological structures; this groundwater takes hundreds of years to recharge and so is not really a sustainable source of freshwater over the relevant time span. That leaves us with rain.

Fortunately, it rains a lot, and despite the headlines, on a *worldwide* basis, the amount of rainfall doesn't vary much from year to year. About two-thirds of the rain falls on the world's oceans, where almost no one lives. But even so, and even taking into account evaporation and the fact that much of the rain over land quickly runs off into the oceans before it can be captured, there is still a lot of usable rainfall every year. Indeed, there is enough every year to yield 5,700 liters per person—about six times as much as the average person actually consumes. Of course, Mother Nature is not particularly evenhanded in the distribution of this usable rainfall. For example, China gets only 5 percent of it, despite having 20 percent of the world's population. Brazil, Canada, and Russia, which together have 6 percent of the world's population, receive 29 percent of the usable rainfall. And although the United States does pretty well on average, picking up 5 percent of the rain and having about 5 percent of the world's population, there are plenty of differences within our borders. Massive amounts of rain fall in southeastern Alaska and on the mountain slopes of Hawaii, while very little falls in Southern California. But the fact that people routinely choose to locate themselves in places where it does not rain highlights one of the fundamental points of this chapter: Water is an **economic good,** and the distribution and consumption of water are fundamentally economic problems, ones that can be solved in markets, just as other economic problems (such as the provision of food, shelter, and clothing) are solved in markets. To focus clearly on this point, let's examine some of the myths that have grown up around water in recent years.

Myth 1: The planet is drying up. As we have suggested earlier, there is nothing to worry about here. The cheapest (and completely sustainable) source of clean freshwater is rainfall, and roughly 113,000 cubic kilometers (3 quadrillion gallons) of the stuff falls every year on land areas around the world, year in and year out. Although small amounts of this are temporarily stored in plants and animals while they are alive, all of it eventually either recharges groundwater or evaporates, forms clouds, and precipitates—all 113,000 cubic kilometers, year after year. Sometimes, more is in Brazil and less in Sudan, and sometimes more of it inconveniently runs off in floods, but because the earth is a closed system, that water stays with us.

Myth 2: We can save water by flushing less and using less in agriculture. Remember the closed system? That applies to toilets and alfalfa, too. Flushing the toilet does not send the water to the moon. It just sends it through the sewer system to a water treatment plant and eventually into aquifers under the ground or back down on our heads in the form of raindrops. So-called low-flow toilets (and showers) have no effect on the amount of water in existence. (Because they may slightly reduce the amount of water running through water and sewer systems, they may conserve a bit on the amount of resources used in these systems. But there are offsets. Such devices are routinely more costly to produce than regular toilets or shower heads, and they occupy people's time—because of double flushes and longer showers. On balance, besides not "saving" water, there is thus no evidence that such devices conserve resources at all.)

Even agriculture, notorious for consuming an enormous amount of (usually subsidized) water around the world, does not destroy the stuff. Most of the water used by agriculture evaporates or runs off into rivers or soaks into underground aquifers. A small amount is temporarily stored in the crops, but this, soon enough, is consumed by animals or humans and simply returns to the same system that delivers 113,000 cubic kilometers of water onto our heads every year. There is no doubt that all of this use of water in agriculture is costly, because it could be used elsewhere. Moreover, agricultural use of water is generally subsidized by taxpayers. Making farmers pay full market value for water would reduce agricultural use and raise our collective wealth by improving the allocation of resources. But it would not alter the amount of water available.

Having said this, agricultural use of water does present two important economic issues. First, as we just noted, government policies around the world routinely cause water for agriculture to be heavily subsidized. Farmers often pay as little as $10 to $20 per acre-foot (about 325,000 gallons) for water that costs anywhere from $500 to $1,000 per acre to provide to them. Because of this huge subsidy, farmers are no doubt richer, but the losses to society are much greater, meaning that our overall wealth is lower.

Second, we not only subsidize water use for agriculture, but we also routinely forbid farmers to sell or lease their water to other users, especially nonagricultural users. This is a particular problem in the relatively arid

American West, where farmers effectively own most of the rights to surface and groundwater but must "use it or lose it"—if they don't put it to beneficial use on their crops, they lose their rights to it. But often this water would be much more productively "used" if it were left in the streams to help support the spawning and other essential life activities of downstream species, such as trout or salmon. Laws are slowly changing to recognize environmental uses as being "beneficial" uses, but existing restrictions on the use of water still yield lower overall wealth for us.

   Myth 3: Water is different from other goods. Many people seem to think that because it is essential to life, water is somehow different from other goods—or at least that it should be treated differently in some very specific ways. Let's first get rid of the notion that water doesn't obey the laws of demand and supply. In fact, although the demand for water in some uses is relatively inelastic, usage of water in *all* uses responds as predicted by the law of demand—when the price of water goes up, people use less of it. Similarly, although getting water from where it is to where people would like it to be is costly, the law of supply still holds true—when the price of water rises, suppliers of water provide more of it to consumers. Sometimes this process is as simple as diverting a stream or capturing rainfall. Sometimes it is as complicated as using reverse osmosis to convert seawater into freshwater. But even if the production technique is as esoteric as recycling urine into fresh, drinkable water (as is done on the international space station), the fact remains that when water becomes more valuable, people are incredibly ingenious in finding ways to make sure it is available.

   Myth 4: Price controls on water protect low-income consumers. Some people claim that water should *not* be treated like other goods, specifically arguing that the price of water received by suppliers and the price paid by consumers should both be kept down by government decree. This, it is said, will protect people, especially those who are poor, from high water prices and will prevent suppliers from earning "excessive" profits. After all, some 1.1 billion people around the world currently do not have ready access to clean water, which makes an inviting target for anyone who might become a monopoly supplier to substantial numbers of these people.

   It is true that governments can reduce the profits of the suppliers of water (or anything else) by limiting the prices they charge. But in reality, this does not protect consumers, particularly not the poorest consumers. Price controls on water *reduce* the amount supplied and, especially for the poor, generally make consumers worse off. They end up with less water than if prices were allowed to reach equilibrium levels, and they are forced to undergo nonprice rationing schemes (ranging from limited hours of service to getting no clean water at all). In fact, if we examine places around the world where the poor have little or no access to clean water, we find that government efforts to "protect" people from potential suppliers of water are in fact a key source of this lack of access. In Brazil, for example, government limits on private water rates forced a major international water project company to cease operations there, reducing the supply of clean water. In India, the widespread insistence by many local governments that water be provided free of charge has effectively stalled most efforts to improve water distribution in that country. And in China, government price controls have discouraged water utilities from developing new water supplies and from upgrading water distribution systems. Government controls on prices make goods *more* scarce, not less, and it is generally the disadvantaged members of society who suffer the most as a result.

Myth 5: The ocean is too salty to drink. As a practical matter, prolonged consumption of saltwater by species not specifically adapted for it is highly deleterious. But the technology for desalination of seawater is advancing rapidly, and the cost of desalination is falling just as rapidly— more than 95 percent over the past twenty years. In relatively arid parts of the earth (including Southern California) desalination has become price-competitive with other sources of supply, and large-scale desalination plants are in operation around the world.

The process yields highly concentrated brine as a by-product. To avoid damage to ocean species that are sensitive to excess salinity, this brine must be dealt with carefully (dispersed widely) when it is returned to the sea. Nevertheless, this is simply a matter of routine care. Moreover, if local conditions make wide dispersal impractical or expensive, the brine can be evaporated, and the resulting solid materials then either used or disposed of in ordinary landfills. The upshot is that with continued technological progress in desalination, water from the ocean will likely become cheaper than collecting rainfall in large portions of the world. Far from running out of water, people everywhere will then find themselves able to secure it as easily as, well, turning on the tap.

DISCUSSION QUESTIONS

1. How much water do people "need"? Is your answer the same if you have to pay their water bills?

2. Evaluate the following: "Although taxpayers foot the bill for federal water sold to farmers at subsidized prices, they also eat the crops grown with that water. Because the crops are cheaper due to the sub-

sidized water, taxpayers get back exactly what they put in, and so there is no waste from having subsidized water for farmers." Would you give the author of this quote an A or an F in economics? Explain.

3. During the droughts that periodically plague California, farmers in that state are able to purchase subsidized water to irrigate their crops, at the same time that many California homeowners have to pay large fines if they water their lawns. Can you suggest an explanation for this difference in the treatment of two different groups of citizens in the state of California?

4. If allocating water through nonprice means generally harms society, can you suggest why governments often do this?

Chapter 13

THE TRASHMAN
COMETH

Is garbage really different? To answer this question, let us consider a simple hypothetical situation. Suppose a city agreed to provide its residents with all the food they wished to consume, prepared in the manner they specified, and delivered to their homes for a flat, monthly fee that was independent of what or how much they ate. What are the likely consequences of this city food-delivery service? Most likely, people in the city would begin to eat more, because the size of their food bill would be independent of the amount they ate. They would also be more likely to consume lobster and filet mignon rather than fish sticks and hamburger because, again, the cost to them would be independent of their menu selections. Soon the city's food budget would be astronomical, and either the monthly fee or taxes would have to be increased. People from other communities might even begin moving (or at least making extended visits) to the city just to partake of this wonderful service. Within a short time, the city would face a food crisis as it sought to cope with providing an ever-increasing amount of food from a city budget that can no longer handle the financial burden.

If this story sounds silly to you, just change "food delivery" to "garbage pickup"; what we have just described is the way most cities in the country have historically operated their municipal garbage-collection services. The result during the 1990s was the appearance of a garbage crisis, with overflowing landfills, homeless garbage barges, and drinking-water wells said to be polluted with the runoff from trash heaps. This seeming crisis—to the extent it existed—was fundamentally no different from the food crisis just described. The problem was not that almost nobody wants garbage or that garbage can have adverse environmental effects or even that we had too much garbage. The problem lay in that we often do not put prices on garbage in the way we put prices on the goods that generate the garbage and that a strange assortment of participants used a few smelly facts to make things seem worse than they were.

First things first. America produces plenty of garbage each year—about 255 million tons of household and commercial solid waste that has to be burned, buried, or recycled. (That works out to 1,600 pounds per person.) About 33 percent of this is paper; yard waste (such as grass trimmings) accounts for another 13 percent. Plastic accounts for about 20 percent of the volume of material that has to be disposed of, but because plastic is relatively light, it makes up only about 12 percent of the weight. More than 85 million tons of this trash is recycled.

Landfills are the final resting place for most of our garbage, although incineration is also widely used in some areas, particularly in the Northeast, where land values are high. Both methods began falling out of favor with people who lived near these facilities (or might eventually), as NIMBY ("not in my backyard") attitudes spread across the land. Federal, state, and local regulations also made it increasingly difficult to establish new waste disposal facilities or even to keep old ones operating. The cost to open a modern 100-acre landfill rose to an estimated $70 million or more, and the permit process needed to open a new disposal facility soared to seven years in some states. Meanwhile, environmental concerns forced the closure of many landfills throughout the country and prevented others from ever beginning operations. By the early 1990s, all but five states were exporting at least some of their garbage to other states. Today, most of the garbage from some densely populated states in the Northeast ends up in other people's backyards: New Jersey ships garbage to six other states, and New York keeps landfill operators busy in nine states. Across the country, some Americans have wondered where all of the garbage is going to go.

Although the failure of America's cities to price garbage appropriately led to an inefficient amount of the stuff, much of the appearance of a garbage crisis has been misleading. Rubbish first hit the headlines in 1987 when a garbage barge named *Mobro,* headed south with New York City trash, couldn't find a home for its load. As it turns out, the barge operator wanted to change his disposal contract after he sailed; when he tried to conduct negotiations over the radio while under way, operators of likely landfills (mistakenly) suspected he might be carrying toxic waste rather than routine trash. When adverse publicity forced the barge back to New York with its load, many people thought it was a lack of landfill space, rather than poor planning by the barge operator, that was the cause. This notion was reinforced by an odd combination of environmental groups, waste-management firms, and the Environmental Protection Agency (EPA).

The Environmental Defense Fund wanted to start a major campaign to push recycling, and the *Mobro* episode gave things the necessary push.

As one official for the organization noted, "An advertising firm couldn't have designed a better vehicle than a garbage barge." Meanwhile, a number of farsighted waste-management companies had begun loading up on landfill space, taking advantage of new technologies that increased the efficient minimum size of a disposal facility. Looking to get firm contracts for filling this space, the trade group for the disposal industry started pushing the notion that America was running out of dump space. State and local officials who relied on the group's data quickly bought into the new landfills, paying premium prices to do so. The EPA, meanwhile, was studying the garbage problem but without accounting for the fact that its own regulations were causing the efficient scale of landfills to double and even quadruple in size. Thus the EPA merely counted landfills around the country and reported that they were shrinking in number. This was true enough, but what the EPA failed to report was that because landfills were getting bigger much faster than they were closing down, total disposal capacity was *growing* rapidly, not shrinking.

For a while, it seemed that recycling was going to take care of what appeared to be a worsening trash problem. In 1987, for example, old newspapers were selling for as much as $100 per ton (in 2009 dollars), and many municipalities felt that the answer to their financial woes and garbage troubles was at hand. Yet as more communities began putting mandatory recycling laws into effect, the prices for recycled trash began to plummet. Over the next five years, 3,500 communities in more than half the states had some form of mandatory curbside recycling; the resulting increase in the supply of used newsprint meant that communities were soon having to pay to have the stuff carted away. For glass, the story is much the same. The market value of the used material is below the cost of collecting and sorting it. Numerous states have acted to increase the demand for old newsprint by requiring locally published newspapers to have a minimum content of recycled newsprint. Because of these mandates, the recycling rate for newsprint has doubled over the past twenty years, but the current rate of 70 percent is thought by many experts to be about the practical maximum.

Recycling raises significant issues that were often ignored during the early rush to embrace the concept. For example, the production of 100 tons of de-inked fiber from old newsprint produces about 40 tons of sludge that must be disposed of somehow. Although the total volume of material is reduced, the concentrated form of what is left can make it more costly to dispose of properly. Similarly, recycling paper is unlikely to save trees, for most virgin newsprint is made from trees planted expressly for that purpose and harvested as a crop; if recycling increases, many of these trees simply will not be planted. In a study done for Resources for the Future, A. Clark Wiseman concluded, "The likely effect of [newsprint recycling] appears to be smaller, rather than larger, forest inventory." Moreover, most virgin newsprint is made in Canada, using clean hydroelectric power. Makers of newsprint in the United States (the primary customers for the recycled stuff) often use higher-polluting energy such as coal. Thus one potential side effect of recycling is the switch from hydroelectric power to fossil fuels.

Some analysts have argued that we should simply ban certain products. For example, Styrofoam cups have gotten a bad name because they take up more space in landfills than paper hot-drink cups and because Styrofoam remains in the landfill forever. Yet according to a widely cited study by Martin B. Hocking of the University of Victoria in British Columbia, Canada, the manufacture of a paper cup consumes 36 times as much electricity and generates 580 times as much wastewater as the manufacture of a Styrofoam cup. Moreover, as paper degrades underground, it releases methane, a greenhouse gas that may contribute to global climate change. In a similar vein, consider disposable diapers, which have been trashed by their opponents because a week's worth generates 22.2 pounds of post-use waste, whereas a week's worth of reusable diapers generates only 4 ounces. Because disposable diapers already amount to 1 percent of the nation's solid waste, the edge clearly seems to go to reusable cloth diapers. Yet the use of reusable rather than disposable diapers consumes more than three times as many BTUs (British thermal units) of energy and generates ten times as much water pollution. It would seem that the trade-offs that are present when we talk about "goods" are just as prevalent when we discuss "bads" such as garbage.

It also appears that more government regulation of the garbage business is likely to make things worse rather than better, as may be illustrated by the tale of two states, New Jersey and Pennsylvania. A number of years ago, to stop what was described as price gouging by organized crime, New Jersey decided to regulate waste hauling and disposal as a public utility. Once the politicians got involved in the trash business, however, politics very nearly destroyed it. According to Paul Kleindorfer of the University of Pennsylvania, political opposition to passing garbage-disposal costs along to consumers effectively ended investment in landfills. In 1972, there were 331 landfills operating in New Jersey; by 1991, the number had fallen to 50, because the state-regulated fees payable to landfill operators simply didn't cover the rising costs of operation. More than half of the state's municipal solid waste is now exported to neighboring Pennsylvania, in part because only about twenty landfills remain open in New Jersey.

Pennsylvania's situation provides a sharp contrast. The state does not regulate the deals that communities make with landfill and incinerator

THE TRASHMAN COMETH 77

operators; the market takes care of matters instead. For example, despite the state's hands-off policy, tipping fees (the charges for disposing of garbage in landfills) are below the national average in Pennsylvania, effectively limited by competition between disposal facilities. The market seems to be providing the right **incentives;** in one recent year, there were thirty-one pending applications to open landfills in Pennsylvania but only two in New Jersey, despite the fact that New Jersey residents are paying the highest disposal rates in the country to ship garbage as far away as Ohio and Georgia.

Ultimately, two issues must be solved when it comes to trash. First, what do we do with it once we have it? Second, how do we reduce the amount of it that we have? As hinted at by the Pennsylvania story and illustrated further by developments elsewhere in the country, the market mechanism can answer both questions. The fact of the matter is that in many areas of the country, population densities are high and land is expensive. Hence a large amount of trash is produced, and it is expensive to dispose of locally. In contrast, there are some areas of the country where there are relatively few people around to produce garbage, where land for disposal facilities is cheap, and where wide-open spaces minimize any potential air-pollution hazards associated with incinerators. The sensible thing to do, it would seem, is to have the states that produce most of the trash ship it to states where it can be most efficiently disposed of—for a price, of course. This is already being done to an extent, but residents of potential recipient states are (not surprisingly) concerned, lest they end up being the garbage capitals of the nation. Yet Wisconsin, which imports more than a million tons of garbage each year, is demonstrating that it is possible to get rid of the trash without trashing the neighborhood. Landfill operators in Wisconsin are now required to send water-table monitoring reports to neighbors and to maintain the landfills for forty years after closure. Operators have also guaranteed the value of neighboring homes to gain the permission of nearby residents and in some cases have purchased homes to quiet neighbors' objections. These features all add to the cost of operating landfills, but as long as prospective customers are willing to pay the price and neighboring residents are satisfied with their protections—and so far these conditions appear to have been met—it would seem tough to argue with the outcome.

Some people might still argue that it does not seem right for one community to be able to dump its trash elsewhere. Yet the flip side is this: Is it right to prevent communities from accepting trash if that is what they want? Consider Gilliam County, Oregon (population 1,950), which wanted Seattle's garbage so badly that it fought Oregon state legislators' attempts to tax out-of-state trash coming into Oregon. Seattle's decision to use the Gilliam County landfill generated $1 million per year for the little community—some 25 percent of its annual budget and enough to finance the operations of the county's largest school.

Faced with the prospect of paying to dispose of its garbage, Seattle had to confront the problem of reducing the amount of trash its residents were generating. Its solution was to charge householders according to the amount they put out. Seattle began charging $16.55 per month for each can picked up weekly. Yard waste that has been separated for composting costs $5.35 per month, and paper, glass, and metal separated for recycling are hauled away at no charge. In the first year that per-can charges were imposed, the total tonnage that had to be buried fell by 22 percent. Voluntary recycling rose from 24 percent of waste to 36 percent—a rate almost triple the national average at the time. The "Seattle stomp" (used to fit more trash into a can) became a regular source of exercise, and the city had trouble exporting enough garbage to fulfill its contract with Gilliam County.

The Seattle experience is paralleled by a similar program in Charlottesville, Virginia. A few years ago, this university town of forty thousand began charging 80 cents per 32-gallon bag or can of residential garbage collected at the curb. The results of the city's new policy suggest that people respond to garbage prices just as they do to all other prices: When an activity becomes more expensive, people engage in less of it. In fact, after controlling for other factors, the introduction of this unit-pricing plan induced people to reduce the volume of garbage presented for collection by 37 percent.

Where did all of the garbage go? Well, some of it didn't go anywhere because many residents began practicing their own version of the Seattle stomp, compacting garbage into fewer bags. Even so, the total weight of Charlottesville's residential garbage dropped by 14 percent in response to unit pricing. Not all of this represented a reduction in garbage production because some residents resorted to "midnight dumping"—tossing their trash into commercial Dumpsters or their neighbors' cans late at night. This sort of behavior is much like the rise in gasoline thefts that occurred in the 1970s when gas prices jumped to the equivalent of over $3 per gallon. But just as locking gas caps ended most gas thefts, there may be a simple way to prevent most midnight dumping. Economists who have studied the Charlottesville program in detail suggest that property taxes or monthly fees could be used to cover the cost of one bag per household each week, with a price per bag applied only to additional bags. According to these estimates, a one-bag allowance would stop all midnight dumping by most one-person households and stop almost half the dumping by a hypothetical three-person household. Moreover, such a scheme would retain most of the environmental benefits of the garbage-pricing program.

The message beginning to emerge across the country, then, is that garbage is no different from the things we consume in the course of producing it. As long as the trashman is paid, he will come, and as long as we must pay for his services, his burden will be bearable.

DISCUSSION QUESTIONS

1. How do deposits on bottles and cans affect the incentives of individuals to recycle these products?

2. Why do many communities mandate recycling? Is it possible to induce people to recycle more without requiring that all residents recycle?

3. How do hefty per-can garbage pickup fees influence the decisions people make about what goods they will consume?

4. A community planning on charging a fee for trash pickup might structure the fee in any of several ways. It might, for example, charge a fixed amount per can, an amount per pound of garbage, or a flat fee per month without regard to amount of garbage. How would each of these affect the amount and type of garbage produced? Which system would lead to an increase in the use of trash compactors? Which would lead to the most garbage?

Chapter 14

BYE-BYE, BISON

The destruction of animal species by humans is nothing new. For example, the arrival of human beings in North America about twelve thousand years ago is tied to the extinction of most of the megafauna (very large animals) that then existed. The famous La Brea Tar Pits of Southern California yielded the remains of twenty-four mammals and twenty-two birds that no longer exist. Among these are the saber-toothed tiger, the giant llama, the 20-foot ground sloth, and a bison that stood 7 feet at the hump and had 6-foot-wide horns.

Although many experts believe that human hunting was responsible for the demise of these species and that hunting and habitat destruction by humans have led to the extinction of many other species, the link is not always as clear as it might seem at first glance. For example, it is estimated that only about 0.02 percent (1 in 5,000) of all species that have ever existed are currently extant. Most of the others (including the dinosaurs) disappeared long before humans ever made an appearance. The simple fact is that all species compete for the limited resources available, and most species have been outcompeted, with or without the help of *Homo sapiens.* Just as important is that basic economic principles can help explain why various species are more or less prone to meet their demise at the hands of humans and what humans might do if they want to delay the extinction of any particular species.[1]

Let's begin with the passenger pigeon, which provides the most famous example of the role of human beings in the extinction of a species. At one time, these birds were the most numerous species of birds in North America and perhaps in the world. They nested and migrated in huge flocks and probably numbered in the billions. When flocks passed

---

1. We say "delay" rather than "prevent" extinction because there is no evidence to date that any species—*Homo sapiens* included—has any claim on immortality.

overhead, the sky would be dark with pigeons for days at a time. The famous naturalist John James Audubon measured one roost at 40 miles long and 3 miles wide, with birds stacked from treetop down to nearly ground level. Although the Native Americans had long hunted these birds, the demise of the passenger pigeon is usually tied to the arrival of the Europeans, who increased the **demand** for pigeons as a source of food and sport. The birds were shot and netted in vast numbers; by the end of the nineteenth century, an animal species that had been looked on as almost indestructible because of its enormous numbers had almost completely disappeared. The last known passenger pigeon died in the Cincinnati Zoo in 1914.

The American bison only narrowly escaped the same fate. The vast herds that roamed the plains were easy targets for hunters; with the advent of the railroad and the need to feed crews of workers as the transcontinental railroads were built, hunters such as Buffalo Bill Cody killed bison by the thousands. As the demand for bison hides increased, the animals became the target of more hunting. Like the passenger pigeon, the bison had appeared to be indestructible because of its huge numbers, but the species was soon on the road to extinction. Despite the outcries of the Native Americans who found their major food source being decimated, it was not until late in the nineteenth century that any efforts were made to protect the bison.[2]

These two episodes, particularly that of the bison, are generally viewed as classic examples of humans' inhumanity to our fellow species, as well as to our fellow humans, for many Native American tribes were ultimately devastated by the near demise of the bison. A closer look reveals more than simply wasteful slaughter; it discloses exactly why events progressed as they did and how we can learn from them to improve modern efforts to protect species threatened by human neighbors.

Native Americans had hunted the bison for many years before the arrival of Europeans and are generally portrayed as both carefully husbanding their prey and generously sharing the meat among tribal members. Yet the braves who rode their horses into the thundering herds marked their arrows so that it would be clear who had killed each bison. The marked arrows gave the shooter rights to the best parts of the animal. Tribal members who specialized in butchering the kill also received a share as payment for processing the meat. Indeed, the Native American hunting parties were organized remarkably like the parties of the

---

2. For the bison's cousin, the eastern buffalo—which stood 7 feet tall at the shoulder, was 12 feet long, and weighed more than a ton—the efforts came too late. The last known members of the species, a cow and her calf, were killed in 1825 in the Allegheny Mountains.

Europeans who followed: Once an animal was killed, its ownership was clearly defined, fully enforced, and readily transferable. Moreover, the rewards were distributed in accordance with the contribution that each person had made to the overall success of the hunt.

Matters were different when it came to the ownership rights to living bison. Native Americans, like the white hunters and settlers who came later, had no economically practical way to fence in the herds. The bison could (and did) migrate freely from one tribe's territory into the territory of other tribes. If the members of one tribe economized on their kill, their conservation efforts would chiefly provide more meat for another tribe, who might well be their mortal enemies. This fact induced Native Americans to exploit the bison, so that the herds disappeared from some traditional territories on the Great Plains by 1840—before Buffalo Bill was even born.

Two factors made the efforts of the railroad hunters more destructive, hastening the disappearance of the bison herds. First, the white population (and thus the demand for the meat and hides) became much larger than the Native American population. Second, white hunters used firearms—a technological revolution that increased the killing capacity of a given hunter by a factor of 20 or more, compared to the bow and arrow. Nevertheless, the fundamental problem was the same for whites and Native Americans alike: The **property rights** to live bison could not be cheaply established and enforced. To own a bison, one had to kill it, and so too many bison were killed.

The property rights to a **scarce good** or **resource** must be clearly defined, fully enforced, and readily transferable if that resource is to be used efficiently—that is, in the manner that yields the greatest net benefits. This is true whether the resource in question is the American bison, the water in a stream, or a pepperoni pizza. If these conditions are satisfied, the resource will be used in the manner that best benefits both its owner and society.[3] If they are not satisfied—as they were not for bison on the hoof or passenger pigeons on the wing—the resource will generally not be used in the most efficient manner. In the case of animal species that are competing with human beings, this sometimes means extinction.

In modern times, the government has attempted to limit hunting and fishing seasons and the number of animals that may be taken by imposing state and federal regulations. In effect, a rationing system (other than

---

3. This does not mean that all species will be permanently protected from extinction, for reasons that are suggested in Chapter 3, "Flying the Friendly Skies?" It does mean that extinction will be permitted to occur only if the benefits of letting it occur exceed the costs.

prices) is being used in an attempt to induce hunters and fishermen to act as though the rights to animals were clearly defined, fully enforced, and readily transferable. The results have been at least partly successful. It is likely, for example, that there are more deer in North America today than there were at the time of the colonists—a fact that is not entirely good news for people whose gardens are sometimes the target of hungry herds. The threatened status of many species of whales illustrates that the problem is far from resolved. The pattern of harvesting whales has been the subject of international discussion ever since World War II, for migratory whales are like nineteenth-century bison: To own them, one must kill them. It was readily apparent that without some form of restraint, many species of whales were in danger of extinction. The result was the founding in 1948 of the International Whaling Commission (IWC), which attempted to regulate international whaling. But the IWC was doomed from the start, for its members had the right to veto any regulation they considered too restrictive, and the commission had no enforcement powers in the event that a member nation chose to disregard the rules. Moreover, some whaling nations (such as Chile and Peru) refused to join the IWC, so commission quotas had little effect on them. Some IWC members have used nonmember flagships to circumvent agreed quotas, while others have claimed that they were killing the whales solely for exempt "research" purposes.

The story of the decimation of a species is well told in the events surrounding blue whales, which are believed to migrate thousands of miles each year. A blue whale, which can weigh almost 100 tons, is difficult to kill even with the most modern equipment; nevertheless, intensive hunting gradually reduced the stock from somewhere between 300,000 and 1 million to, at present, somewhere between 3,000 and 4,000. In the 1930–1931 winter season, almost 30,000 blue whales were taken, a number far in excess of the species' ability to replenish through reproduction. Continued intense harvesting brought the catch down to fewer than 10,000 by 1945–1946, and in the late 1950s, the yearly harvest was down to around 1,500 per year. By 1964–1965, whalers managed to find and kill only 20 blue whales. Despite a 1965 ban by the IWC, the hunting of blues continued by nonmembers such as Brazil, Chile, and Peru.

Humpback whales were also hunted to near-extinction. From an original population estimated at 300,000, stocks plunged to 5,000 or fewer, although as many as 60,000 to 80,000 humpbacks are alive today. It is generally agreed that the IWC ban on hunting humpbacks has played a key role in the species' ongoing recovery.

Whales are not the only seagoing creatures to suffer from an absence of clearly defined, cheaply enforceable, and transferable property rights.

Codfish off the New England and eastern Canadian coasts were once so abundant, it was said, that a person could walk across the sea on their backs. The fish grew into 6-foot-long, 200-pound giants, and generations of families from coastal communities knew they could count on the fish for a prosperous livelihood. The problem was that the fish had to be hauled from the sea before rights to it could be established. The result was overfishing, which led to declining yields and shrinking fish. Between 1970 and 2000, the catch dropped more than 75 percent, and the typical fish caught these days weighs but 20 pounds. As a result, the Canadians have closed down their cod fishery, and the American fleet is a ghost of its former self.

The cod is not alone in its demise. The world's ocean fisheries are in decline. Since 1950, nearly 30 percent of all fisheries have collapsed, and some scientists project that in forty years, *all* of the world's fisheries could disappear. The problem, it is widely agreed, is a failure of humans to manage fisheries in a way that is consistent with both maximum economic benefit and long-term survival of ocean fish stocks. But it is now becoming increasingly apparent that a simple property-rights system has the power to stop and even reverse these declines.

A system of catch shares called individual transferable quotas (ITQs) is stunningly successful in protecting fisheries. Where such rights have been assigned, there is no evidence of collapse. In fact, the assignment of catch share rights often halts and even reverses potential collapse. And in fisheries where they are used, ITQs have permitted the return of economically viable fishing activities.

Command-and-control systems of fisheries management have historically held sway around the world. These systems limit, for example, fishing gear and season length, in an effort to keep total harvests within **quotas.** But even the best of them suffer from a profound misalignment of **incentives:** the self-interest of the individual harvester is generally inconsistent with actions that would both maximize the value of the fishery and ensure its sustainability. Because individuals lack secure rights to part of the harvest, they are motivated to "race to fish" to outcompete others. The results are poor stewardship and lobbying for ever-larger harvest quotas, causing excessive harvests, reduced stocks, and eventual collapse.

In recent years, the failure of command-and-control fishery management has become increasingly clear, but the question has been, is there a viable alternative? Economists have suggested that catch shares assigned to individual harvesters (such as ITQs) offer such an alternative, because property-rights systems, of which ITQs are an example, are generally the most effective way to conserve resources.

Catch-share systems combine two features. First, based on biological and other scientific criteria, an allowable catch size is determined. Then members of the fishing community (individuals or cooperatives, for example) are assigned shares of the total allowable catch. These shares can then be used or be sold or leased to others; no one is allowed to harvest in excess of the amount specified in the harvester's quota. The ITQs give fishermen de facto property rights in the catch, much as they have rights in their boats and gear. Collectively, these rights owners then have an incentive to protect and maintain the value of the fishery, just as they do to maintain their other property.

Case studies of the use of ITQs suggest that catch shares can dramatically improve both the biological and the economic health of fisheries. Alaska, British Columbia, Iceland, and New Zealand all represent locations where ITQs are regarded as having succeeded. But recent research covering more than eleven thousand fisheries around the world reveals that ITQs are effective worldwide. In fact, the outcomes for fisheries with and without catch-share systems have been studied systematically, accounting for factors (such as ecosystem characteristics and fish species) that might have played a role in the health and viability of the fish stocks. This amounts to conducting a statistically controlled experiment—and the results are striking.

A conventional measure of collapse for a fishery is a decline in catch to a level that is less than 10 percent of the maximum recorded catch for that fishery. By this criterion, an average of more than fifty fisheries has reached collapse each year since 1950, in a worldwide pattern that seems to be pointing toward the demise of all fisheries. But in fisheries where a catch-share system is implemented, the process of collapse halts—completely. Moreover, in many of the ITQ fisheries, recovery of fish stocks begins soon after implementation, even as fishermen continue to profitably catch fish.

It is now estimated that had ITQs been implemented in all fisheries beginning in 1970, the incidence of collapse would have been cut by two-thirds. Moreover, instead of watching fisheries collapse today, we would be seeing them getting healthier, even as they were supporting fishermen and nourishing consumers. Most important, it appears that the power of ITQs to prevent and even reverse fishery collapse applies to species and ecosystems throughout the world.

Until now, skeptics of the property-rights approach to solving environmental problems have argued that fisheries are profoundly different from other resources, somehow immune to the benefits of instituting catch shares. That argument is no longer viable. Catch shares are being implemented in growing numbers around the world. It is now clear that an expansion of ITQs and other catch-share systems can lead to the recovery of fish stocks and of the profits from harvesting them—one more illustration that the clear assignment of enforceable, transferable property rights remains the most effective way we know to protect other species from the depredations of *Homo sapiens*.

DISCUSSION QUESTIONS

1. Has there ever been a problem with the extinction of dogs, cats, or cattle? Why not?

2. Some people argue that the best way to save rare species is to set up private game reserves to which wealthy hunters can travel. How could this help save endangered species?

3. Is government *ownership* of animals needed to protect species from extinction?

4. In the United States, most fishing streams are public property, with access available to all. In Britain, most fishing streams are privately owned, with access restricted to those who are willing to pay for the right to fish. Anglers agree that over the past thirty years, the quality of fishing in the United States has declined, while the quality of fishing in Britain has risen. Can you suggest why?

PART FOUR

Macroeconomic Variables

CHAPTER 15

Measuring GDP

Overall business activity in any country never stays the same. There are "booms" and "busts"—**expansions** and **recessions**—even though the long-term trend may be up. Even noneconomists can agree on some of the obvious signs of an "up" in business activity (expanding corporate **profits,** higher employment, rising business investment spending) and the obvious signs of "down" periods (rising unemployment, falling profits, more idle production capacity). But the one traditional *overall* measure of business activity is being seriously questioned. This measure is **gross domestic product (GDP),** which is a measure of the total market value of final goods and services produced in a country in any one year.

Unless you have a deep and abiding love of accounting, you may be wondering, why should I read this chapter? There are two reasons. First, almost all macroeconomic policy is driven by policymakers' perceptions of what is happening to a few key variables, perhaps the most important of these being GDP. So if you want to understand the policies now in place or being contemplated, you must start by understanding how GDP is calculated and what it does and does not measure. Second, the human condition varies dramatically around the globe. Radical differences in prosperity and poverty from one nation to the next can be understood only if we begin with a clear awareness of what is being measured. And that awareness starts with measuring GDP.

WHAT DOES GDP MEASURE?

The way GDP is measured has been under attack for some time. There are two separate issues here. First, does GDP measure what the U.S.

Department of Commerce *claims* it measures? For example, if someone were to produce and sell you an illegal good, the transaction has resulted in a new, domestically produced final good and should be counted in GDP as a matter of definition. But because neither you nor the producer of the good is likely to report this trade to the Department of Commerce, it is unlikely that the transaction will make it into the official statistics.

The second issue has to do with whether GDP measures *welfare* (the general level of satisfaction), which is what some people seem to think it measures. News commentators, for example, often speak of the latest GDP numbers as though they are the definitive measure of "how America is doing." But GDP is a measure of the *market value* of newly produced final goods and services. It can change when the *quantities* of those products increase or decrease or when the *prices* of those products go up or down. If the prices of goods and services change in the absence of a corresponding change in the quantity or quality of those items, GDP will change. Yet the level of satisfaction of individuals is unlikely to have changed under such circumstances. Hence this is a case where a change in GDP clearly does *not* signal a change in the level of satisfaction (or welfare) of individuals.

It is possible to adjust GDP for changes in the **price level.** Doing so results in something called **real GDP.** Whether this number is good as a measure of welfare is itself subject to debate, but at least the effects of changes in price levels have been eliminated, giving us a concrete measure of the amount of goods and services that are newly produced in the economy. In this chapter, we focus on the strengths and weaknesses of real GDP and use this term to describe what we are measuring. But be warned: Not all commentators and journalists are careful in distinguishing between *GDP* and *real GDP,* so you will have to be on the alert when you read or listen to news reports.

ACCOUNTING FOR MISSING INFORMATION

As a general rule, to "correct" real GDP, we should *add* what is not measured but should be and *subtract* what is included but should not be. Interestingly enough, the Department of Commerce already devotes considerable effort to making sure that real GDP is as accurate as possible when it comes to measuring what it claims to measure. For example, even though there is no "market" in owner-occupied housing, the Commerce Department has devised methods of estimating the implicit rental value of houses occupied by their owners, and it includes the aggregate value of these services in its published measure of real GDP.

In a similar vein, farmers consume some of the food items they produce before those items ever get to the market. Again, the Commerce

Department has devised ways to estimate the market value of such food, using methods that take into account typical **consumption** patterns, family size, and the like. As with owner-occupied housing, these estimates are included in the official GDP numbers.

WHAT IS STILL MISSED

Despite the government's best efforts, there are some major omissions from published measures of real GDP. For example, do-it-yourself activities are not included in the official measures, even though they constitute the production of a service. If you take your car to a mechanic, the services performed on the car end up as part of measured real GDP. But if you and a friend repair your car, these services are not included in the statistics. (We need to be careful here: Any parts or tools you buy from local stores *are* included in measured real GDP. It is the labor component—the value of the time you and your friend put into the repairs—that escapes detection and thus inclusion in real GDP. And because labor typically accounts for about two-thirds of the value of output, this means that in cases such as this, more may be excluded than included.)

The biggest category of do-it-yourself services left out of the official GDP statistics consists of those performed in the house by homemakers. The value of the services performed by homemakers who are not explicitly paid can indeed be large. Every year, various sources estimate the value of these services based on the going wage rates that would have to be paid to provide the services if the homemaker did not. By now, the *weekly* value of a homemaker's services is estimated at over $800. With many millions of such individuals spread across the country, the implied undermeasurement of newly produced final goods and services is huge. We should note, however, that homemakers' services counted in real GDP have been steadily increasing over the past thirty years. This is because women have poured into the paid workforce and now purchase in the market more and more of the services that they used to perform themselves. Each time a (former) homemaker hires another individual or firm to do something, that activity will be counted in real GDP.

Then there is the matter of the huge volume of transactions—hundreds of billions of dollars per year—in markets for illegal and underground activities. In some "true" measure of real GDP, we should probably add the value of these activities, which include prostitution and the illegal drug trade, because such goods and services presumably generate satisfaction to the individuals purchasing them. We should also include "underground" income that is the result of legal activities but is not reported. Some of this income goes unreported by individuals hoping to evade income taxes. But it also includes much of the income earned by illegal immigrants, who do not report their incomes simply because they do not wish to be deported.

The final bit of "income" that we should account for, especially if we are interested in closing the gap between official income measures and the well-being of the citizenry, is the amount of time people have for leisure. After all, leisure is a good, and it is scarce. It has value and generates satisfaction. For the civilian economy, average weekly hours worked have fallen from over forty-eight in 1943 to under thirty-four in 2009, a definite increase in the real **standard of living** for the individuals enjoying this added leisure time.

SUBTRACTIONS NEEDED TOO

What about things that are newly produced but don't really belong in real GDP? The most important of these are **intermediate goods**—goods that contribute to present or future consumer welfare but are not direct sources of utility themselves. Here again, the accountants at the Department of Commerce have done much of the work for us, because most of these goods are handled in the normal construction of the real GDP figure. For example, the steel, plastic, aluminum, rubber, and other components that go into making a car end up being counted only once—in the form of the car itself. All of the earlier market transactions involving the components that make up the car are subtracted before the official figures for real GDP are published. Nevertheless, there are still some intermediate goods that *should* be deducted but are not, including such items as personal business expenses and commuting costs. For example, the government statisticians treat as equivalent the $5 you spend on gasoline to go on a date in the evening and the $5 you spend on gasoline for your trip to work in the morning.

The next category of expenditures that might be considered worthy of subtraction is sometimes referred to as "regrettable necessities." This includes spending for diplomacy, national security, police and fire protection, and prison facilities. Unlike sports cars and prom dresses, battle tanks and body armor are not produced because they yield consumer satisfaction in and of themselves. They are produced because they make it possible for us to enjoy the consumption of other goods. For example, during World War II, automobile assembly lines were converted into assembly lines used to make military vehicles that helped us win the war—and thus resume our way of life afterward. In this sense, we can think about regrettable necessities as intermediate goods that go into the production of other goods. As such, they probably should be subtracted from real GDP, but the government statisticians won't hear of it.

It is also important to recognize that the urbanized, industrialized society that makes it possible for us to have many of the goods we consume has some drawbacks. Big cities make large-scale commercial activities (and thus more market goods) feasible. But they also bring with them a variety of urban disamenities, such as congestion, noise, and litter. If we want to narrow the gap between the official statistics and some measure of welfare, we should make deductions from real GDP for such sources of dissatisfaction. It is difficult to put a precise numerical value on them, however, and so none of the official statistics are adjusted. Similar considerations apply when economic activity causes a reduction in environmental quality. Air, water, and view pollution all reduce consumer welfare, but they are sufficiently difficult to quantify that the accountants make no deductions when pollution increases and no additions when pollution control measures yield environmental improvements.

WHAT DO WE KNOW WHEN?

If you have been following closely thus far, you can appreciate the fact that keeping track of GDP is a huge undertaking. There are, after all, more than 23 million businesses in the United States, producing vast numbers of goods and employing more than 140 million people. Perhaps for this reason it often takes quite a while before we really know what's going on with GDP.

The Commerce Department constructs estimates of GDP every calendar quarter (three-month period), reporting numbers as *annual rates,* that is, what GDP would be for a year if it continued at its level for that quarter. Here is where it gets interesting (or tedious, if you hate numbers). One month after the end of each quarter, the Commerce Department issues an "advance" report on GDP; a month later, it issues a "preliminary" report; and after another month, it announces its "final" estimate of GDP for that quarter. But it is not over yet: Frequently, sometimes many months later, the Commerce Department issues a "revised" estimate of GDP. And every once in a while it will go back a few years later and revise the revisions!

There are two consequences of all this estimating and revising. The first is that there is a steady stream of numbers coming out on GDP, some for the latest quarter, some for an earlier quarter, and some for quarters or years past. Unless you look at the fine print, it is sometimes hard to tell exactly what the bureaucrats are trying to tell us about the state of the economy. This brings us to our second point. As we discuss more fully in the next chapter, although measures of GDP are *not* the basis on which economic expansions and recessions are officially classified, many of the components of GDP go into the determination of whether the economy is expanding or contracting. And with all of the revisions of these numbers, it is easy to see why it gets pretty hard to pin down exactly where we are and where we might be going. Thus it was that it took fully a *year* for the number crunchers to decide that the latest recession started in December 2007 and not, say, six months before or twelve months after that date.

What Does It All Mean?

For centuries, macroeconomic policymakers have sought to understand how the economy is doing and where it is headed next. Not until the twentieth century, with the first systematic measurements of GDP, did they begin to develop such an understanding. We have seen that GDP sometimes doesn't measure what it is designed to measure, it often doesn't measure what some people think it ought to measure, and it usually doesn't measure it when we'd like it to. Most important, it is crucial when making comparisons over time or across nations to account for differences in the price level—to focus on real GDP. Even once we do this, we have seen that ambiguities and errors remain—illegal goods, underground markets, disamenities, and regrettable necessities, to name but a few. Nevertheless, for all its weaknesses, real GDP continues to be used by policymakers, reported on by journalists, and editorialized about by commentators for one simple reason: It beats all the alternatives in helping us understand how the economy is doing and where it is headed next.

For Critical Analysis

1. How does one determine what is a final good or service and what is a regrettable necessity or an intermediate good? In other words, where does one draw the line?

2. Why can't we conclude that welfare is proportional to annual national consumption?

3. Would you categorize each of the following expenditures as intermediate goods, regrettable necessities, or consumption goods: (a) a spare tire, (b) surgery to repair a badly broken arm, (c) a Botox injection to remove forehead wrinkles, (d) voice lessons, and (e) expenditures on your college education? Explain your reasoning in each case. Would your answers to (c) and (d) change if you knew that the purchaser was a professional singer who made many public appearances? Why or why not?

CHAPTER 16

What's in a Word? Plenty, When It's the "R" Word

Incumbent presidents (and members of their political party) hate the "R" word. We speak here of **recession,** a word used to describe a downturn or stagnation in overall, nationwide economic activity. Politicians' attitudes toward recessions are driven by the simple fact that people tend to "vote their pocketbooks." That is, when the economy is doing well, voters are likely to return incumbent politicians to office, but when the economy is doing poorly, voters are likely to "throw the bums out." Interestingly, although *recession* is the word most commonly used to describe a period of poor performance by the economy, most people don't really know what the word means.

THE NBER

Ever since its founding in 1920, a private organization called the National Bureau of Economic Research (NBER) has sought to accurately measure the state of overall economic conditions in the United States. (It also sponsors research on other economic issues.) Over time, the NBER developed a reputation for measuring the economy's performance in an evenhanded and useful way. As a result, most people now accept without argument what the NBER has to say about the state of the economy. And most notably, this means that it is the NBER that we rely on to tell us when we are in a recession.

If you are an avid reader of newspapers, you may well have heard a recession defined as any period in which there are at least two quarters (three-month periods) of declining **real gross domestic product (real GDP).** In fact, the NBER's recession-dating committee places little reliance on the performance of real (inflation-adjusted) GDP when deciding on the state of the economy. There are two reasons for this. First, the government measures GDP only on a quarterly basis, and the NBER prefers to focus on more timely data that are available at least monthly. Second, the official GDP numbers are subject to frequent and often substantial revisions, so what once looked like good economic performance might suddenly look bad, and vice versa.

Looking back at 2001 (a turbulent year), for example, the initial figures showed that real GDP declined in only one quarter during the year. But when the government finally finished all of its revisions to the data, it turned out that real GDP actually fell during *three* quarters of 2001. In 2007, the government issued a revision of its revised GDP figures for 2004–2006. Of the twelve quarters covered by this "revision of the revisions," the numbers for all twelve were changed: Two were revised upward and ten downward. One can easily see why an organization such as the NBER, which prides itself on reliability and accuracy, might be reluctant to place too much weight on measures of real GDP.

So what does the NBER use as its criteria in measuring a recession? Its official definition of a recession gives us some insight: "A recession is a significant decline in activity spread across the economy, lasting more than a few months, visible in industrial production, employment, real income, and wholesale-retail sales." Those are a lot of words to define just one term, but it's not too difficult to get a handle on it. The point to note at the outset is that the NBER focuses chiefly on four separate pieces of information:

- Industrial production
- Employment
- Real income (measured by inflation-adjusted personal income of consumers)
- Sales at both the wholesale and retail levels

All of these figures are reliably available on a monthly basis, and so every month, the NBER uses the latest figures on each to take the pulse of the economy. When all four are moving upward, that's generally good news. When all are moving downward, that's definitely bad news. And when some are moving in one direction and some in another direction, that's when expert judgment comes into play.

THE THREE *D*'S

If the NBER recession-dating committee uses a strict formula to time the onset or end of a recession, the committee members don't reveal what it is. What they do reveal is that they are looking for three crucial elements, all starting with the letter *D*, when they officially announce the start or end of a recession:

1. *Depth.* If there is a downturn in one or more of the four key variables, the NBER focuses first on the magnitude of that downturn. For example, in an economy like ours with total employment of over 140 million, a drop in employment of 50,000 would not be crucial; an employment drop of, say, one million surely would be considered significant.

2. *Duration.* Month-to-month fluctuations in economic activity are the norm in our economy. These fluctuations occur partly because our measures of economic activity are imperfect and partly because, in an economy as complex as ours, many things are happening all the time that have the capacity to affect the overall performance of the economy. Thus if real personal income moves up or down for a month or even two months in a row, the recession-dating committee is likely to determine that such a change is well within the bounds of normal variation. But if a trend persists for, say, six months, the committee is likely to place a much heavier weight on that movement.

3. *Dispersion.* Because the NBER is trying to measure the overall state of the economy, it wants to make sure it is not being misled by economic developments that may be important to many people but are not reliable indicators of the overall state of the economy. For example, America is becoming less dependent on industrial production and more reliant on service industries. In addition, it is well known that industrial production is sensitive to sharp movements not shared by sectors elsewhere in the economy. So the NBER tempers the importance of industrial production by simultaneously relying on measures such as wholesale and retail sales to make sure it has a picture of what is happening throughout the economy.

A PRECISE ANSWER

Having blended its four measures of the economy in a way that reflects its focus on the three *D*'s, the recession-dating committee makes its decision. A recession, in its view, begins "just after the economy reaches a peak of activity" and ends "as the economy reaches its trough" and starts expanding again. Between trough and peak, the economy is said to be in an **expansion.** Historically, the normal state of the economy is expansion; most recessions are brief (usually ending within twelve to eighteen months), and in recent decades, they have been rare. Our most recent recession began in December 2007 after six years of economic expansion.

The four measures used by the NBER to date recessions generally move fairly closely together. Although individually they sometimes give conflicting signals for short periods of time, they soon enough start playing the same song. Nevertheless, some contention about the NBER's decisions remains. There are two sources of debate. One focuses on *potential* growth of economic activity, and the other highlights the importance of population growth.

The NBER defines a recession as an absolute decline in economic activity. But some economists note that at least for the past couple of centuries, growth in economic activity from year to year has been the norm in most developed nations, including the United States. Hence, they argue, a recession should be declared whenever growth falls significantly below its long-term potential. This dispute becomes more important when there is reason to believe that potential growth has shifted for some reason or when comparing the current performance of two nations that are growing at different rates. For example, suppose nation X has potential growth of 4 percent per year while nation Y has potential growth of only 2 percent per year. If both are actually growing at 2 percent, the unemployment rate in X will be rising, and some people would argue that this fact is sufficient to declare that X is in a state of recession. The biggest problem with this proposed measure of recession is that it is difficult to declare with confidence exactly what the potential growth rate of any country is.

The second point of contention starts with the observation that the population is growing in most countries. Hence even if economic activity is growing, the well-being of the average citizen might not be. For example, suppose the population is growing 3 percent per year but real personal income is growing only 2 percent a year. Assuming that the other measures of activity were performing like personal income, the NBER would say the economy was in an expansion phase, even though **real per capita income** was declining. Some economists would argue that this state of affairs should be declared a recession, given that the term is supposed to indicate a less-than-healthy economy. This point has some validity. Nevertheless, there have not been many prolonged periods when the NBER has said the economy was expanding while real per capita income was falling.

Ultimately, of course, even if the recession-dating committee somehow tinkered with its methods to better acknowledge the importance of potential growth and population changes, some other issue would undoubtedly be raised to dispute the NBER's conclusions. For now, most economists are content to rely on the NBER to make the call. Most politicians are, too—except, of course, when it suits them otherwise. As for ordinary voters, well, even if they don't know how a recession is defined, they surely know what one feels like—and are likely to vote accordingly.

FOR CRITICAL ANALYSIS

1. Why is it important, both for the political process and for our understanding of the economy, for the NBER to resist the temptation to change its definition of a recession to fit the latest political pressures or economic fads?

2. Do you think that voters care more about whether the NBER says the economy is in a state of recession or whether they and their friends and family members are currently employed in good jobs? Why do politicians make a big deal over whether the economy is "officially" in a recession or an expansion? (*Hint:* Is it hard for the average voter to tell what is going on in the economy outside his or her community, leaving the voter dependent on simple measures—or labels—of what is happening elsewhere in the economy?)

3. Examine the data from the last six recessions. (Good sources for data are www.nber.org/cycles/recessions.html, www.bea.gov, and www. globalindicators.org.) Rank them on the basis of both duration and severity. The first is easy; the second is more difficult: Is it possible that some people—either politicians or other citizens—might disagree about how to measure the severity of a particular recession? How would you measure it?

CHAPTER 17

The Panic of '08

The risk is small—1 in 10,000 over a ten-year period. That is the chance that a borrower will default on the highest-grade, so-called triple A (AAA) debt according to Moody's, one of the three government-approved investment-rating agencies in the United States. Trillions of dollars of debt instruments rated AAA were floating around the world in 2008. By the end of that year, about a half a trillion dollars of that AAA-rated "paper" was in default. That meant that millions of individuals, **mutual funds, hedge funds,** banks, city governments, and state governments ended up losing hundreds of billions of dollars—and this was just on the "low-risk" **bonds.** Losses on riskier **assets** were even greater.

To understand how the United States and the world suffered the greatest financial meltdown since the 1930s, we have to go back at least fifteen years.

THE BIG FEDERAL PUSH TO EXPAND HOME OWNERSHIP

As you will see in Chapter 35, "Credit Chaos," starting in 1995, both Congress and the Clinton administration began pushing hard for banks and other mortgage-lending institutions to relax the standards applied to anyone seeking a home **mortgage.** The goal was to increase home ownership, particularly among lower-income U.S. residents.

Mortgage-lending institutions got the message. They began relaxing standards for down payments, credit histories, and other barometers of financial risk. Many of the new home loans they made were labeled subprime or Alt-A (so-called borderline mortgages). After the recession of 2001–2002, the two giant government-sponsored mortgage corporations,

Fannie Mae and Freddie Mac, began pushing lenders to offer even more mortgage loans of dubious quality. Soon almost anyone could get a mortgage, and within a short period of time, a housing boom took flight. Low- and even no-income individuals were realizing the American dream of home ownership—with lots of debt to pay back.

TAKING THE RISK OUT OF SUBPRIME MORTGAGES: MBSs, ABSs, AND CDOs

No lending institution, even the most risk-loving, would continue to make a larger and larger share of its loans to risky borrowers if it could not shift some or all of the risk elsewhere. Enter the **mortgage-backed security,** or **MBS.** Back in the 1970s, Fannie Mae and Freddie Mac had begun buying up mortgage loans and packaging them as MBSs. Every lending institution that sold its high-risk mortgages for use in MBSs reduced its risk. During the 1980s, **investment banks** got involved in MBSs. They started selling packages of MBSs throughout the world, albeit on a modest scale at that time.

Then investment banks came up with something called an **asset-backed security,** or **ABS.** First created by investment banks in the 1990s, these **investment security** "packages" really took off in 2003 when subprime mortgage loans and other risky loan assets were packaged together. Even this packaging was not enough to distribute all of the risk, so investment bankers resurrected an investment vehicle called a **collateralized debt obligation,** or **CDO.** These investment securities were created by mixing asset-backed securities, subprime loans, and other credit-related contracts all into one package.

NO DATA, NO PROBLEM

With all these new investment entities floating around, Wall Street investment bankers had a hard time assessing their respective risks. These were new financial instruments, and many purchasers simply bought and held them. The result was that the market for these assets was relatively illiquid. Lacking market-based data on risks, the investment banks relied on their programmers to create computer models of potential risk. But the programmers (often called "quants" because they constructed quantitative numerical models) had limited data on which to base the accuracy of their risk models. And what was worse, the data that they did have on subprime mortgage defaults were deceiving: Yes, it was true that during the period 2003–2005 many subprime borrowers were paying their mortgages on time. But the whiz kids of Wall Street did not realize that these subprime mortgage borrowers were paying their debts with *additional* borrowing. Borrowers' debts were growing, not shrinking, as the Wall Street quants had mistakenly thought.

So at the same time, based on fundamentally flawed assumptions, the rating agencies (such as Moody's) were bestowing triple A ratings on vast quantities of subprime-mortgage-related investment securities—hundreds of billions of dollars' worth. At the peak, 90 percent of **securitized** subprime loans had magically turned into investment securities with a top rating of AAA (or the equivalent).

THE MARKET TURNS

Many of the mortgage loans made in 2003–2005 entailed relatively low initial monthly payments that sharply escalated after two to three years. When these payments began rising on a wide scale in late 2005 and early 2006, many borrowers could not make those increased payments, and the housing **bubble** burst with a vengeance. Individuals who had purchased homes hoping to sell them for a quick **profit** found themselves "underwater," referring to the fact that the market values of their properties were suddenly less than what they owed. A lot of individuals just walked away from their mortgage debts and their houses.

All of the entities that owned MBSs, ABSs, and CDOs were suddenly receiving billions of dollars less in monthly mortgage payments. Moreover, it was clear that the market value of these securities and obligations was going to turn out to be less than people had anticipated. But how much less would it be?

MARK TO MARKET MEANT MANY MARKDOWNS

Suppose you are trying to determine how much you are worth. In one column, you write down the values of your assets—cars, houses, savings accounts, stocks, and bonds. In the other column, you add up all of your **liabilities**—mortgages, car loan outstanding, credit-card balances, and so on. When you subtract the latter from the former, you end up with your **net worth.**

Now suppose that one of your assets is a ten-year U.S. Treasury bond for which you paid $10,000 seven years ago. There are three years to go before it will mature—meaning that the federal government will pay off the bond then. If you look in the newspaper today, you might find that the market value of that ten-year bond with three years remaining is, say, $9,500. Or the market value might be $10,300. What should you do when figuring out your actual assets? Should you **mark to market,** that is, value it at current "market" value? Or should you just figure that because you are going to get your $10,000 in three years (plus interest in the intervening period), you will assess the value at $10,000? Your answer depends on the purpose for which you want the estimate of your net worth.

Among accountants, an archaic principle holds that you should mark to market, or use what is called **fair-value accounting.** In other words, you should adjust your **balance sheet** (assets and liabilities) when the market values of your financial assets or liabilities change. This seems like a harmless and sensible accounting principle. For financial institutions, it requires them to adjust their balance sheets when the market values of the financial assets that they own change. Many of those financial institutions do in fact hold ten-year Treasury bonds, as noted earlier. They also hold **shares of stock** in IBM, General Electric, Microsoft, and other corporations. When the market values of those bonds and stocks change, the mark-to-market accounting principle does not raise any issues.

But what about assets for which there is no real day-to-day market? In other words, what about assets that are highly **illiquid?** Many of the assets based on subprime and Alt-A mortgages—all those MBSs, ABSs, and CDOs—were extremely illiquid. Beginning late in 2007, it became clear that some of the underlying mortgages on which those investment securities were based were not going to be paid off in full. But no one knew how many would not be paid off or which ones would go into **default.** And because there was little trading in securities that were based on the mortgages, no one really knew how much they were worth.

Regulators started pressing investment banks and other financial institutions to mark to market. But how was this to be done without any real markets in many of these securities? Enter the computer-modeling wizards again. They put new parameters into their computer valuation models, and presto—they came up with massive downward revaluations of the assets (and thus net worth) of financial institutions. Overnight, some of these financial institutions publicly announced that they had just lost billions of dollars. They actually had not yet lost them, but the computer models, using the mark-to-market accounting principle, generated "paper losses" that staggered the minds of investors throughout the world.

Auditors of financial institutions were worried about overstating the market values of any investments based on subprime mortgage loans. So they continued to drastically reduce the **book value** of anything that resembled a subprime mortgage. Thus the use of the mark-to-market accounting principle quickly became a weapon of mass destruction in the world's financial sector. Within a short period of time, investors lost confidence in some of the largest financial institutions around the world.

THE END OF INVESTMENT BANKING

Many financial institutions went below their required **capital ratios**—the ratio of assets to debt. They needed to raise new capital. They did so by offering new shares of stock for sale. Once the national investment-rating agencies saw those companies in need of new capital, the agencies started reducing these companies' credit ratings, making it more difficult for them to obtain financing and putting more pressure on them to sell assets. These sales in turn reduced the value of their assets, which reduced their ratings. A vicious circle ensued.

Wall Street investment banks—Bear Stearns, Goldman Sachs, Lehman Brothers, Merrill Lynch, and Morgan Stanley—were major players in the mortgage-securities markets. Rising defaults on mortgages, combined with the widespread application of the mark-to-market principle, caused a rapid decline in the values of the securities based on mortgages. Much of this accelerated in 2007 and early 2008 when the investment banks still had positive **cash flows.** But the rapidly declining book value of the assets of investment banks caused other market participants to lose confidence in them. In short order, Bear Stearns found itself no longer a viable entity (and was ultimately purchased by JP Morgan Chase, a **commercial bank**). Not long thereafter, Merrill Lynch sold out to Bank of America. Lehman Brothers went bankrupt. The remaining two large investment banks, Goldman Sachs and Morgan Stanley, became commercial banks. In a matter of weeks, the U.S. investment-banking industry ceased to exist.

In the end, U.S. financial institutions had to **write off** many *hundreds* of billions of dollars, calling them losses. But most of these losses were based solely on computer models rather than on asset transactions. As one analyst pointed out, if the mark-to-market accounting principle had been in effect during the early 1990s when commercial banks found themselves in trouble, every major commercial bank in the United States would have collapsed.

The mark-to-market rule was eased a bit in 2009, but the basic principle remains in place.

BRINGING DOWN AN INSURANCE GIANT

One of the largest insurance companies in the world, American International Group (AIG), also fell victim to overreliance on computer modeling. AIG became a big player in selling a type of insurance against defaults (nonpayment of interest or principal) on all sorts of debts. This insurance is known as **credit-default swaps.** AIG (and many other insurance companies) devised computer models to gauge the risk in its $400 billion portfolio of credit-default swaps.

But these computer models did not take into account abrupt changes in market conditions. In December 2007, the head of AIG, Martin Sullivan, assured AIG's investors that they need not be concerned about exposure to credit-default swaps. Why? Because the company's computer models gave it "a very high level of comfort."

As the master investor Warren Buffett once said, "Beware of geeks bearing formulas." And indeed, AIG's computer formulas turned out to be dead wrong. The federal government had to swoop in to keep AIG afloat. Initially, the government said it was guaranteeing $83 billion of debt at AIG, only later to explain that it had to guarantee more than $200 billion. By 2009, a horde of other insurance companies were asking the federal government for help.

THE WOBBLY STOCK MARKET

Some analysts say that the wildest month in the history of Wall Street ended on October 31, 2008. What no one disputes is that October was the worst month in twenty-one years, as measured by the Standard & Poor's Index of 500 stocks. In contrast, the final week of October 2008 was the best week for the market in thirty-four years. And overall, October 2008 will go down as the most volatile in the eighty-year history of the S&P 500, capping a year that also ranks among the worst in history in terms of both performance and volatility. The most important single factor driving this volatility was this concern: What were trillions of dollars of assets tied to the housing market really worth?

Of course, no one could have reliably predicted what was going to happen to stock prices in 2008. What is certain, though, is that investors reading about hundreds of billions of dollars in losses (even if they were just on paper) could not be expected to have much confidence in the short-term business future in America or elsewhere. And certainly investors were anticipating that declining housing prices were likely to help push the economy into a recession that would likely last for much more than a few months.

The full history of the Panic of '08 is yet to be written. Here is what we do know. There is no doubt that there was a massive downward revision in asset values of all types in 2008, and there was a financial panic of the sort not seen since the 1930s. But the long-run impact of the Panic of '08 on the U.S. and world economies remains uncertain. We can be pretty sure, nonetheless, that a new Great Depression is not around the corner. During the Great Depression of the 1930s, the Federal Reserve allowed the **money supply** in circulation to decrease by one-third. Under Herbert Hoover's leadership, the federal government implemented the Smoot-Hawley Tariff Act, which helped reduce world trade and depressed the economy of the United States. Under President Franklin Roosevelt's leadership, the federal government created legislation and **institutions** that actually raised prices and suppressed private employment.

The federal government has yet to do any of these in response to the Panic of '08—at least so far.

FOR CRITICAL ANALYSIS

1. When might it be important for you, as an individual or household, to use the mark-to-market accounting principle in assessing your own net worth?

2. Do you think that the rating agencies, all of which had bestowed AAA ratings (or the equivalent) on many financial assets that dropped dramatically in value in 2008, should be held liable for investors' losses? Why or why not?

3. The financial meltdown in the United States quickly spread to the rest of the world, particularly to western Europe. It turns out that many large financial institutions throughout the world had invested heavily in mortgage-backed securities, asset-backed securities, and collateralized debt obligations. They, too, had to start writing down the values of these investments, just as financial institutions had done in the United States. What could have enticed so many institutions throughout the world to invest so heavily in securities based on subprime mortgages in the United States?

CHAPTER 18

The Case of the Disappearing Workers

Every month, the Bureau of Labor Statistics (BLS) goes out into the labor market to determine how many unemployed people there are in the United States. With the data it acquires, the BLS calculates the **unemployment rate.** This number is a key indication of how well the economy is doing. The unemployment rate is calculated in a seemingly straightforward way: It is the percentage of the total **labor force** that is (1) over age sixteen but not institutionalized or in school and (2) actively seeking employment but has not found it.

The reelection chances of incumbent presidents often hinge on the estimated rate of unemployment. Historically, when the unemployment rate is rising, the president's chances of reelection have been far worse than when the rate is stable or falling. As the old saying goes, "people vote their pocketbooks" (or in this case, their pay stubs).

For this and a variety of other reasons, understanding how the unemployment rate is measured is important for politicians and ordinary citizens alike. Remarkably, however, there is little consensus about the accuracy of unemployment statistics in the United States. First, consider the period when the United States had its greatest measured rate of unemployment—the Great Depression, which started in 1929 and did not end until the start of World War II a decade later.

25 PERCENT UNEMPLOYMENT—HARD TO IMAGINE

If you look at official government statistics on the unemployment rate during the Great Depression, you will find that in some statistical series, the rate hit 25 percent—meaning that one of every four Americans who were part of the labor force could not find a job during the depth of the depression. That high unemployment rate, of course, makes any **recession** since then seem insignificant in terms of the number of people adversely affected.

Some economists, though, are not so sure that one-fourth of the labor force was actually unemployed during the Great Depression. The reason is simple: At that time, the federal government had instituted numerous programs to "put people back to work." These included the Works Progress Administration (WPA), the Civilian Conservation Corps (CCC), and various lesser programs. Government statisticians decided that everyone working in these federally sponsored "make-work" programs would have been unemployed otherwise. Consequently, they decided to count these millions of Americans as unemployed. Michael Darby, an economist at UCLA, subsequently recalculated unemployment statistics for the depth of the Great Depression. After adjusting for people who were actually working but were counted as unemployed, he found a maximum unemployment rate of 17 percent. This number is still the highest we have had in modern times, but it is certainly not one-fourth of the labor force.

How much sense does Darby's adjustment make? The argument against the official government statistics is straightforward: The federal government taxed individuals and businesses to pay workers at the WPA and CCC. Had the federal government not taxed individuals and businesses to pay these new government employees, the private sector would have had more disposable income, more spending, and higher employment. Whether all of those people would have gotten private-sector jobs is impossible to know, but it is clear that the official numbers greatly overstated the true unemployment rate during the Great Depression.

Discouraged Workers: A Cover for a Higher "True" Unemployment Rate?

Certain individuals, after spending some time in the pool of the unemployed, may become discouraged about their future job prospects. They may leave the labor market to go back to school, to retire, to work full-time at home without pay, or just to take some time off. Whichever path they choose, when interviewers from the Bureau of Labor Statistics ask these individuals whether they are "actively looking for a job," they say no. Individuals such as these are often referred to as **discouraged workers.** They might seek work if labor market conditions were better and potential wages were higher, but they have decided that such is not the case, so they have left the labor market. For years, some critics of the officially measured unemployment rate have argued that during recessions, the rising numbers of discouraged workers cause the government to grossly underestimate the actual rate of unemployment.

To get a feel for the labor market numbers, let's look at the 1990s, perhaps one of the greatest periods of rising employment in U.S. history. During that decade, the number of Americans who were unemployed fell by over 5 million. Moreover, far fewer workers settled for part-time jobs. Many who had been retired came back to work, and many of those about to retire continued to work. There were even large numbers of students who left school to take high-paying jobs in the technology sector.

The onset of the 2001 recession produced a turnaround in all of those statistics. The number of unemployed rose by about 2.5 million individuals. The number of part-time workers who indicated that they would like to work full-time rose by over a million. And the proportion of those out of work for more than half a year increased by over 50 percent.

According to some economists, another 2 million workers dropped out of the labor force—the so-called discouraged-worker problem. For example, University of Chicago economist Robert Topel claims, "The unemployment rate does not mean what it did twenty years ago." He argues that employment opportunities for the least skilled workers no longer exist in today's labor market, so such individuals simply left the labor force, discouraged and forgotten by the statisticians who compile the official numbers.

Are Discouraged Workers a Problem?

Other economists argue differently. They note that the labor market is no different from any other market, so we can examine it using **supply** and **demand** analysis, just as we do with any other good or service. The **labor supply curve** is upward-sloping. That means that as overall wages rise (corrected for inflation, of course), the quantity of labor supplied would be expected to increase. After all, when the inflation-corrected price of just about anything else goes up, we observe that the quantity supplied goes up, too. Therefore, argue these economists, the concept of discouraged workers is basically flawed. They say it makes no more sense to talk of discouraged workers than it would to talk of "discouraged apples" that are no longer offered for sale when the price of apples falls.

Because of the upward-sloping supply curve of labor, when **real wages** rise economywide, we expect retirees and those just about to retire to return to or remain in the labor market. We expect students to quit school early if the wages they can earn are relatively high. The opposite must occur when we go into a recession or the economy stagnates. That is to say, with reduced wage growth (or even declines in economywide real wages) and reduced employment opportunities, we expect more young people to stay in school longer, retirees to stay retired, and those about to retire to actually do so. In other words, we expect the same behavior in response to incentives that we observe in all other markets.

DISABILITY INSURANCE AND LABOR FORCE PARTICIPATION

It is also worth noting that some, perhaps many, of the departures from the labor force by low-skill individuals may actually be prompted by certain government programs. We refer here to a portion of the Social Security program that has expanded dramatically over the past twenty years. It involves **disability payments.** Originally established in 1956 as a program to help individuals under age sixty-five who are truly disabled, Social Security Disability Insurance (SSDI) has become the federal government's second-fastest-growing program (after Medicare). The real value of benefits has steadily risen as the Social Security Administration gradually made it easier for individuals to meet the legal criteria for "disabled" status. SSDI now accounts for over $100 billion in federal spending per year. Under SSDI, even individuals who are not truly disabled can receive payments from the government when they do not work.

In addition, because Social Security also offers Supplemental Security Income (SSI) payments for disabled people who have little or no track record in the labor force, some people are calling disability insurance the centerpiece of a new U.S. welfare state. Just consider that since 1990, the number of people receiving disability payments from the Social Security Administration has more than tripled to over 8 million—perhaps not surprising when you consider that the real value of the monthly benefits a person can collect has risen almost 60 percent in the past thirty-five years. The federal government now spends more on disability payments than on food stamps or unemployment benefits.

What does this mean? Simply that people who might have worked through chronic pain or temporary injuries—particularly those without extensive training and education—have chosen to receive a government disability benefit instead. The average Social Security disability payment is about $1,000 a month, tax-free. For many at the lower echelons of the job ladder, $1,000 a month tax-free seems pretty good. Indeed, those receiving disability payments make up the largest group of the 2 million or so who left the labor force during the 2001–2002 recession. And because people respond to incentives, we can be sure of one thing: Whatever happens to the economy in the future, if the real value of disability payments keeps rising, so will the number of people with disabilities.

FOR CRITICAL ANALYSIS

1. To what extent do you believe that the existence of unemployment benefits increases the duration of unemployment and consequently the unemployment rate? (*Hint:* Use demand analysis and **opportunity cost.**)

2. Is it possible for the unemployment rate to be "too low"? In other words, can you conceive of a situation in which the economy would be worse off in the long run because there is not enough unemployment?

3. It is believed that much of the increase in the number of people collecting SSDI has resulted from decisions by workers at the Social Security Administration (SSA) to make it easier to qualify for benefits. How are the disability rules set by SSA workers likely to change depending on (a) whether the SSA budget is held constant or expands when the number of SSDI recipients rises; (b) the overall state of the economy, especially the unemployment rate; and (c) the likelihood that individuals with disabilities will be discriminated against in the workplace?

CHAPTER 19

Poverty, Wealth, and Equality

In 1960, the poorest 20 percent of households in the United States received a bit over 4 percent of total income. Today, after half a century of government efforts to relieve poverty, the bottom 20 percent receives a bit less than 4 percent of total income. Almost 40 million Americans lived in poverty in 1960; almost 38 million U.S. citizens *still* live in poverty, despite the expenditure of hundreds of billions of dollars in aid for the poor. In the richest country in the world, poverty seems remarkably resilient.

FIRST, THE FACTS

If we are to understand why, we must begin by getting the facts straight. First, even though the *absolute* number of Americans living in poverty has not diminished over the past half-century, population growth has brought a sizable reduction in the *proportion* of impoverished Americans. As conventionally measured, more than 22 percent of Americans lived in poverty in 1960; by 2009, about 13 percent of the population was below the official poverty line.

Second, traditional methods of measuring poverty may be misleading, because they focus solely on the *cash incomes* of individuals. In effect, government statisticians compute a "minimum adequate" budget for families of various sizes—the "poverty line"—and then determine how many people have cash incomes below this line. Yet major components of the federal government's antipoverty efforts come in the form of **in-kind transfers** (transfers of goods and services, rather than cash) such as Medicare, Medicaid, subsidized housing, food stamps, and school lunches. When the dollar value of these in-kind transfers is included in measures of *total* income, the **standard of living** of persons at lower income levels has improved substantially over the years. There is disagreement over how much of these in-kind transfers should be included in measures of the total income of recipients.[1] Nevertheless, most observers agree that these transfers, plus the **Earned Income Tax Credit** (which gives special **tax rebates** to low-income individuals), are major sources of income for people at the bottom of the income distribution. Adjusting for these transfers and tax credits, it seems likely that over the past fifty years, the proportion of Americans living below the poverty line has been cut almost in half. Just as important, the standard of living for the poorest 20 percent of the population has doubled since the mid-1960s. In short, the incidence of poverty in this country has declined markedly over the past half-century, and individuals who remain officially classified as "poor" have a far higher real standard of living than the poor of the 1960s.

THE IMPACT OF INCOME MOBILITY

Whatever measure of income we use, it is crucial to remember that most Americans exhibit a great deal of **income mobility,** tending to move around in the income distribution over time. The most important source of income mobility is the "life-cycle" pattern of earnings: New entrants to the workforce tend to have lower incomes at first, but most workers can enjoy rising incomes as they gain experience on the job. Typically, annual earnings reach a maximum at about age fifty-five. Because peak earnings occur well beyond the **median age** of the population (now about age thirty-seven), a "snapshot" of the current distribution of earnings will find most individuals "on the way up" toward a higher position in the income distribution. People who have low earnings now are likely, on average, to have higher earnings in the future.

Another major source of income mobility stems from the operation of Lady Luck. At any point in time, the income of high-income people is likely to be abnormally high (relative to what they can expect on average) due to recent good luck—say, because they just won the lottery or

---

1. There are two reasons for this disagreement. First, a given dollar amount of in-kind transfers is generally less valuable than the same dollar amount of cash income, because cash offers the recipient a greater amount of choice in his or her consumption pattern. Second, medical care is an important in-kind transfer to the poor. Inclusion of all Medicaid expenditures for the poor would imply that the sicker the poor got, the richer they would be. Presumably, a correct measure would include only those medical expenses that the poor would have to incur if they were *not* poor and so had to pay for the medical care (or medical insurance) out of their own pockets.

just received a generous bonus. Conversely, the income of people who currently have low incomes is likely to be abnormally low due to recent bad luck—for example, because they are laid up after an automobile accident or have become temporarily unemployed. Over time, the effects of Lady Luck tend to average out across the population. Accordingly, people with high income today will tend to have lower income in the future, while people with low income today will tend to have higher future income; equivalently, many people living below the poverty line are there temporarily rather than permanently.

The importance of income mobility is strikingly revealed in studies examining the incomes of individuals over time. During the 1970s and 1980s, for example, among the people who were in the top 20 percent (quintile) of income earners at the beginning of the decade, fewer than half were in the top quintile by the end of the decade. Similarly, among the people who were in the bottom quintile at the beginning of the decade, almost half had moved out of that bracket by the end of the decade. Despite news stories that suggest otherwise, income mobility remains robust. From 1996 to 2005 (the decade most recently studied), *more than half* of the people who were in the bottom 20 percent income bracket in 1996 had moved out of that bracket by 2005.

APPEARANCES VERSUS REALITY

Nothwithstanding the data just cited, several forces have either increased income inequality in the United States or have given the appearance of such an increase, so it is best to be clear about these. Consider first that a rising proportion of the population is *far* above the poverty line. In 1969, for example, only about 4 percent of all people in America had incomes seven times greater than the poverty-line level. Today, about 20 percent of Americans have incomes that high (above $150,000 for a family of four). Much of this jump in incomes at the top of the income distribution has come at the very top. Thirty years ago, for example, people in the top 10 percent of earners in America pulled in about 31 percent of total income; today, they garner 37 percent. In even more rarified company, the top 1 percent of earners used to account for 9 percent of total income; today, they take in 16 percent of income. So even though inflation-adjusted incomes are rising across the board, they appear to be rising the fastest at the very top. Economists are seeking to explain this pattern, which first became apparent during the 1990s. Much work remains to be done, but a few answers are emerging.

First, some key demographic changes are occurring in America. The nation is aging, and an older population tends to have more income inequality than a young population because older people have had more time to experience rising or falling fortunes. Americans are also becoming better educated, and this tends to increase income inequality. People with little education have incomes that tend to cluster together, while the incomes of well-educated people spread out: Some choose to convert their **human capital** into much higher incomes, while others convert it into added leisure time. Taken together, these two demographic changes, aging and education, can account for more than 75 percent of the *appearance* of greater income inequality.

Second, a substantial part of the rapid income growth at the top has really been a matter of accounting fiction rather than reality. Until the late 1980s, there were substantial tax advantages for the very wealthy to have a large portion of their incomes counted as corporate income rather than personal income; in effect, a big chunk of income for the wealthy used to be hidden not from the tax authorities but from the policymakers who worry about the distribution of income. Subsequent changes in the tax laws have since encouraged people to report this income as personal rather than corporate income. Their incomes haven't really changed; it just looks to policymakers like they have.

The third factor we need to account for is the difference in consumption bundles of those near the top of the income distribution and those near the bottom. High-income individuals tend to spend a larger proportion of their incomes on labor-intensive services (such as investment advice, personal care, and domestic help). Low-income individuals tend to spend a larger share of their incomes on nondurable goods, such as food, clothing, shoes, and toiletries. As it turns out, over the past twenty-five years, the items consumed by lower-income individuals have fallen markedly in cost relative to the items consumed by the wealthy. Rising **real wages** have pushed up the costs of service-intensive consumption, while growing international trade with China, India, and other developing nations has pushed down the relative costs of items important to low-income individuals. Overall, this difference in **inflation** rates between the people at the top and those at the bottom of the income distribution has effectively wiped out *all* of the seeming change in their relative incomes over this period.

Life at the Bottom

Nevertheless, it is clear that many people at the bottom of the income distribution are struggling, so we need to take a look at what is going on here. One point is clear: Between 1990 and 2007, the United States experienced a huge influx of immigrants. Newcomers typically earn far less than long-term residents. When large numbers of them are added to the mix of people whose incomes are being measured, *average* income can fall, even when the incomes of all individuals are rising. Thus immigration has created downward pressure on *measured* incomes at the bottom of the distribution. But new immigrants have also added to competitive pressures in labor markets for less skilled individuals. On balance, it appears that immigration has probably lowered the wages of high school dropouts in America by 4 to 8 percent. And although this seems small, remember that it is occurring among people whose incomes are already low. Both of these effects are likely to lessen and perhaps even reverse due to the recession of 2007–2009 because deteriorating economic conditions in America caused many recent immigrants to return to their homelands.

Public policy has also taken its toll on the incomes of people at the bottom. The war on drugs, for example, has saddled millions of individuals with criminal records, and the impact has been disproportionately greatest on African Americans, whose incomes were lower to begin with. For example, since 1990, more than 2 million African American males have served time in jail on serious (felony) drug charges. Once they return to the workforce, they find that their felony records exclude them from a great many jobs—and not just jobs at the top. Often convicted felons cannot find positions that pay more than $8 per hour. The result is that the incomes of such individuals are sharply diminished, which means more poverty.

There is one bright spot on the poverty policy front, however. It is the "welfare reform" program undertaken in 1996. Previously, low-income families had been eligible to receive—for an unlimited duration—federal payments called Aid to Families with Dependent Children (AFDC). The program was converted in 1996 into Temporary Assistance to Needy Families (TANF). Limits were placed on the length of time individuals could receive payments, and all recipients were given additional incentives and assistance to enhance their job skills and to enter or reenter the **labor force**. The full impact of this policy change is still being studied, but it now appears that it has modestly raised incomes among those at the bottom of the income distribution.

Although the resilience of poverty in America is discouraging to the poor and to those who study their plight, it is useful to consider these issues in an international context. In other industrialized nations, such as Japan and most countries in Europe, people at the bottom of the income distribution sometimes (but not always) fare better than the poor in America. Although the poor typically receive a somewhat larger *share* of national income than in America, the national income they share is lower.

Hence compared to America, the poorest 10 percent of the population has a higher average income in Japan and Germany but a lower average income in the United Kingdom and Italy.

In developing nations—which is to say, for the vast majority of people around the world—poverty has a completely different meaning than it does in America. In Africa and much of Asia, for example, it is commonplace for people at the bottom of the income distribution to be living on the equivalent of $400 per *year* or less—in contrast to the $10,000 to $15,000 per year they would earn in America. This staggering difference in living standards is due to the vast differences in legal and economic **institutions** that are observed around the world. In America, as in many other industrialized nations, these institutions give people the incentives to put their talents to work and also protect the fruits of their labors from expropriation by the government. Thus the best antipoverty program anyone has ever seen is the creation of an institutional environment in which human beings are able to make maximum use of the talents with which they are endowed.

FOR CRITICAL ANALYSIS

1. Why do most modern societies try to reduce poverty? Why don't they do so by simply passing a law that requires that everybody have the same income?

2. How do the "rules of the game" help determine who will be poor and who will not? (*Hint:* How did the Civil Rights Act of 1964, which forbade discrimination on the basis of race, likely affect the incomes of African Americans compared to the incomes of white Americans?) Explain your answer.

3. Which of the following possible in-kind transfers do you think raises the "true" incomes of recipients the most: (a) free golf lessons, (b) free transportation on public buses, or (c) free food? Why?

4. Consider three alternative ways of helping poor people obtain better housing: (a) government-subsidized housing that costs $6,000 per year; (b) a housing **voucher** worth $6,000 per year toward rent on an apartment or a house; or (c) $6,000 per year in cash. Which would you prefer if you were poor? On what grounds might you make your decision?

CHAPTER 20

Will It Be Inflation or Deflation?

During the summer of 2008, when gas prices were skyrocketing, the Department of Labor issued a frightening statistic: The **consumer price index (CPI)** had risen more than 5 percent over the prior twelve months, the biggest jump in nearly twenty years. A few months later, the average price of gasoline paid in the United States had dropped from over $4 per gallon to well under $2 per gallon. And as the price of gas was plummeting, **inflation** among primary commodities (such as lumber, metals, and grain) was collapsing as well. As a result, in the late summer and early fall, the overall inflation rate shrank to almost nothing; in fact, during several months in late 2008 and early 2009, overall consumer prices actually *fell*—there was **deflation.** This rapid turn of events quickly switched the Web site and news channel chatter about the problems of inflation into chatter about the prospects for sustained deflation. Before we try to sort out whether inflation or deflation is in your future, let's first make sure we know to what we are referring.

A FORMAL DEFINITION OF INFLATION AND DEFLATION

Inflation is defined as a rise in the average of all prices, appropriately weighted for their importance in the typical consumer's budget. Inflation is not a change in one price. If the CPI rises by 3 percent over a twelve-month period, what we know is that the appropriately weighted average of prices of goods and services in the United States went up by 3 percent relative to a year before. (Sometimes you will see references to **core inflation.** This is a measure of the overall change in prices *excluding energy and food.*)

If the rate of change in the **price level** is negative rather than positive, we have deflation—on average, prices are falling rather than rising. As our brief introduction suggests, people worry a lot about inflation, but they also worry about deflation. So we must ask, are these concerns misplaced?

THE DOWNSIDE OF DEFLATION

Deflation can be troublesome for the economy. One reason is that most of the debts in a modern society like ours are expressed in terms of dollars. When there is deflation, the **real purchasing power** of those dollars goes up. For creditors, this is good news, because it means that people now owe them more, measured in terms of the goods and services those dollars will buy (so-called *real* terms). But for debtors, this is bad news, for exactly the same reason. Deflation raises the real burden of the debts they owe. Debtors have to pay back the sums owed with dollars that have a higher purchasing power than the dollars that were lent. In effect, during times of deflation, the inflation-corrected rate of interest (the **real interest rate**) goes up, imposing an added burden on debtors. Although it is possible that deflation's positive effects on creditors and negative effects on debtors could exactly cancel out, often it doesn't happen this way. The result can be significant economic dislocations.

There is also another problem with deflation. It never proceeds evenly and smoothly. During the Great Depression, when prices fell an *average* of about 8 percent per year for four straight years, this deflation did not proceed uniformly over time; some months and years were worse than others. Moreover, the deflation did not proceed uniformly across all goods; house prices, for example, fell much more than clothing prices. Because of the erratic and unpredictable progression of deflation, individuals and businesses had to focus much of their attention on trying to predict the magnitude and timing of changes in the prices of goods and services. Had there been no deflation, they could have been producing new goods and services instead. The result was that the U.S. economy had fewer goods and services available for **consumption.**

THE COSTS OF INFLATION

Inflation acts as a tax on people's holdings of money—that is, their holdings of **currency** and **checkable deposits.** All of us hold some currency and checkable deposits because of the convenience they provide. As a result, each of us loses **wealth** whenever there is inflation, because the purchasing power of our money balances decreases at the rate of inflation.

Assume that you have $20 stashed in your wallet as an emergency cash reserve; that is, you have no immediate expectation of spending it. If at the end of one year there has been a 10 percent rise in the price level, the purchasing power of that $20 note will only be $18, measured in terms of taxi rides or sandwiches. You will have lost value equal to 10 percent times the amount of currency you kept in your wallet.

In essence, then, the purchasing power, or real value, of the money we hold depreciates when there is inflation. The only way we can avoid this type of **inflation tax** on the money we hold is to reduce our holdings of money. But doing this is not an easy matter. It is beneficial—productive— to have money on hand to pay for the things that we want when we want them rather than trying to purchase everything at the beginning of a pay period so as to minimize the dollars in our checkable accounts or in our wallets.

Thus one cost to society of inflation is that it increases the cost of holding money. For society as a whole, we therefore use *too little* money during periods of inflation. This effect is greatest for currency, because its real value falls one-for-one with each rise in the price level. The tax is much less for checkable deposits, because many of these accounts pay some interest, and that **nominal interest rate** rises when the expected inflation rate rises.

We should also add that periods of inflation generate exactly the sort of prediction problems that arise when there is deflation. Inflation never proceeds evenly across time or across goods. As a result, during periods of inflation, consumers and businesses must spend some of their time trying to predict exactly how the inflation is likely to proceed. And this in turn means they are spending less time producing output that is available for consumption.

INFLATION, DEFLATION, AND THE MONEY SUPPLY

Throughout the history of the world, there has been a fairly consistent long-run relationship between the change in the price level over time and the change in the **money supply**—money in circulation. This relationship does not move in lockstep fashion in the short run. But it does hold, on average, over longer periods of time, and it is *sustained* inflation or deflation that is a cause for the greatest concern.

There are several ways to define a country's money supply; for our purposes, let's treat it as currency plus all of the funds in accounts that can be used for transactions, such as those accessible with debit cards. As already noted, a predictable long-term relationship has been observed between changes in the money supply and changes in the general price level: sustained, rapid monetary growth yields inflation, and sustained shrinkage in the money supply causes deflation. **Expansive monetary policy** on the part of the **Federal Reserve** caused the money supply to increase quite rapidly after the short **recession** in 2001–2002, for example. The expansion in the money supply continued through the decade. Not surprisingly, inflation crept upward, from 1.6 percent in 2001 to over 4 percent in 2007. And as inflation rose, so did concerns over how bad it would get.

DEFLATION DISCUSSIONS FRONT AND CENTER

The talk of inflation came to a screeching halt at the end of the summer of 2008. Partly it was those plummeting gas and commodity prices that took the steam out of the inflation talk. But the financial panic of 2008 also changed sentiments about the likely course of the price level in 2009 and beyond.

Indeed, all of Washington, D.C., and the financial world suddenly started worrying about deflation. According to Professor Frederic Mishkin of Columbia University, "If inflation expectations were to decline sharply, that would greatly increase the risk of deflation." Further, according to American Enterprise Institute researcher Desmond Lachman, "A deep and prolonged recession could raise the specter of deflation of the sort that plagued the Japanese economy." Lachman was referring to the 1990s, when Japan experienced a flat or declining price level (some economists refer to this as Japan's "lost decade").

Will this talk of deflation turn out to be reality as you are reading these words? We are skeptical. Among other things, the Fed reacted to the Panic of '08 with much easier credit policies, injecting more money into the economy. Initially, banks were not very amenable to lending out these new funds, so there were few signs of inflationary pressure early in 2009. But unless the Fed manages to move these funds out of the system as the economy recovers from the recession, inflationary trouble lies ahead.

So here is our prediction, notwithstanding the dire predictions of falling prices. Deflation may be in your future, but if so, only for a relatively short time. Inflation, at least in the long run, is more likely. Eventually, all the increases in the money supply that were made possible by the Fed's credit expansion in 2008 will be realized in 2010 and beyond. Once the economy starts moving again, particularly the financial sector, banks will start lending their **excess reserves.** The money supply will be growing again, and the price level will be rising. So in the short run, you may see a bit of both rising and falling prices, but over the long haul, we would bet that you have mostly inflation to look forward to.

FOR CRITICAL ANALYSIS

1. When the price of a barrel of petroleum increased greatly in 2008, every news article about rising oil prices had a negative slant. When the price of petroleum dropped by more than half later in the year, the press said little, and much of what the press said was negative. Those negative comments focused on fears that there would not be enough new exploration for oil in the future. Is it really possible for a rise in the price of a good to be "bad" and also for a drop in the price of that same good to be "bad"?

2. If the inflation rate is fully anticipated, what are the ways in which consumers and businesses can protect against the resulting loss of purchasing power?

3. Who are the people who are most affected by unanticipated inflation? Why?

CHAPTER 21

Is It Real, or Is It Nominal?

Every few years, some important commodity, such as gasoline, electricity, or food, experiences a spike in prices. Reporters examine such price spikes and plaster newspapers, magazines, and Web sites with the appropriate headlines—sometimes relentlessly, day after day. TV commentators interview frustrated and worried Americans who spout the expected negative reactions to the higher prices of essential items in their budgets. The world, it would seem, is coming to an end.

WAS GAS REALLY EXPENSIVE?

Let's just take one often-in-the-press example, gasoline prices. The authors of the book you are reading are old enough to remember the TV interviews that ensued when the price of gas first hit the unprecedented level of $1 per gallon, back in 1980. The same types of interviews occurred when the price of a gallon of gas broke the $2 barrier, early in 2005, and lodged above $3 in 2007. Not surprisingly, virtually the same types of interviews occurred when the price of a gallon of gas rose above $4 in the summer of 2008. At each point in time, everyone interviewed had the same response, even though years had passed between the different price spikes: "I guess I'll just have to stop driving." "I'm going to get a bike." "I'm selling my big car and getting a small one." And of course, each time there was an accompanying story about how record numbers of people were (or soon would be) flocking to their neighborhood motor scooter dealerships.

If we wish to sensibly analyze the effects of higher prices on the quantity demanded and the quantity supplied of any good or service in this world, we can rely neither on what journalists report nor on what

Americans say when they are interviewed. After all, what is important is not what people say but what they do. As economists, we best understand consumers by their **revealed preferences.** Similarly, businesspeople are best understood by their actions, not their words. What people do is reflected in how much they actually buy of any good or service after its price changes, not by their complaints to a TV reporter or what they post on their blog or on Facebook or MySpace.

RELATIVE PRICES, NOMINAL PRICES, AND INFLATION

For both microeconomic and macroeconomic analysis, the relevant price is the price *relative to* all other prices, because people's decisions are based on **relative prices,** not **nominal prices.** The latter simply tell us the number of pieces of paper (dollar bills) you must hand over for a good. Nominal prices tell us nothing about the real sacrifice (measured in terms of goods or labor services) that one must make to obtain those goods. Relative prices reflect the real sacrifice involved in acquiring a good because they tell us the price of a good or service relative to the price of another good or service or to the average of all other prices. Relative prices tell us how much of other goods we must sacrifice.

Said another way, we have to separate out the rise in the general price level, called **inflation,** and the rise in the nominal price of a particular good or service. If *all* nominal prices went up exactly 3 percent, there would be no change in relative prices. This inflation of 3 percent per year would not change the real sacrifice entailed in acquiring any particular good. In the real world, even during periods of inflation, some prices go up faster than others and some prices even go down—witness the price of computing power, DVD players, and MP3 players. Nevertheless, if we want to predict people's behavior, we must know what has happened to the *relative* price of a good, and to determine this, we must adjust for inflation.

GAS PRICES REVISITED

Now let's get back to our example of gasoline prices. Your grandparents might be able to talk about buying gas for 30 cents a gallon (its average nominal price most of the time between 1956 and 1964). Today, what you pay in dollars per gallon is many times that level. People still drive nonetheless—indeed, the use of gasoline for cars and trucks in the United States is roughly triple what it was when the nominal price of gas was only 30 cents. Something must have happened. The most important "something" is a general rise in all prices, including gasoline prices.

In the summer of 2008, the price of gasoline spiked over $4 per gallon. Presidential candidate Barack Obama argued that the government should intervene on gas prices to "give families some relief." Two-thirds of American voters at that time said they thought that the price of gas was "an extremely important political issue." (Of course, when gas prices started tumbling in the fall of 2008, there were not many front-page articles or TV interviews with happy consumers. And the politicians simply became silent on this subject.) Consider, though, that at its nominal price at the beginning of 2009, the *relative* price of gas was back down to about what it had been in 1960—after correcting for overall inflation. For many people, this is a shocking revelation. But correcting for inflation is absolutely essential if you want to sensibly analyze the price of anything over time. Often we talk about the **real price** of a good or service. This refers specifically to subtracting the rate of inflation from the change in a nominal price over time. Not surprisingly, we also do the same exercise when we want to go from **nominal income** to **real income** over time.

THE IMPORTANCE OF HIGHER DISPOSABLE INCOME

Another fact is particularly relevant when thinking about the real burden of gasoline. People are becoming more productive over time because they are getting better educated and because ongoing technological change enables us to produce more with a given input of our time. As a result of this higher **productivity,** U.S. consumers' **disposable incomes** generally rise from one year to the next—and certainly rise on average over longer periods of time. As Americans become richer on average, they are financially able to handle even higher relative prices of those items they wish to purchase, gasoline included.

To help us understand this point better, researchers Indur Goklany and Jerry Taylor came up with an "affordability index." They compared family income to the price of gas from 1949 to 2008. They arbitrarily set 1960 at an affordability index of 1; relative to this, a higher affordability index number means that something is more affordable. Even when gas was $4.15 per gallon, the affordability gas index was 1.35. In other words, the ratio of the average person's disposable income to the price of gasoline was higher by about 35 percent in 2008 than it was in 1960— gasoline was *more* affordable than it had been back in 1960, when your grandparents were filling up their tanks at 30 cents a gallon. That's hard to believe for some of us but true nonetheless. And once gas prices started going down at the end of 2008, the gas affordability index rose even more, passing 2, meaning that gasoline was more than twice as affordable at the beginning of 2009 as it had been in 1960.

PRODUCT QUALITY CHANGES

The quality of gasoline typically does not change much over time. But the quality of many other products often changes significantly over time, usually for the better. Often we forget about this crucial aspect when we start comparing prices of a good or service over time. If you ask senior citizens today how much they paid for their first car, you might get prices in the range of $2,000 to $5,000. The average new car today costs around $24,000 (in nominal dollars). By now, of course, you know that if you want to compare these numbers, you have to first account for the inflation that has occurred over whatever time period you are examining. In this case, adjusting for inflation still means that the relative price of a car appears to be about 30 percent higher than it was, say, fifty years ago.

Does that necessarily mean that a car is really 30 percent more expensive than it was in 1960? Probably not. We must take into account improved quality features of cars today compared to those of fifty years ago. Today (unlike fifty years ago), the average car has the following:

- Antilock computer-controlled power brakes
- Power steering
- Digital radio with CD or MP3 player
- Air conditioning
- Steel-belted radial tires
- Cruise control
- Power windows and locks
- Air bags
- Forty percent better fuel economy

The list of improved and new features is actually much longer. Today, the average car is safer, breaks down less often, needs fewer tune-ups, has a host of amenities that were not even dreamed of fifty years ago—and almost certainly lasts for at least twice as many miles. If you correct not only for inflation but also for these quality increases, the relative price of cars today has almost certainly *fallen* appreciably in the past fifty years, in spite of the "sticker shock" that you may experience when you go shopping for a new car. That is, appearances to the contrary, the inflation-corrected **constant-quality price** of automobiles is actually lower today than it was five decades ago.

DECLINING NOMINAL PRICES

The necessity of adjusting for inflation and quality changes continues to apply even when we are examining goods whose nominal prices have declined over time. A good example is computing power. The nominal price of the average personal computer has gone down in spite of general inflation over the past several decades. These days, a Windows-based desktop computer has an average price of about $550; for a laptop, the average price is a bit over $700. A decade ago, the average machines in each category would have had nominal prices of twice as much. You might be tempted to conclude, then, that the price of personal computing has fallen by 50 percent. You'd be wrong: The price has actually fallen by more than 50 percent.

Why? There are two reasons. First, over the past ten years, the average dollar prices of all goods increased by 30 percent; that is how much overall inflation there has been. That means that the *relative* price of the average computer has fallen by two-thirds, which, of course, is greater than 50 percent. But even here we are missing something extremely important: The quality of what you are buying—computing power—has skyrocketed. The processor speed of the average computer today is at least ten times greater than it was ten years ago and is increasing exponentially. Moreover, hard drives are bigger, monitors are flat-screen LCDs instead of bulky old cathode ray tubes, laptops are lighter, RAM is larger—the list of improvements goes on and on. And despite people's frustrations with both the hardware and software of the personal computer today, longtime users can tell you that both are vastly more reliable than they were a decade ago. Thus if you only look at the inflation-corrected decrease in computer prices, you will be underestimating the *true* decrease in the relative price of computers.

The moral of our story is simple. At some point in your education, you learned that "what goes up must come down." Now you know that when it comes to prices, it is often the case that "what goes up has actually gone done." It is a lesson worth keeping in mind if you really want to understand the behavior of consumers and businesses alike.

FOR CRITICAL ANALYSIS

1. Create a list of goods (or services) whose quality has improved over time in such a way that the current prices of these commodities do not accurately reflect their real prices, even after adjusting for inflation. Now see if you can come up with a list of items whose quality has systematically *decreased* over time. Can you suggest why it is easier to find examples of the former than the latter?

2. The demand for small-engine motor scooters jumped when the price of gasoline started moving up in the summer of 2008. Make a prediction about the demand for this form of transportation in, say, two years from today. Explain your answer.

3. Explain why you will make more accurate predictions if you focus on the changing incentives people face rather than listening to what they say they are going to do.

PART FIVE
Economic Growth

CHAPTER 22

Rich Nation, Poor Nation

Why do the citizens of some nations grow rich while the inhabitants of others remain poor? Your initial answer might be "because of differences in the **natural-resource endowments** of the nations." It is true that ample endowments of energy, timber, and fertile land all help increase **wealth.** But natural resources can be only a very small part of the answer, as witnessed by many counterexamples. Switzerland and Luxembourg, for example, are nearly devoid of key natural resources, and yet decade after decade, the real income of citizens of those lands has grown rapidly, propelling them to great prosperity. Similarly, Hong Kong, which consists of but a few square miles of rock and hillside, is one of the economic miracles of modern times, while in Russia, a land amply endowed with vast quantities of virtually every important resource, most people remain mired in economic misery.

Unraveling the Mystery of Growth

A number of recent studies have begun to unravel the mystery of **economic growth.** Repeatedly, they have found that it is the fundamental political and legal **institutions** of society that are conducive to growth. Of these, political stability, secure private property rights, and legal systems based on the **rule of law** are among the most important. Such institutions encourage people to make long-term investments in improvements to land and in all forms of **physical** and **human capital.** These investments raise the **capital stock,** which in turn provides for more growth long into the future. And the cumulative effects of this growth over time eventually yield much higher **standards of living.**

Table 22–1 Differing Legal Systems

Common Law Nations	Civil Law Nations
Australia	Brazil
Canada	Egypt
India	France
Israel	Greece
New Zealand	Italy
United Kingdom	Mexico
United States	Sweden

Professor Paul Mahoney of the University of Virginia, for example, has studied the contrasting effects of different legal systems on economic growth. Many legal systems around the world today are based on one of two models: the English **common law system** and the French **civil law system.** Common law systems reflect a conscious decision in favor of a limited role for government and emphasize the importance of the judiciary in constraining the power of the executive and legislative branches of government. In contrast, civil law systems favor the creation of a strong centralized government in which the legislature and the executive branch have the power to grant preferential treatment to special interests. Table 22–1 shows a sample of common law and civil law nations.

THE IMPORTANCE OF SECURE PROPERTY RIGHTS

Mahoney finds that the security of property rights is much stronger in nations with common law systems, such as the United Kingdom and its former colonies, including the United States. In nations such as France and its former colonies, the civil law systems are much more likely to yield unpredictable changes in the rules of the game—the structure of **property and contract rights.** This, in turn, makes people reluctant to make long-term fixed investments in nations with civil law systems, a fact that ultimately slows their growth and lowers the standard of living of their citizens.

The reasoning here is simple. If the police will not help you protect your rights to a home or car, you are less likely to acquire those **assets.** Similarly, if you cannot easily enforce business or employment contracts, you are much less likely to enter into those contracts—and thus less likely to produce as many goods or services. Furthermore, if you cannot plan for the future because you don't know what the rules of the game will be ten years or perhaps even one year from now, you are far less likely to make productive long-term investments that require years to pay off. Common law systems seem to do a better job at enforcing contracts and securing property rights and thus would be expected to promote economic activity now and economic growth over time. When Mahoney examined the economic performance of nations around the world from 1960 until the 1990s, he found that economic growth has been one-third higher in the common law nations, with their strong property rights, than it has been in civil law nations. Over the years covered by his study, the increase in the standard of living—measured by **real per capita income**—was more than 20 percent greater in common law nations than in civil law nations. If such a pattern persisted over the span of a century, it would produce a staggering 80 percent differential in terms of real per capita income in favor of nations with secure property rights.

THE IMPORTANCE OF OTHER INSTITUTIONS

The economists William Easterly and Ross Levine have taken a much broader view, both across time and across institutions, assessing the economic growth of a variety of nations since their days as colonies. These authors examine how institutions such as political stability, protection of persons and property against violence or theft, security of contracts, and freedom from regulatory burdens contribute to sustained economic growth. They find that it is key institutions such as these, rather than natural-resource endowments, that explain long-term differences in growth and thus present-day differences in levels of real income. To illustrate the powerful effect of institutions, consider the contrast between Mexico, with a real per capita income of about $12,000 today, and the United States, with a real per capita income of about $48,000. Easterly and Levine conclude that if Mexico had developed with the same political and legal institutions that the United States has enjoyed, per capita income in Mexico today would be equal to that in the United States.

THE HISTORICAL ROOTS
OF TODAY'S INSTITUTIONS

In light of the tremendous importance of institutions in determining long-term growth, Easterly and Levine go on to ask another important question: How have countries gotten the political and legal institutions they have today? The answer has to do with disease, of all things. The seventy-two countries Easterly and Levine examined are all former European colonies in which a variety of colonial strategies were pursued. In Australia, New Zealand, and North America, the colonists found geography and climate that were conducive to good health. Permanent settlement in such locations was attractive, and so the settlers created institutions to protect private property and curb the power of the state. But when Europeans arrived in Africa and South America, they encountered tropical diseases—such as malaria and yellow fever—that produced high mortality among the settlers. This discouraged permanent settlement and encouraged a mentality focused on extracting metals, cash crops, and other resources. This, in turn, provided little incentive to promote democratic institutions or stable long-term property rights systems. The differing initial institutions helped shape economic growth over the years, and their persistence continues to shape the political and legal character and the standard of living in these nations today.

No Property Rights, No Property

Recent events also illustrate that the effects of political and legal institutions can be drastically accelerated—at least in the wrong direction. When Zimbabwe won its independence from Great Britain in 1980, it was one of the most prosperous nations in Africa. Soon after taking power as Zimbabwe's first (and thus far only) president, Robert Mugabe began disassembling that nation's rule of law, tearing apart the institutions that had helped it grow rich. He reduced the security of property rights in land and eventually confiscated those rights altogether. Mugabe has also gradually taken control of the prices of most goods and services in his nation and even controls the price of its national currency, at least the price at which Zimbabweans are allowed to trade it. The Mugabe government has also confiscated large **stocks** of food and most other things of value that might be exported out of or imported into Zimbabwe. In short, anything that is produced or saved has become subject to confiscation, so the incentives to do either are—to put it mildly—reduced. As a result, between 1980 and 1996, real per capita income in Zimbabwe fell by one-third, and since 1996 it has fallen by an additional third. Eighty percent of the workforce is unemployed, investment is nonexistent, and the annual inflation rate reached *231 million percent* in 2008. Decades of labor and capital investment have been destroyed because the very institutions that made progress possible have been eliminated. It is a lesson we ignore at our peril.

FOR CRITICAL ANALYSIS

1. Consider two countries, A and B, and suppose that both have identical *physical* endowments of, say, iron ore. But in country A, any profits that are made from mining the ore are subject to confiscation by the government, while in country B, there is no such risk. How does the risk of expropriation affect the *economic* endowments of the two nations? In which nation are people richer?

2. In light of your answer to question 1, how do you explain the fact that in some countries there is widespread political support for government policies that expropriate resources from some groups for the purpose of handing them out to other groups?

3. Going to college in the United States raises average lifetime earnings by about two-thirds, given our current political and economic institutions. But suppose that ownership of the added income generated by your college education suddenly became uncertain. Specifically, suppose a law was passed in your state that enabled the governor to select 10 percent of the graduating class from all of the state's colleges and universities each year and impose a tax of up to 50 percent on the difference between the earnings of these people in their first job and the average earnings of people in the state who have only a high school education. What would happen to immigration into or out of the state? What would happen to attendance at colleges and universities within the state? If the governor were allowed to arbitrarily decide who got hit with the new tax, what would happen to campaign contributions to the governor? What would happen to the number of people "volunteering" to work in the governor's next campaign? Would your decision to invest in a college education change? Explain your responses.

CHAPTER 23

Return of the Luddites: Technophobia and Economic Growth

In March 1811, General Ned Ludd and his Army of Redressers began the attacks. The objects of their rage were factories in Nottingham, England, that were using newly installed weaving machines. The **Luddites,** as they came to be known, feared that the new machines would take away their jobs and leave them unemployed. Passage of the Frame Breaking Act (which specified the death penalty for anyone who destroyed industrial machinery) soon brought a halt to the Luddites' activities. But their spirit is resurgent today in people who see catastrophe in every new technology.

TECHNOLOGY AND WEALTH

There is no doubt that technological advances have fueled **economic growth** and thereby markedly improved the lives and lengthened the life spans of human beings. Whether we look at the wheel, which drastically reduces transportation costs, or vaccines and antibiotics, which save the lives of millions of people every year, technology has raised our **wealth.** Higher wealth, in turn, enables us to make a broader range of decisions regarding the use of a wider range of **resources.** People who are wealthy can choose to have improved health for their children or higher environmental quality, or—if they are wealthy enough—both. People who are poor must watch their offspring die of preventable childhood diseases, are powerless to improve the environmental conditions in which they live, and face the prospect of never doing anything about either outcome. It is no accident that the residents of technologically advanced nations have longer life spans; they live longer because the technology has raised their wealth and enabled them to choose more healthful diets and higher-quality health care. Likewise, it is no accident that the average life span around the world rose to sixty-seven years from thirty during the twentieth century. Longevity increased because the spread of technology raised wealth and enabled people to make life-preserving and health-enhancing choices that simply were not feasible in 1900. And note finally that higher wealth, spurred by technological advances, has enabled us to choose better outcomes everywhere in our lives, including education, environmental quality, cultural amenities, and charitable activities.

To be sure, not every technological advance has made us unambiguously better off. Nuclear weapons, for example, have threatened human survival since their invention. More recently, improved knowledge of how to refine anthrax spores was used to kill people and poses the possibility of killing still more. Nevertheless, on balance, the overwhelming impact of technological advance has been to spur economic growth and, in so doing, vastly improve the economic condition of humankind.

Despite the huge benefits created by technological advances, many people in addition to Ned Ludd's Army of Redressers have objected to the introduction of new technology. Because these objections are both persistent and loudly voiced, it is important that we examine them carefully to assess their validity.

THE FEAR OF COMPETITION

The Luddites' actions were driven by one motive, pure and simple: They were hand weavers who objected to the competition offered by the new mechanized weaving machines of the day. They perceived, quite correctly, that the new machines would reduce the **demand** for hand weavers, and so they sought to prevent this competition. But the new technology did more than compel many hand weavers to learn how to use the machines or to find employment in other pursuits. It also drastically reduced the price of textiles, enabling people to own more than one set of clothes, worn all day, every day—a "luxury" that reduced deaths from cold weather in the winter and hot weather in the summer. Moreover, the rapid spread of the textile industry helped spur the development of other technology that led to the creation of new industries, such as chemicals, which have further raised our wealth. To be sure, the hand weavers were worse off, but the gains then and later to the rest of society have been staggeringly greater.

In more recent times, the fear of competition has spurred numerous other objections to technological advances. For example, when vegetable-oil-based margarine was invented around the middle of the twentieth century, the dairy industry claimed that the new product was a threat to human health (this from the purveyors of animal-fat-based butter!) and a fraud as well because the new stuff was made to look like butter. Dairy lobbyists were successful in persuading many state legislatures to outlaw yellow margarine, forcing consumers to take home white margarine from the store and mix it with yellow food coloring in their own kitchens. The substantially lower price of the new product was enough to overcome dairy industry resistance, however, and margarine became a commercial success long before the health *benefits* of vegetable oil over animal fat became apparent.

Somewhat later in the twentieth century, the development of electronic typesetting offered competition for Linotype machines, which required skilled workers to set metal type before newspapers and books could be printed. The first of these electronic typesetters, called the Photon, was four times as fast as the Linotype and could be operated by lower-wage clerical workers rather than by expensive members of the International Typographical Union (ITU). The competitive threat posed by the Photon led the ITU to call a four-month strike against all New York City newspapers in 1962–1963. The strike ended the life of the *New York Mirror,* but the remaining newspapers won from the union the right to use the Photon—in return for guaranteeing all existing ITU typesetters lifetime employment contracts. The new machines drastically reduced the costs of printing newspapers, books, and other materials, thereby raising society's wealth. Within a few decades, of course, the Photons themselves were made obsolete by yet another technological advance, the relatively low-cost but high-powered personal computer—a development no doubt objected to by Photon operators.

THE FEAR OF ADVERSE EFFECTS

It has become commonplace in recent years to object to specific new technology on the grounds that it has or *might have* adverse effects on human, animal, or plant life. This, for example, is the source of objections to irradiated food and to genetically modified food.

Fear of adverse effects stems largely from scares over DDT and other pesticides, which arose during the 1960s. It was asserted, for example, that DDT caused cancer in humans and should be banned. Despite the claims of dangers to humans, the World Health Organization has found that "the only confirmed cases of injury have been the result of massive accidental or suicidal ingestion." Moreover, the use of DDT was enormously successful in wiping out malaria in many nations around the world, saving the lives of millions of people. DDT even significantly cut the costs of raising fruits and vegetables, thereby increasing the consumption of these important cancer-fighting foodstuffs. Despite the evidence, however, most countries have banned DDT. The result has been a resurgence of malaria, the deaths of millions of people living in tropical climates, and an unequivocal threat to the lives of hundreds of millions of other human beings.

On the other side of the coin, there is evidence that indiscriminate use of DDT threatened the health and existence of numerous animal species, including the bald eagle. It is perhaps instructive, though, that recent research reveals that this harm to animal life resulted from excessive applications of DDT, that government agencies (rather than farmers) were responsible for almost all such applications, and that if the government agencies had followed the manufacturers' instructions, it is likely that no animal species would ever have been threatened.

THE FEAR OF WEALTH

Strange as it may seem, the third objection to technological advances is that they stimulate economic growth and make us richer! There are two complaints here. First, there is the argument that economic growth promotes population growth, which will eventually overwhelm our supposedly fixed resource base and thereby lead to widespread starvation and misery. Second, there is the claim that economic growth inevitably leads to environmental degradation, which in turn threatens the existence not just of humans but of all species. Whatever the plausibility of these arguments to some people, the evidence clearly refutes these notions.

Technological advances that raise our wealth *do* tend to promote population growth. After all, it takes resources to live. But the positive effect of wealth on population is much less than you might think because as people get richer, they generally have fewer children per family. Instead of pouring resources into a larger number of children, they put those resources into a higher-quality experience for the fewer children that they do rear—for example, by spending more funds on education. More important, a crucial way that technological advances raise our wealth is by enabling us to extract resources more effectively and to use those resources more efficiently. Just consider some seemingly mundane examples:

- Steam injection wells permit more complete extraction of petroleum.
- Improved machinery and designs have cut the weight of aluminum beverage cans by 40 percent.
- Advances in chemistry have created stronger, lighter plastics and longer-lasting paints and finishes.

As the result of these and thousands of other inventions, the world's reserves of oil, natural gas, aluminum, zinc, and many other commodities have *risen* over time, despite our continued use of these resources. So to be concerned that growing prosperity will cause population growth that outstrips our resources is to fail to understand the sources of that growing prosperity.

But what impact does higher wealth have on the environment? After all, more consumption necessitates more production, and that, it seems, must lead to more pollution. This reasoning would be correct if it did not ignore two crucial facts. Technological advances do help promote production, but they make it possible to produce goods with fewer inputs per unit of output, and they also make possible the development of cleaner processes, such as hybrid cars and solar power. Moreover, although early stages of economic development are often accompanied by environmental degradation, the effect is soon overwhelmed by another one. Environmental quality is a **normal good,** that is, a good that people want to consume more of as they get richer. The result is that soon after technological advances begin pushing up incomes, people begin insisting that more and more resources be devoted to protecting and enhancing environmental amenities. Indeed, once **per capita income** reaches about $8,000 in a country, environmental quality begins improving dramatically, and incomes rise even more. Thus technological advances don't merely bring us lighter beverage cans; they ultimately bring us a better environment.

THE BOTTOM LINE

The lesson of history—emphatically and unmistakably—is that technological change raises our wealth and improves the lot of humankind. Yes, there is always the *possibility* that some new technology could cause more harm than good. But what is certain is that systematic attempts to suppress technological change *almost always* cause more harm than good. It is sensible to consider carefully the potential adverse effects of new technologies and to make sure that all of the costs of those technologies are taken into account. But it is foolhardy—and impoverishing—to let unfounded fears blind us to the benefits of those technologies.

FOR CRITICAL ANALYSIS

1. If we want to obtain the maximum possible good for humankind, why is it important to take into account both the benefits and the costs of new technology, rather than simply focusing on one or the other?

2. Some people argue that a special government agency should assess, pass judgment on, and either permit or prevent the introduction of all new technological advances. Are there any reasons to think a government agency would do a better job at this (that is, benefit humankind more) than the private-sector inventors of those technologies? Are there any reasons to think such a government agency would do an inferior job?

3. Analyze the economic consequences of outlawing the wheel, which was, at the time, a major technological innovation. First, select some specific markets, and see how making the wheel illegal would affect demand and **supply** and affect the economic well-being of producers and consumers in those markets. Second, consider the economy as a whole: Is the level of real income likely to be higher or lower as a result of abolishing the wheel? How does the wheel differ from other major technological innovations, past or present?

CHAPTER 24

The Lion, the Dragon, and the Tigers: Economic Growth in Asia

In the 1980s, a group of economies in Asia came to be known as the "Asian tigers" because of their aggressive approach to **economic growth.** Among the tigers were Singapore, Malaysia, Thailand, and Indonesia. All took the view that a combination of low wages and high export sales represented the fast track to economic growth and prosperity. Now these tigers have been overtaken by the "dragon" of Asia, China—which is following the same path with perhaps even greater success.

THE GUANGDONG EXPERIMENT

For decades after the Communists' rise to power in 1949, China was best known for poverty and repression, and its aggression came mostly on the military front. But in recent years, *economic* aggression has become the Chinese byword. Although both poverty and repression are still the norm, both are changing for the better. China, it seems, is trying to learn from capitalism, even if not converting to it.

China's economic offensive began thirty years ago in its southeastern province of Guangdong. The Chinese leadership decided to use this province as a test case to see if capitalist **direct foreign investment** could stimulate economic growth in a way that could be politically controlled. The experience was deemed a success—economic growth soared amid political stability. What the government learned from the experience helped it smooth the 1997 transition of Hong Kong from British to Chinese control. Most important in terms of China's long-term economic aspirations, many foreign investors came to view the Guangdong experiment as solid evidence that they could invest in China without fear that the Communist government would confiscate their capital. Around 1992, foreign investment began to flow into China. Today, the annual rate of such investment is more than twenty times greater than it was at the beginning of the 1990s.

THAT SAME OLD SONG: DEMAND AND SUPPLY

Economic investment is being attracted to China by two powerful forces: **demand** and **supply**. On the demand side, 1.3 billion people live there, some 20 percent of the world's population. Although **per capita income** is still low by world standards, it has been growing by about 7 percent per year, after adjusting for inflation. At that rate, the **standard of living** for the Chinese people—and hence their **purchasing power** in world markets—is doubling every decade. China is already the world's largest cell-phone market, with 500 million customers. It is estimated that within a few years, China will account for 25 percent of the world's purchases of personal computers. Indeed, China now spends over $100 billion a year on information technology and services, and this amount is growing at an annual rate of 20 percent. Within two decades, the Chinese economy will likely surpass the U.S. economy and become the world's largest.

With its population of 1.3 billion individuals, China also offers attractions on the supply side. Highly skilled workers have been plentiful in the Chinese labor market. China's universities produce hundreds of thousands of engineering graduates each year. The fact that the Chinese workforce is generally well educated and often English-speaking has helped make the country attractive to foreign employers. Collaborative scientific ventures between Chinese researchers and U.S. firms are becoming increasingly common. A research team at Beijing University played a role in deciphering the genetic makeup of rice, for example. The American computer hardware and software firms Intel, IBM, Oracle, and Microsoft have shifted some key components of their research to China in recent years. Indeed, American firms of all types are setting up operations in China.

WORRIED TIGERS

Malaysia, Thailand, and Singapore are increasingly concerned by the competition they face from their neighbor to the north. Chinese medium- and high-tech industries have cut into the market share of the very sectors that helped fuel the growth of the Asian tigers. The situation is even more critical in Japan: Wages are much higher there than in China, but the Japanese technological lead over China is gradually eroding. "Are we to become a vassal of the Chinese dynasty again?" asked one Japanese official, clearly concerned that his nation's manufacturers were having trouble competing with Chinese firms. Eventually, Japan and China's other neighbors will adjust to the growing economic presence of China, but the transition may not be pleasant.

THE IMPORTANCE OF LABOR

Most observers agree that labor market developments will play a key role in the future. To this point, an important element of China's competitiveness in world markets has been the low wages there. Even though American and European firms operating in China choose to pay their workers more than state-owned enterprises pay, the firms still enjoy considerable savings. Only a few years ago, unskilled and semiskilled labor in China cost only 25 percent as much as in Europe. Moreover, in the past, foreign firms were able to hire engineers for salaries that were only 10 to 20 percent of the cost of hiring engineers in America or Europe.

Labor markets in China are changing rapidly, however. Between 2000 and 2008, average wages rose 50 percent, with bigger increases among higher-skilled workers. Many firms were unable to hire as many workers as they would have liked, and most had to upgrade their fringe benefits and other on-the-job amenities just to retain existing workers. Wages are still well below American and European levels, but the gap has closed, undercutting the competitive advantage of many Chinese firms. The most recent worldwide recession has altered labor market conditions as significantly in China as anywhere, but it is unlikely to permanently impede China's march to economic superpower status.

THE AWAKENING LION

Just to China's southwest, another giant is stirring. Around 1990, the lion of India began to throw off the self-imposed shackles of nearly a half-century of markets largely closed to international competition. The central government began opening many state-owned companies to competition from private-sector rivals. FedEx and United Parcel Service (UPS) have made huge inroads on the Indian postal service, and numerous foreign firms are now competing with the state-owned telephone service, which had long been a complete **monopoly.**

Entry into the Indian market brought familiarity with its workforce, many of whose members are fluent in English. The technical capabilities of graduates of top Indian universities, combined with their English skills and low wages, made them perfect staffers for a proliferation of call centers that have opened up across India. Tens of thousands of technical and customer-relations jobs that used to go to Middle America are now held by the growing middle class in India.

But India, too, has struggled with growth. The talent pool at the top is thin: Only a dozen or so of India's seventeen thousand universities and colleges can compete with America's best, and the wages of graduates of these top schools have soared. Moreover, India suffers from overwhelming infrastructure problems: Much of its road system is either overcrowded or in disrepair, and its port facilities are in desperate need of modernization. For the time being, such transportation problems are likely to keep India from becoming a major manufacturing powerhouse. India has also been hampered by its huge and seemingly permanent government bureaucracy. For example, despite the fact that the postal service there has lost more than half of its business to newcomers such as FedEx and UPS, none of the 550,000 postal service employees can be fired.

WHAT DOES THE FUTURE HOLD?

At least India is a democracy, and its legal system, inherited from the British, who ruled there for so long, is in close conformity with the legal systems of most developed nations. Matters are rather different in China. As you saw in Chapter 22, "Rich Nation, Poor Nation," political and legal **institutions** are crucial foundations for sustained economic growth. Despite China's advances over the past thirty years, its future may be clouded unless it can successfully deal with two crucial institutional issues.

First, there is the matter of resolving the tension inherent when a Communist dictatorship tries to use capitalism as the engine of economic growth. Capitalism thrives best in an environment of freedom and itself creates an awareness of and appreciation for the benefits of that freedom. Yet freedom is antithetical to the ideological and political tenets of the Communist government of China. Will the government be tempted to confiscate the fruits of capitalist success to support itself? Or will growing pressure for more political freedom force the government to repress the capitalist system to protect itself? Either route would likely bring long-term economic growth to a halt.

The second potential problem involves China's cultural attitude toward intellectual property. In a land where imitation is viewed as the sincerest form of flattery, people routinely use the ideas of others in their own pursuits. As a result, patent and copyright laws in China are far weaker than in Western nations. Moreover, actions elsewhere considered to be commercial theft (such as software piracy) are largely tolerated in China. If foreign firms find that they cannot protect their economic **assets** in the Chinese market, foreign investment will suffer accordingly, and so will the growing dragon that depends on it so heavily.

FOR CRITICAL ANALYSIS

1. Currently, AIDS is spreading in China and India. If the governments of these nations fail to stop the spread of AIDS, what are the likely consequences for future economic growth in China and India?

2. In 1989, a massive protest against political repression in China was halted by the government's massacre of more than 150 individuals at Tiananmen Square in Beijing. What impact do you think that episode had on foreign investment and growth in China during the years immediately thereafter?

3. Presumably, the residents of China are consumers of goods as well as producers of them. Hence as growth takes place in China, not only will the worldwide supply of some goods increase, but so will the worldwide demand for other goods. What impact will Chinese economic growth have on the prices of the goods it supplies on world markets, relative to the goods it demands on world markets? Do *all* producers of goods in foreign nations lose as a result of Chinese economic growth? Do *all* consumers in foreign nations gain as a result of China's economic growth?

4. Explain how each of the following factors will influence India's ability to succeed in a highly competitive, rapidly changing global marketplace: (a) an educational system that is largely state-operated and that emphasizes job security for teachers and professors; (b) a transportation infrastructure that is largely antiquated and in disrepair; and (c) a political system that is adept at protecting favored constituents from competition and handing out favors that have concentrated benefits and widely dispersed costs.

CHAPTER 25

Outsourcing and Economic Growth

One prominent business commentator keeps a "hit list" of corporations that send jobs overseas. Such actions are decidedly un-American, he opines, whenever he gets a chance to express his views against **outsourcing.** A recent Democratic presidential nominee had a name for heads of companies that outsourced telemarketing projects, customer services, and other white-collar jobs to foreign countries: He called them "Benedict Arnold CEOs."

Congress even tried to pass a bill to prevent any type of outsourcing by the Department of State and the Department of Defense. Republican representative Don Manzullo of Illinois said, "You can't just continue to outsource overseas time after time after time, lose your strategic military base, and then expect this Congress to sit back and see the jobs lost and do nothing." When an adviser to the president publicly stated that the foreign outsourcing of service jobs was not such a bad idea, numerous politicians lambasted him for even the suggestion that outsourcing could be viewed in a positive light.

WHAT IS THIS "OUTSOURCING"?

The concept of outsourcing is simple: Instead of hiring American workers at home, American corporations hire foreign workers to do the same jobs. For example, some of these foreign workers are in India and do call-center work, answering technical questions for computer purchasers. Another job such workers do well (and cheaply) is software development and debugging. Because of low-cost communication, especially over the Internet, software programmers can be just about anywhere in the world and still work for U.S. corporations.

Besides the fear that outsourcing "robs Americans of jobs," it is also claimed that outsourcing reduces **economic growth** in the United States. (Presumably, that must mean that it increases economic growth in, say, India.) Because outsourcing is part and parcel of international trade in goods and services, the real question becomes, can the United States have higher growth rates if it restricts American corporations from "sending jobs abroad"?

As we set out to answer this question, we must keep one simple fact in mind: Outsourcing is nothing more or less than the purchase of labor services from the residents of a foreign nation. When the Detroit Red Wings host the Vancouver Canucks, fans at the game are outsourcing: They are purchasing labor services from Canadians. In this sense, Canadian hockey players are no different from Indian software engineers; they are citizens of foreign nations who are competing with citizens of the United States in the supply of labor services. Just as important, outsourcing is no different from any other form of international trade.

THE LINK BETWEEN ECONOMIC GROWTH AND OUTSOURCING

International trade has been around for thousands of years. That means that the concept of outsourcing is certainly not new, even though the term seems to be. After all, the exchange of services between countries is a part of international trade. In any event, if we decide to restrict this type of international trade in services, we will be restricting international trade in general. Experts who study economic growth today have found that the openness of an economy is a key determinant of its rate of economic growth. Any restriction on outsourcing is a type of **trade barrier,** one that will reduce the benefits we obtain from international trade.

There is a clear historical link between economic growth and trade barriers. Figure 25–1 shows the relationship between the openness of an economy—fewer or more trade barriers—and the rate of economic growth. At the bottom of the graph is a trade barrier index, which for the United States is equal to 100. On the vertical axis, you see the average annual growth of **per capita income** in percentage terms.

It is evident from this graph that countries that have fewer international trade barriers have also had higher rates of economic growth. The lesson of history is quite clear: International trade increases economic growth, and growth boosts economic well-being. Government efforts to restrict outsourcing will restrict international trade, and this will make Americans poorer, not richer.

Figure 25–1 Relationship between Economic Growth and Barriers to International Trade

Trade Barrier Index (United States = 100)

WILL THE UNITED STATES BECOME A THIRD WORLD COUNTRY?

In spite of the evidence just shown, Paul Craig Roberts, a former Reagan administration treasury official, declared at a Brookings Institution conference that "the United States will be a Third World country in twenty years." His prediction was based on the idea that entire classes of high-wage service-sector employees will eventually find themselves in competition with highly skilled workers abroad who earn much less than their U.S. counterparts. He contended that U.S. software programmers and radiologists, for example, will not be able to compete in the global economy. Thus, he argued, the United States will lose millions of white-collar jobs due to outsourcing of service-sector employment to India and China.

Jeffrey E. Garten, former dean of the Yale School of Management, reiterated and expanded on this prediction. He believes that the transfer of jobs abroad will accelerate for generations to come. He argues that in countries from China to the Czech Republic, there is a "virtually unlimited supply of industrious and educated labor working at a fraction of U.S. wages." Similarly, according to Craig Barrett, board chair at the chip maker Intel, American workers today face the prospect of "300 million well-educated people in India, China, and Russia who can do effectively any job that can be done" in the United States.

Still other commentators have claimed that India alone will soak up 3 to 4 million jobs from the U.S. labor market by 2015. Some even believe that this number may exceed 10 million. If true, one might expect American software developers and call-center technicians to start moving to India!

SOME OVERLOOKED FACTS

Much of the outsourcing discussion has ignored two simple facts that turn out to be important if we really want to understand what the future will bring.

1. *Outsourcing is the result of trade liberalization in foreign nations.* After decades of isolation, the markets in China, India, and eastern Europe have begun to open up to international trade. As is often the case when governments finally allow their people to trade internationally, these governments have pushed hard to stimulate exports— of labor services as well as goods. But this cannot be a long-term equilibrium strategy because the workers producing those goods and supplying those services are doing it because they want to become consumers. Soon enough, and this is already happening, they want to spend their hard-earned income on goods and services, many of which are produced abroad. Thus today's outsourcing of jobs to those nations must eventually turn into exports of goods and services to those same nations.

2. *Prices adjust to keep markets in balance.* The supply curve of labor is upward-sloping. Thus as U.S. corporations hire foreign workers (either directly by outsourcing or indirectly by importing goods), market wages in foreign lands must rise. Between 2003 and 2008, for example, Indian labor-outsourcing companies saw wages rise more than 40 percent. Over a longer span, real wages in southern China (which has been open to trade far longer than India) are now *six times higher* than they were just twenty years ago. These higher wages obviously reduce the competitiveness of the firms that must pay them. Moreover, it is not just wages that adjust: The relative values of national currencies move, too. Between 2003 and 2007, the value of the dollar fell more than 25 percent, making foreign goods (and workers) more expensive here and making U.S. goods and workers more attractive in foreign markets.

Of course, adjustments are never instantaneous. Moreover, they are occurring because some American firms are moving output and employment abroad; hence at least some U.S. workers are having to move to lower-paying jobs, often with a spell of unemployment along the way. How big is the impact in the short run, before all of the price adjustments take place? According to the Bureau of Labor Statistics, in a typical recent year, the number of jobs lost to outsourcing is measured in the thousands—out of a workforce of over 150 million. So if you are currently a U.S. software developer, you don't have to worry about packing your bags for Mumbai, at least not soon.

INSOURCING BY FOREIGN FIRMS

U.S. firms are not the only ones that engage in outsourcing. Many foreign firms do the same. When a foreign firm outsources to the United States, we can call it **insourcing.** For example, Mexican firms routinely send data to U.S. accounting businesses for calculation of payrolls and for maintaining financial records. Many foreign hospitals pay our radiologists to read X-rays and MRI images. Foreign firms use American firms to provide a host of other services, many of which involve consulting. Also, when a foreign automobile manufacturer builds an assembly plant in the United States, it is in effect outsourcing automobile assembly to American workers. Thus American workers in the South Carolina BMW plant, the Alabama Mercedes-Benz plant, or the Toyota or Honda plants in Tennessee and Ohio are all beneficiaries of the fact that those foreign companies have outsourced jobs to the United States. Indeed, all across the country and around the world, hundreds of millions of workers are employed by "foreign" corporations—although it's becoming difficult to tell the nationality of any company, given the far-flung nature of today's global enterprises.

WHAT REALLY MATTERS: THE LONG RUN

If you own the only grocery store in your small town, you are clearly harmed if a competing store opens across the street. If you work in a small telephone-equipment store and a large company starts taking away business via Internet sales, you will obviously be worse off. If you used to be employed at a call center for customer service at Wal-Mart and have just lost your job because Wal-Mart outsourced to a cheaper Indian firm, you will have to look for a new job.

These kinds of "losses" of income or jobs have occurred since the beginning of commerce. They will always exist in any dynamic economy. Indeed, if we look over the American economy as a whole, in a typical year roughly *one million workers lose their jobs every week.* But slightly *more* than one million people find a new job every week. So on balance, employment in the United States keeps growing, even though the average person will change jobs every three years—some, no doubt, because of international competition. But job turnover like this is an essential component of a labor market that is continually adjusting to economic change. It is a sign of health, not sickness, in the economy. If you find this hard to believe, you can look west or east. In Japan, efforts to "protect" workers from international trade resulted in economic stagnation and depressed real income growth from 1989 to 2006. In Europe, similar efforts to "preserve" the jobs of existing workers have resulted in *higher,* not lower, unemployment because firms are unwilling to hire people that they cannot fire later.

It is true that the pattern of job losses and gains in a given year are altered during an economic recession, such as the latest one. In particular, during the early stages of a recession, additional people lose their jobs in a given week and fewer people find a job each week, with the result being higher unemployment in the short run. But international trade is not the cause of recessions in the United States (although an economic recession can be made worse by *restrictions* on international trade, as it was in the early 1930s). On the contrary, international trade is an important source of economic prosperity.

If you are still wondering, simply look back at Figure 25–1. The lessons of history and of economics are clear: Trade creates **wealth,** and that is true whether the trade is interpersonal, interstate, or international. The reality is that labor outsourcing is simply part of a worldwide trend toward increased international trade in both goods and services. As international trade expands—assuming that politicians and bureaucrats allow it to expand—the result will be higher rates of growth and higher levels of income in America and elsewhere. American workers will continue to enjoy the fruits of that growth, just as they always have.

FOR CRITICAL ANALYSIS

1. What, if any, differences exist between competition among service workers across the fifty states and competition among service workers across nations?

2. When BMW decides to build a plant in the United States, who gains and who loses?

3. International Business Machines Corporation (IBM) recently stated that it expected to save almost $170 million annually by shifting several thousand high-paying programming jobs overseas. Explain why IBM would undertake this move. Then explain the short-run and long-run effects of this outsourcing.

CHAPTER 26

Poverty, Capitalism, and Growth

Fifty years ago, nearly half of the world's population lived in poverty; today, the proportion is about 17 percent. In fact, compared to fifty years ago, even though the world's population has doubled, there are actually fewer people now living below the poverty line. Despite the human misery that is evident to varying degrees in virtually every nation of the world, there is little doubt that economic prosperity has made great strides.

THE SWEEP OF HISTORY

The past half-century is but a small part of a story that has evolved over the course of 250 years. In the middle of the eighteenth century, perhaps 90 percent of the world's population lived in a state of **abject poverty,** subsisting on the equivalent of less than $1 per person per day, measured in today's terms. In fact, for most of human history, abject poverty—including inadequate nutrition and rudimentary shelter—was the norm for almost everyone, everywhere. This began to change in the eighteenth century with the **Industrial Revolution** and its associated mechanization of tasks that had always been laboriously done by humans or animals. Stimulated in the early years by the invention and application of the steam engine, the Industrial Revolution initiated a massive cascade of innovations in transportation, chemistry, biology, manufacturing processes, communications, and electronic technology. This continuing process of invention and innovation has made little headway in many parts of the world, but where it has taken hold, there has been a sustained rise in average **real per capita income** and a corresponding decline in poverty. By 1820, the extent of abject poverty had fallen from 90 percent to 80 percent; by 1900, it had dipped below 70 percent; and it has continued to decline since. Before the Industrial Revolution, more than five out of six people lived in abject poverty; today, it is one out of six.

UNEVEN PROGRESS

This story of human progress has been uneven across countries. Europe, North America, and a few other locations have witnessed the greatest increases in real per capita income and the greatest decreases in poverty. By contrast, the **standard of living** and the extent of poverty in most nations in Africa have changed little over the past 250 years. Even within given countries, progress has sometimes been erratic. Ninety years ago, for example, the standard of living in Argentina was the sixth highest in the world; today, that nation ranks seventieth in living standards. In contrast, thirty years ago, 250 million people in China lived in abject poverty; that number has since been cut to one-tenth that number.

In Chapter 22, "Rich Nation, Poor Nation," you saw the key institutional factors that determine average levels of **per capita income**. Secure **property and contract rights** and the **rule of law** were the **institutions** under which the Industrial Revolution flourished best, and it is thus in nations that have embraced these institutions that people are most likely to be prosperous. These same institutions are the ones typically associated with *capitalism,* economic systems that depend primarily (though not necessarily completely) on markets to allocate scarce **resources.** Of course, no country in the world is completely capitalist; in the United States, for example, less than two-thirds of resources are allocated by the private sector, while the rest are allocated by federal, state, or local governments. At the other end of the spectrum, even in Communist countries such as Cuba, Vietnam, and North Korea, markets play at least some role in allocating resources.

Despite a few ambiguities, then, it is possible to measure the degree of capitalism (or, as some would term it, economic freedom) in each country around the world. Doing so yields measures that seem to correspond reasonably well with what many people would think is true about the economies of those countries. For example, using the measures constructed by Canada's Fraser Institute, Hong Kong's economy is rated the most capitalist, while the United States is tied for third (with Switzerland and New Zealand). Singapore, Canada, Ireland, and Australia are other nations whose economies are judged among the ten most capitalist in the world. If you know much about economic prosperity around the world, you will be aware that these countries are also among the world leaders in real per capita income. Indeed, the association of capitalism with prosperity is everywhere quite strong.

Capitalism and Prosperity

It is convenient for our purposes to divide all the nations in the world into five groups, ranging from "most capitalist" to "least capitalist." Data limitations prevent doing this with every single nation. Nevertheless, it is possible to do it for about 125 of them, putting 25 nations into each of the five groups. Thus among the top 25 "most capitalist" nations, in addition to the countries we mentioned earlier, many (but not all!) of the original members of the **European Union (EU)** would be included, along with Chile, Costa Rica, and Kuwait. At the other end of the spectrum, the economies of Russia, Algeria, Venezuela, and Zimbabwe would all fall into the group of the 25 "least capitalist" nations.

As we suggested earlier, people who live in the most capitalist nations in the world also tend to have the highest average income. For example, average per capita income for people living in the group including the 25 most capitalist nations averages over $23,000 per year. For people living in the next most capitalist group of nations, per capita income averages about $13,000 per year. Once we get down to the 25 least capitalist nations, average income has dropped to but $3,300 per year. And because rates of economic growth are *also* higher in more capitalist nations, the differences in income between the most and least capitalist nations are growing over time.[1]

Of course, this is a chapter about poverty, and the *average* income in a nation may bear little relation to the income earned by its poorest residents. Many people believe, for example, that capitalist nations promote excessively competitive behavior so that people who are not good at competing end up much poorer in capitalist than in noncapitalist nations. If the rich get richer in capitalist countries while the poor get poorer, then even if the average person in capitalist nations is doing well, the same might not be true for people at the bottom of the income distribution. As it turns out, however, the poor do *not* do worse in capitalist countries; in fact, they do better.

Capitalism and Poverty

Consider the 25 most capitalist nations in the world. On average, the poorest 10 percent of the population receives about 2.5 percent of total income in these countries. Indeed, if we look across *all* countries, we see

---

1. All income comparisons are made using a method called **purchasing power parity (PPP),** generally acknowledged to be the most accurate means of making comparisons across nations with very different income levels and consumption bundles.

that although there is some variation from nation to nation, the poorest 10 percent of the population typically gets between 2.0 and 2.5 percent of total income. One way to put this is that on average, capitalism does *not* lower the share of total income going to the people at the bottom of the income distribution. Capitalist or Communist, in Africa or in the Americas, the per capita income of the poorest 10 percent of the population in a nation ends up being about one-quarter of what it is in the middle of the income distribution for that country.

Now if you followed the numbers earlier about average income and capitalism, you may already have figured out the next point: Because capitalism raises total income in a nation without reducing the *share* of income going to the poor, capitalism ends up raising income at *all* points in the income distribution. Thus for the poorest 10 percent of the population in highly capitalist countries, average per capita income is about $5,900 per year (or just under $24,000 per year for a family of four). For the poorest 10 percent of the population in the least capitalist countries, average income is under $750 per year (about $3,000 for a family of four). Expressed somewhat differently, poor people in the most capitalist nations can expect average income levels *eight times higher* than poor people in the least capitalist nations.

The radically better standard of living experienced by the poor in capitalist nations is reflected in many other statistics indicative of quality of life. For example, life expectancy in the 25 most capitalist nations is about seventy-seven years; in the least capitalist, it is about fifty-seven. Similarly, infant mortality rates are *eight times higher* in the least capitalist countries than in the most capitalist. Moreover, because people at the top of the income distribution have access to health care in both rich and poor nations, these differences in life expectancy and infant mortality are chiefly due to differences among people at the bottom of the income distribution. In capitalist nations, compared to noncapitalist countries, it is the poor whose newborns are surviving infancy and whose adults are surviving to old age.

There is another compelling difference between capitalist and noncapitalist countries that sheds light on what the future may bring. In the 25 most capitalist countries of the world, fewer than 1 percent of children under the age of fifteen are working rather than in school. In the 25 least capitalist nations, one child of every six under the age of fifteen is working rather than in school—a rate nearly twenty times higher. Thus in capitalist nations, children are much more likely to be getting the education necessary for them to learn the skills of the future. This in turn means that **economic growth** is likely to be higher in capitalist than in noncapitalist nations, and this is exactly what we observe. Growth in per capita income in the 25 most capitalist countries averages about 2.3 percent per year, enough to double income at all levels over the next thirty years. In contrast, average per capita incomes are actually *falling* in the least capitalist countries, implying that the misery of today's poor in these nations is likely to get worse.

More than Numbers

It is easy to get too wrapped up in numbers, so it may be useful to make a few simple head-to-head comparisons. Consider North Korea and South Korea. Both emerged from World War II with shattered economies, only to fight each other in the Korean War. When the war was over, South Korea embraced capitalism, building an economy based on the rule of law, secure property rights, and a reliance on the market as the primary means of allocating scarce resources. North Korea rejected all of these, choosing instead a Communist system that relied on centralized command and control to allocate resources—a system ruled not by law but by one man at the top. South Korea became a world economic powerhouse, with per capita income of almost $25,000 per year. North Korea stagnated and, with a per capita income of only $1,900 per year, must now rely on foreign aid to feed many of its people.

If we were to look at East Germany and West Germany between World War II and the fall of the Berlin Wall in 1989, we would see the same story repeated. West Germany embraced the central principles of a market-based capitalist economy and prospered. East Germany rejected those principles, and its people were impoverished. A similar tale of two countries can be told in comparing the economies of Taiwan and China between 1950 and 1980: Capitalist Taiwan prospered while Communist China stagnated—and people at the bottom of the income distribution suffered the most.

Indeed, as noted in Chapter 24, China itself presents us with a tale of two countries: the Communist version before 1980 and the increasingly capitalist one of the years since. After decades of post–World War II stagnation under communism, the gradual move toward market-based resource allocation in China since 1980 is transforming life for people at all levels of income. Overall, real per capita income has roughly doubled every decade since 1980. Moreover, at least in those areas of the country where the Communists have let the capitalists try their hand, this economic progress has been widespread and sustained. So even though political freedom in China is not yet to be had, the growing economic freedom in that nation is having the same impact it has had around the world and over time: When people are able to enjoy secure property rights, the rule of law, and a reliance on markets as allocators of scarce resources, people at *all* points in the distribution benefit.

FOR CRITICAL ANALYSIS

1. The income measures discussed in this chapter do not include non-cash benefits that are often available to low-income individuals, such as food stamps and Medicaid. Do you think such noncash benefits are more likely to be made available to poor people in a rich nation or in a poor nation? Explain your answer. Hint: Do people get more or less charitable as their incomes rise? Then ask yourself, how will the difference in noncash benefits in rich nations versus poor nations affect your conclusions regarding relative incomes of poor individuals in capitalist nations compared to noncapitalist nations? Explain this answer as well.

2. How would a political system in which there is the rule of law (that is, in which the same rules apply to everyone) serve to protect people at the bottom of the income distribution most strongly?

3. In light of the analysis in Chapter 1 and the information presented in this chapter, what are some ways that people in developed nations might help people in developing nations achieve higher income levels? Explain, giving specific examples, if you can.

PART SIX

Fiscal Policy

CHAPTER 27

The Growth of Big Government

In 1996, the forty-second president of the United States, William Jefferson Clinton, declared, "The era of big government is over." Whatever else President Clinton may have been, he was not a prophet. Shortly after he made this declaration, **discretionary spending** by the federal government accelerated at a torrid pace.

DISCRETIONARY VERSUS NONDISCRETIONARY GOVERNMENT SPENDING

Spending by the federal government and some state governments can be divided into two types: discretionary and nondiscretionary. Discretionary spending is anything that Congress decides to spend for which it has to appropriate monies in its **appropriation bills** each **fiscal year.** A good example of discretionary spending is the $30 billion spent to help New York City and various private firms that suffered greatly from the terrorist attacks on September 11, 2001. Nondiscretionary spending is usually driven by **entitlement programs.** These are *formula-driven* expenditures. The best examples are Social Security and Medicare, which provide specific formulas, or rules, that automatically decide who is eligible and the amount for which they are eligible. Once the law is passed that dictates the amount to which individuals are entitled, Congress no longer controls the amount of funds spent on these programs. The only way such nondiscretionary spending can be slowed down or speeded up is if Congress changes the formulas that dictate who gets what and how much they get.

At the time Bill Clinton made his pronouncement, discretionary spending had indeed fallen slightly from 1994 through part of 1995. It was hovering around $550 billion per year. But by 2008, such spending was in the neighborhood of *double* that amount. And that was *before* the $800 billion economic bailout plan or the new infrastructure and other "stimulus" spending that started in 2009. So much for the end of big government!

Is 9/11 to Blame?

One can reasonably (but misleadingly) argue that since September 11, 2001, the federal government and state and local governments have had to spend more on antiterrorism measures. Though this statement is true in one sense, the overall government-spending picture, particularly at the federal level, is quite different. For six years before the terrorist attacks, total federal discretionary spending had already been rising rapidly. This spending was eventually supplemented by funds that were voted for spending on homeland security and national defense. But these supplements were a small blip on the radar screen of total increases in federal discretionary spending. Roughly $30 billion was spent on homeland security and national defense programs in the months following 9/11. But in fiscal year 2002, Congress voted an additional $90 billion of new discretionary spending, which included funds for medical research and highway construction. Fiscal years 2003 through 2007 all witnessed further additions to federal discretionary spending.

What has been true and will continue to be true into the foreseeable future is that numerous expenditures that have absolutely nothing to do with countering terrorism will be approved in the name of the fight against terrorism. Consider the latest set of "gifts" to the farming sector, one of the most brazen examples of how old-fashioned special interest **subsidies** can be hidden under the cover of the war on terrorism. Since 1978, farmers have received subsidies of $400 billion from the federal government. In recognition of the huge amount of spending going to this tiny **interest group,** Congress in 1996 passed the Freedom to Farm bill, which was intended to phase out subsidies to farmers gradually. Yet not only have the subsidies *increased* since then, but members of Congress from farm states have also used the war on terrorism as a pretext to ask for even more. How have they done this? By including the word *security* in the title of the farm bill to link the "insecurity" that farmers are currently feeling about their future incomes to the insecurity that Americans in general are feeling in the wake of the terrorist attacks.

The latest farm legislation, passed in 2008, is expected to cost U.S. taxpayers and consumers at least $30 billion per year. The Farm Security and Rural Investment Act, its full title, was the largest agricultural subsidy in the history of the United States—foisted on the public in the name of increased "security," of course.

Some observers believe that all manner of spending that is packaged under the banner of homeland security will become a permanent addition to our federal spending apparatus. The federal government will, as a consequence, keep getting larger, not smaller.

THE DEPARTMENT OF HOMELAND SECURITY

When President George W. Bush proposed creation of the Department of Homeland Security (DHS), he argued that it would not make government larger. Almost everyone now thinks that President Bush will turn out to be no better as a prognosticator than his predecessor. In principle, the DHS has simply combined twenty-two agencies and 170,000 workers to create a more efficient way to protect Americans at home. Realize, though, that this department is the most massive new bureaucracy since the Department of Defense (DOD) was created in 1947. The likelihood of the DHS remaining even close to its original size is small, if not zero.

First, many DHS activities, like DOD activities, are secret. This reduces the chances that spending on them will be carefully scrutinized. Second, DHS and DOD activities are supposed to protect us from people who would do us harm. If a member of Congress stops a project on budget grounds and an unfortunate security breach later occurs as a result, that could be the end of a political career. Finally, DHS activities, like DOD activities, are complex and far-reaching. It is easy to claim— and difficult to refute—that a loss of spending on one project will have spillover effects that will irreparably damage many other projects.

The result with the DOD is a budget that seems largely immune to shrinkage. Furthermore, plenty of private-sector firms have an incentive to keep that budget big because they are doing business with the department. Hence they lobby for additional funding so that they, too, can get some of those extra federal dollars. It is likely that these same incentives will work their magic with the DHS budget. Indeed, within a few months after the DHS asked private corporations to propose new technologies to fight terrorism, some fifteen hundred companies had pitched their ideas. Consider one proposal from an enterprising company: Fit every commercial airline seat with metal straps. Why? To snare potential hijackers. Yet another proposal: Teach transcendental meditation to our enemies. Why? Obviously, to calm them down. The list, one imagines, is still growing.

The Impact of Social Security and Medicare Spending on the Federal Budget

So far, we have discussed mainly federal discretionary spending. On the horizon, however, looms a serious and growing problem with two of the most important entitlement programs, Social Security and Medicare. At the beginning of the twenty-first century, actual outlays for Social Security and Medicare were about 6.5 percent of the nation's annual national income, or, as it is commonly called, **gross domestic product (GDP).** That proportion has now risen to 7 percent; by 2025 it will grow to 10 percent and by 2040 to over 12 percent. This increase in spending on these two entitlement programs is due not only to the increased number of retirees from the baby boom generation (born between 1946 and 1964) but also to the aging of the population as a whole, which is projected to continue for the next half-century at least.

The implied burden of this aging and the growing programs is enormous. At the beginning of the twenty-first century, there were 4.3 workers for every person aged sixty-five or over. By 2020, there will be 2.6 workers; by 2050, there will be 2.4; and by 2075, only 2.2. In other words, a working couple will have to provide almost all of the Social Security and Medicare support for each retired person—in addition to supporting themselves and their children. Put somewhat differently, if you think a big piece of your paycheck is going for taxes now, just wait—a much larger piece will be departing in the future.

Bailout at Any Cost

In 2008, federal spending took on an entirely new dimension when, in response to the Panic of '08 (see Chapter 17), Congress passed a $700 billion bailout package for the financial industry. This was followed in 2009 by an additional $800 billion federal stimulus package that was designed, it was said, to pull us out of the recession of 2007–2009. And behind the scenes, the Federal Reserve was busy giving financial institutions more than $1 trillion in government securities in exchange for commercial paper and other risky private-sector debts that could turn out to be largely worthless. Indeed, within a matter of months, Congress and the Fed had committed American taxpayers to $2 *trillion* in potential spending obligations.

Just how much the taxpayer—which is to say, you—will end up paying depends on how many companies default on the various bailout programs. At this point, the exact total is a matter of speculation. It is pretty clear, however, that the sum will be in the many tens of billions of dollars, possibly *hundreds* of billions of dollars. And since 40 percent of all Americans pay *no* federal income taxes, this means that the rest of us will pay plenty. If the **default** rate ends up being as low as 15 percent, a family of four will be hit with an extra tax bill of about $8,000—in addition to its obligation for the rest of the growing government.

THE TRUE SIZE OF GOVERNMENT

Government at any level does not exist independently of the people who live, work, spend, and pay taxes in our society. As an economy, we face a **budget constraint.** Whatever is spent by government—federal, state, and local—cannot be spent by individuals. Fundamentally, when we talk about the "size" of government, we are talking about the proportion, or percentage, of GDP that government commands. Logic dictates that whatever government commands in terms of spending decisions, private individuals do not command. From this perspective (and this is simple arithmetic), federal, state, and local governments command over 40 percent of GDP. In addition, some observers have argued that the various levels of government also compel businesses and individuals to spend an additional 10 percent of total income to comply with government regulations and **mandates.** If we follow this line of reasoning, the implication is that directly or indirectly, government in the United States controls the allocation of over one-half of all **resources**—which leaves less than half for you.

FOR CRITICAL ANALYSIS

1. The Tax Foundation estimated that the direct tax burden of government actually dropped significantly between 2000 and 2004, due chiefly to federal tax cuts in 2003. Based on what you have read in this chapter, do you believe that this decline has continued since 2004 or will continue in the future? Why or why not?

2. Around the world, the percentage of total GDP controlled by the government has a tendency to grow. Why do you think this is so?

3. Although federal taxes were cut twice between 2001 and 2005, federal spending rose over that span, so the amount of debt owed by the federal government increased. What does this higher level of debt imply about the likely tax burden of the federal government in the future?

CHAPTER 28

Debts and Deficits: What's a Trillion More or Less?

How many times have you heard the advice to "stay out of debt"? Certainly, that advice has rarely been followed by your lawmakers in Washington, D.C. Over the past half-century, the federal government has spent within its means during only five years. In the other years, it ran a **federal budget deficit**—that is, it spent more than it received in tax receipts. Now, of course, if you or your family spent more than you earned year-in and year-out, you would eventually go bankrupt. Obviously, this has not happened to the federal government.

DIFFERENT WAYS TO LOOK AT THE FEDERAL BUDGET DEFICIT

The official federal budget deficit can be found in numerous publications, including *The Economic Report of the President.* If you examine the data on the federal deficit for the past twenty years, you see that after shrinking in the 1990s, it has been growing since. To get a handle on the true size of the deficit, though, as you learned in Chapter 12, we must at least take into account changes in the **price level.** When we thus correct for **inflation,** the *real* federal budget deficit from 1989 to 2009 grew by 60 percent less than the nominal value that each year's deficit showed, because the overall price level rose 60 percent.

Over that same time period, something else very important happened. The size of the U.S. economy grew quite handsomely. Consequently, the more revealing statistic concerning the federal budget deficit is how that deficit has changed as a percentage of total economic activity, or **gross domestic product (GDP).** In 1989, the deficit as a share of GDP was 2.8 percent. At the beginning of 2009, it was 2.9 percent. Those two numbers are obviously almost identical—although by the time you read this, the federal deficit will have grown to a *much* larger share of GDP.

THE CRASH OF 2008–2009

Whereas the estimated federal budget deficit was about $450 billion in 2008, by the time you read this, it will have risen to $1 trillion or more. That will represent the largest single one-year increase in the real (inflation-adjusted) deficit in the history of the United States—and the largest jump in the deficit as a share of GDP since World War II. As we write this chapter, we cannot even tell you exactly how big the latest surge in the deficit is because no one yet can predict it.

In response to the financial meltdown of 2008–2009, the federal government legislated so many financial bailouts that the actual amount for which the U.S. taxpayer is on the hook is currently unknowable. Eventually, we will know, of course. To return to our back-of-the-envelope calculations, consider this: Ignoring for the moment the federal takeover of the two enormous government-sponsored mortgage companies, Freddie Mac and Fannie Mae, the 2008 $700 billion bank bailout bill will certainly add another $400 or $500 billion to the 2009 deficit. (The addition to the deficit is less than the official size of the bailout because the government will recoup *something* from the companies we are bailing out.) Add to this President Obama's $800 billion economic "stimulus" package, passed early in 2009, and now you are talking in the trillions, more or less, of course. Thus, realistically speaking, by 2010, the federal budget deficit will be more than *double* what it was in 2008, expressed as a percentage of GDP.

DEFICITS AND DEBT

If you decide to go on an expensive Caribbean vacation, you may not have enough funds currently available to do so. You could borrow at least part of the funds from a consumer finance company or from your bank. This additional borrowing adds to your outstanding debt. The same logic applies to the federal government. Each year that there is a deficit, the **public debt** grows by that amount, because the debt is just the sum of current and past deficits. In the popular press, you often read that the public debt now exceeds $12 trillion. That quoted number is usually meaningless. It refers to the **gross public debt,** which at the beginning of 2009 was $12.7 trillion.

The problem with the gross public debt statistic is that it includes **interagency borrowings.** If one part of the federal government loans funds to another part of the federal government, that loan really has no impact on anybody. Therefore, what we really want to know is the size and growth in the **net public debt**. The net public debt is the gross public debt minus all federal interagency borrowings. At the beginning of 2009, this debt was $8.4 trillion—quite a bit less than the gross public debt.

Are you shocked, even by this smaller number? You might be, but you are still not looking at the most appropriate statistic. As with the federal deficit, we either have to look at the inflation-corrected change in the net public debt over time or at the net public debt as a percentage of GDP. In 1989, the net public debt represented about 40 percent of GDP. At the beginning of 2009, it represented about 50 percent of GDP. What will it be at the beginning of 2010? Well, it is a good bet that it will be substantially more than 50 percent of GDP, but probably not yet at the astronomical 108.6 percent it reached in 1946, just after the end of World War II.

Another way of examining the importance of the net public debt is to first correct for inflation and then correct for the number of Americans. The result is the **per capita real net public debt**. Measured in 2008 dollars, in 1989, this number was $15,500. Early in 2009, it hit $28,000; this is a hefty increase, particularly when you consider that most of the increase occured after 2007.

UNFUNDED TAXPAYER LIABILITIES

For at least a decade, some politicians and many economists examined with a critical eye the activities of Freddie Mac and Fannie Mae. They pointed out that even though these entities were owned by private shareholders, there was an implicit government guarantee of their obligations. In other words, if they got into trouble, the federal government would come to the rescue. That is why they have always been referred to as **government-sponsored enterprises (GSEs)**.

As early as the 1990s, some economists calculated that there was several hundred billion dollars' worth of implicit taxpayer **liabilities** associated with the government's implicit guarantee of these fast-growing mortgage-market institutions. These researchers thought that the implicit future taxpayer liabilities should be added to the net public debt numbers.

As you know by now, the tragic story of the implicit guarantees of their obligations came to be true. The federal government had to take over both companies in the fall of 2008. We're all on the hook, but not for a measly few hundred billion dollars. Rather, it looks as if U.S. taxpayers are committed for these two large organizations to the tune of close to a trillion dollars (that's $1,000,000,000,000). We will not know for several years what the exact number is. What we do know, though, is that the published U.S. government net public debt statistics underestimate the *true* net public debt because of these now obvious and undeniable liabilities.

There is more to this story of **unfunded taxpayer liabilities.** If you look at projected expenditures on Social Security, Medicare, and the federal portion of Medicaid (health care for the poor, partly financed by the state governments), you come up with a number so large you cannot even comprehend it. That number, which is in the tens of trillions of dollars, some 300 or 400 percent of current GDP, represents the unfunded portion of future estimated federal expenditures on the three programs just mentioned.

Because these unfunded federal spending program expenditures are so large, you can be certain of one thing—something will have to give. The long-run problem amounts to an enormous increase in the net public debt—one that is staggering in size, even compared to the massive obligations incurred during the Great Depression and World War II. Eventually, members of Congress, the president, and the public (that would be you) will have to face the music. Only two options are available: Either spending on these programs will have to be cut dramatically, or you will have to sacrifice an unprecedented share of your hard-earned income to pay for the rising retirement and medical expenditures of seniors.

WHO REALLY PAYS FOR CURRENT FEDERAL GOVERNMENT EXPENDITURES?

Some economists believe that discussion of the federal budget deficit is beside the point—a red herring, as it were. Consider a typical year. Total economic activity as measured by GDP is perhaps $16 trillion as you read this. At the local, state, and federal levels of government, numerous expenditures are made. Let's suppose those expenditures equal 40 percent of GDP. Now ask yourself this question: For a typical resident, does the method of paying for government expenditures matter? For example, assume that all of these expenditures are paid for by tax revenues; there are no deficits. You know *explicitly* that as the average U.S. resident, you have given up 40 percent of your annual income to pay for government at all levels.

Consider another scenario. Suppose taxes pay for only a portion of that 40-plus percent of GDP spent by government. Deficit financing pays for the rest. As a typical U.S. resident, you still do not have control over the part of GDP the government spent during the year. Even if only a portion of the 40-plus percent controlled by government is financed via current taxes, you are still on the hook for the rest of it—plus interest, of course. Moreover, however the spending is financed this year, it is still government employees, not you, who get to decide how 40-plus percent of your income is used.

Consider an earlier example when government spending also skyrocketed. During World War II, Americans fought in two simultaneous wars, in the Pacific and in Europe. Not surprisingly, government spending increased dramatically. Many history books talk about how Americans continued paying for World War II for years thereafter because the net public debt rose so much due to high wartime federal borrowing.

But can that really be true? No, it cannot. The people in this country who lived during World War II effectively paid for World War II each year when government expenditures took place. As a percentage of GDP, they ended up with less for themselves. Indeed, the inflation-corrected per capita rate of consumption expenditures dropped during World War II and did not start rising until several years after the end of that war.

In a sentence, the real burden of government is the **resources** it uses, and that burden occurs at the point in time when the resources are used, deficits and debts notwithstanding.

For Critical Analysis

1. If you cannot continue to spend more than you earn, why can the federal government?

2. Some economists estimate that if you add the unfunded tax liabilities of just Social Security and Medicare, they add up to about $80 trillion. Do you think that in the long run, this $80 trillion estimate can continue to hold true? Why or why not? (*Hint:* Who pays for unfunded tax liabilities?)

3. Why will the U.S. government never go bankrupt?

CHAPTER 29

Higher Taxes Are in Your Future

"These road improvements of $241,000,000 were paid for:

86 percent from the Federal Highway Trust Fund
12 percent from state funds
2 percent from local funds."

Most of you have seen at least one sign similar to this while driving somewhere in the United States. If you have ever driven anywhere in Europe, you see comparable signs, but they usually have a longer list of "contributors." The parallel, though, is that the "contributors" are government agencies, not *you*. Now, it would be nice to think that funds for highway improvement projects come from the moon or Mars or even from the bank account of some foreign oil mogul. But they do not.

THOSE PESKY BUDGET CONSTRAINTS

Government does not exist independently of those who live, work, spend, and pay taxes in our society. As an economy, we face a **budget constraint.** Whatever is spent by government—federal, state, or local—is not and cannot be spent by individuals in the nation. Whatever government commands in terms of spending decisions, private individuals do not command. All of those dollars available for spending on final goods and services in the United States can be controlled either by you, the private citizen, or by government. Otherwise stated, what the government spends, you don't spend. It is as simple as that, despite the periodic efforts of government (especially at the national level) to conceal the truth of this budget constraint.

FEDERAL SPENDING PROGRAMS ON THE HORIZON

Throughout the latter weeks of the presidential campaign in 2008, the two candidates offered an increasingly costly and often mind-boggling array of proposed new federal programs. At one point, John McCain said, if elected, he would "help out" 3 million Americans who were at risk of losing their homes. McCain also supported more government help for people in paying for health insurance.

Soon-to-be-elected Barack Obama argued in favor of even more new government spending. He said that he would create 2 million new jobs by rebuilding our crumbling infrastructure and "laying broadband lines that reach every corner of the country." He promised to spend $15 billion a year over the next ten years on renewable energy. He had a plan to "make health care affordable and accessible for every American." He said he would invest in early childhood education and "recruit an army of new teachers." And in an editorial in the *Wall Street Journal* the day before the election, he said that he was willing to make a deal with every young American: "If you commit to serving your community or your country, we will make sure you can afford your tuition."

At the same time that these new government programs were being promised, Congress was separately considering an additional multibillion-dollar "economic stimulus" plan. Moreover, many nongovernment organizations had their own ideas for more federal spending. For example, in November 2008, the Campaign for America's Future organized a convention in which the theme was the creation of a government-funded investment fund for public works projects. Simultaneously, the Center for American Progress released a two-year, $100 billion plan for producing renewable energy. The latter group argued that increased government spending should also go to schools, health care, job training, and technology innovation. Another group, Realizing the Dream, Inc., wanted the federal government to commit the necessary funds to reduce poverty by 50 percent in the next ten years.

Even as the chorus of voices in favor of additional federal government spending on new programs was growing, Secretary of the Treasury Henry Paulson was already doling out the hundreds of billions of dollars authorized under the $700 billion "bailout" bill (officially called the Emergency Economic Stabilization Act of 2008). Almost simultaneously, even more federal spending was being pushed hard by Representative Charles Rangel (D., N.Y.). When asked about the effect these additional programs would have on the deficit, Rangel said that he did not want to hear about that. "For God's sake," he said, "don't ask me where the money will come from. I'm going to the same place Paulson went."

Where is "the same place Paulson went"?

INCREASED SPENDING, INCREASED TAXES

When Congress passes legislation to spend more, whether it is for bailing out the financial sector, improving education and public infrastructure, or attempting to reduce poverty, there is ultimately only one place it can obtain the resources. That place is you and everyone else who earns income each year in the United States. Having the ability to run a larger federal government deficit (and thus increase the net national debt) does not change the fundamental budget constraint facing our society.

What government spends, the rest of us do not spend. Perhaps without your realizing it, your **real tax rate** has already gone up in the last several years. Why? Because federal government spending has increased as a percentage of **gross domestic product (GDP)**. Your real tax rate is easily calculated. It is the percentage of GDP controlled by the government. The observed taxes that you pay through automatic withholding of federal income taxes on your wages or salary will eventually catch up. The budget constraint guarantees that.

BUT WHAT ABOUT ALL THOSE TAX CREDITS?

During the heat of the 2008 presidential campaign, Barack Obama said he wanted to give tax relief to 95 percent of all households. Let's look at these numbers. Currently, only about 60 percent of American households pay federal income taxes (down from about 80 percent in 1984). Almost 59 million tax filers do not pay any federal income taxes. So how can the government reduce income taxes for an individual or a household that does not pay any? It can (and does) do this by what is known as a **tax credit,** or a *refundable tax credit,* as it is known at the IRS. Under a tax credit, people who pay no federal income taxes effectively get a check from the federal government, which they can use to pay other federal taxes they might owe (such as Social Security) or to pay *future* federal tax liabilities, should they arise. And if there are no current or likely future tax liabilities, well, they get to keep the cash. Consider some of the proposed tax credits that might already be in place by the time you read this:

- A $500 refund to low- and middle-income workers to offset Social Security taxes
- A tax credit covering 50 percent of child care expenses up to $6,000 a year
- A $4,000 tax credit for college students paying tuition if they perform "community service"

- A refundable 10 percent mortgage-interest tax credit for taxpayers who fill out the simplified tax form (Form 1040A)
- A $3,000 tax credit for businesses that hire new workers in 2009 and 2010

So, you might be asking, if so many Americans are going to get tax credits, what is the basis for our prediction that taxes will nonetheless increase? The answer goes back to the first paragraph of this chapter. No government obtains funding from the moon or from Mars. Every single penny that government spends, someone in the private sector does not spend. We already saw in 2008 and 2009 an increase in federal government spending of trillions of dollars on "bailing out" the economy and "stimulating" the economy. If we add to those expenditures additional ones creating more renewable energy, reducing poverty, subsidizing for college attendance, and more, the share of government spending as a percentage of total annual national spending will continue to rise. Thus total taxes must rise.

If, in addition, 95 percent of taxpayers see "tax relief" as Obama promised during the 2008 campaign, the remaining 5 percent of taxpayers will receive a bill for much more than they are currently paying in federal income taxes. Yet higher taxes on the very richest Americans are not going to be sufficient to pay for all of the increased government spending, especially if other people are getting their taxes cut. The highest 5 percent of income earners in the United States already pay over 60 percent of all federal income taxes. As you will read about in the following chapter, sending them a bill for a larger proportion of a larger total tax bill is likely to cause them to change their behavior in ways that will reduce the growth of total income and possibly even reduce the level of total tax receipts.

IS ARGENTINA SHOWING THE WAY?

Argentina was one of the ten richest countries in the world a hundred years ago. It has since slipped to about seventieth on that list. Over the same period of time, government spending (and taxes) in Argentina has been growing relative to the overall size of the economy. Most recently, Argentine president Cristina Kirchner announced that the nation's private pension system was being taken over by the national government. While she claimed that it was for the "good of the people," because the market was too risky for retirement savings, in fact President Kirchner wanted to use those assets to fund more government spending. Technically, the government will "borrow" from the retirement system. But because the Argentine government has a track record of defaulting on its borrowings, many people expect that they will get back few, if any, of their hard-earned retirement pesos. As you might expect, contributions into the private pension plan plummeted as soon as the government announced its plan. Some Argentine citizens quietly began moving other **assets** out of the country, hoping to protect them from similar confiscation. Still others began making plans for moving *themselves* out of the country, on the grounds that emigration was the ultimate form of protection.

The Argentine government's nationalization of the private pension system is simply a once-and-for-all increase in taxes. While it is unlikely that the U.S. government would seek to take control of private pension plans here, the Argentine story illustrates the key point of this chapter. What the government spends, we must pay for. Sometimes the government must be creative in making that happen, but happen it will. Hence our prediction: Higher taxes are in your future.

FOR CRITICAL ANALYSIS

1. The government now owns shares of stock and warrants in many banks, insurance companies, some auto companies, and in other sectors of the economy. (Warrants are rights to own future shares of stock.) If the value of the shares owned by the federal government increases because the market price per share rises, in what way could this increase actually permit a reduction in future taxes? Explain.

2. If you are a lower-income-earning individual and receive enough tax credits so that you pay no income taxes, should you care about tax increases for other individuals? Explain.

3. Is it *possible* that in, say, ten years, the real tax rate paid by U.S. residents will be lower than it is today? What circumstances would have to change to make this occur? Explain.

CHAPTER 30

Soak the Rich

"The art of taxation consists in so plucking the goose as to obtain the greatest possible amount of feathers with the smallest possible amount of hissing." So said Jean-Baptiste Colbert (1619–1683), minister of finance under French King Louis XIV. About three hundred years later, the thirty-fifth president of the United States, John F. Kennedy, said, "An economy hampered by restrictive taxes will never produce enough revenue to balance our budget, just as it will never produce enough jobs or enough profits."

Although Colbert and Kennedy both recognized the costs of taxation, they were focused on two very different kinds of costs. Colbert sought to minimize political opposition to taxes he proposed. Kennedy was interested in reducing the *economic* costs of taxes, which arise because higher taxes induce people to produce less output. At various times in America's history, the politicians in power have sometimes taken the Colbert approach to taxation and at other times the Kennedy approach. Most recently, in both Europe and America, politicians have argued that we should "make the rich pay their 'fair' share." Before we can establish whether the rich do or do not pay their fair share of taxes, we must first examine the different types of taxing systems. We can then also get some notion of whether an effort to concentrate taxes on a narrow segment of the population (the "rich") is more in the spirit of Colbert or of Kennedy.

Proportional, Regressive, and Progressive Taxation Systems

A **proportional tax system** is the easiest to understand. If the income **tax rate** is, say, 20 percent, every taxable dollar earned is taxed at 20 percent. If you have taxable income of $50,000 a year, you pay $10,000 in income taxes. If you have taxable income of $1 million a year, you pay $200,000 in income taxes.

A **regressive tax system** involves collecting a smaller percentage of taxes as one's income rises. Suppose you are taxed 18 percent on the first $100,000 and 3 percent on everything thereafter. If you make $100,000, you pay $18,000 in income taxes. If you make $200,000, you pay $21,000 in income taxes ($18,000 on the first $100,000 plus $3,000 on the next $100,000).

Many economists argue that sales taxes on food are regressive. Why? Because everyone pays the same percentage tax on food, but higher-income-earning people spend a smaller *share* of their incomes on food. Therefore, the effective average tax rate (taxes divided by income) for food is lower for higher-income-earning individuals.

With a **progressive tax system,** the more you earn, the higher your **marginal tax rate.** Suppose you are taxed 20 percent on the first $50,000 and 30 percent on the next $50,000. If you make $50,000, you will pay $10,000 in taxes. If you make $100,000, you will pay $25,000 in taxes ($10,000 on the first $50,000 plus $15,000 on the next $50,000). Thus the proportion of your income that goes to taxes rises as your income rises.

Notice one important fact: *No matter what taxation system is in place, the more income you make, the more you pay in taxes.* What is at issue in the distinction between tax systems is the size of the *additional* income taxes you pay as your income rises. If the percentage stays the same, we have a proportional tax system; if the percentage drops, we have a regressive tax system. Finally, if the percentage increases, we have a progressive tax system. But whatever the system, as long as the tax rate is positive, the higher your income, the higher your taxes. If you have ever earned a paycheck, this is presumably a lesson you already have seen in action.

Do the Rich Pay More?

The Internal Revenue Service (IRS) keeps extensive data on how much different groups pay in income taxes. In 1979, the IRS started looking at what share of the nation's tax bill the most affluent individuals paid. In that year, the top 1 percent of income earners made 9.3 percent of the nation's income but paid 18.3 percent of its income taxes. At the time, the highest-income-earning U.S. residents were in the 70 percent **tax bracket**—that is, their marginal tax rate was 70 cents on the dollar.

Flash forward to current times. Based on IRS data published in 2007, the top marginal tax rate for the big income earners was about 35 percent.

Table 30–1 Shares of Income and Taxes Paid for Top Earners

Share of Earners	Share of Income	Share of Federal Income Taxes
Top 1%	19%	37%
Top 5%	33%	57%
Top 10%	44%	68%
Top 25%	66%	85%

The top 1 percent of income earners made almost 19 percent of the nation's total annual income. But their share of total federal personal income taxes paid was 37 percent. That's not a typo—the top 1 percent of income-earning U.S. residents paid more than *one-third* of all federal personal income taxes in the United States. The fact that high-income individuals pay a large proportion of U.S. federal personal income taxes is reflected also in Table 30–1. In fact, if we look at those people whose income put them in the top 40 percent of all income earners, we see that they paid 99.1 percent of all federal personal income taxes. And what about the tax burden on the other 60 percent of the people? They paid less than 1 percent of federal income taxes.

Other numbers reveal the same pattern. Over the past few years, the richest 1.3 million tax filers, those with adjusted gross incomes of more than $365,000, paid more federal income taxes than all of the 66 million U.S. filers below the **median income** in the United States—to the tune of *ten times* more.

No matter how you wish to analyze the federal personal income tax system in the United States, there is no doubt that it is highly progressive. You may have read or heard about a rich person somehow avoiding taxes, and that surely does happen. But as a group, the highest-income-earning U.S. residents pay the bulk of federal personal income taxes.

THE FEW PAYING FOR THE MANY

What has been happening over the past several decades is rarely discussed on the TV news or during political debates: A shrinking number of Americans are bearing a larger and larger share of the nation's income tax burden. The flip side of the coin is that a growing share of U.S. residents pay little or no taxes whatsoever. If, when you fill out your federal tax return, you owe *any* income tax, you are still in the majority—but not by much. At least 44 million U.S. resident adults pay *no* federal income taxes (including Social Security taxes).

By the time you read this, many of the **tax rebate** proposals discussed by politicians in 2008 and 2009 may have turned into law. If so, then just about half of all adult Americans will be paying no federal personal income taxes. Consider also that an increasingly large number of Americans actually receive more income through the federal income tax system than they pay. Specifically, about 25 million families and individuals with incomes less than about $40,000 now receive payments through their tax filing as part of the **earned income tax credit** program: They pay *negative* **taxes.**

TAX RATE CUTS FOR THE RICH

Whenever there have been tax rate cuts, the charge has been heard that these were "tax cuts for the rich." That charge, of course, *must* be true. Because the highest-income individuals pay most of the federal income taxes, any effective tax rate cut will benefit them. We could eliminate all of the federal personal income taxes assessed on the bottom 50 percent of income earners in the United States and the U.S. Treasury would see almost no change in total tax revenues received.

We see similar phenomena everywhere in our lives. For example, a small percentage of drivers (such as long-haul truckers and people who commute long distances to work) consume a disproportionately large amount of the gasoline and diesel fuel used in America. When the price of fuel falls, most of the savings go to these truckers and commuters. The little old lady who drives only to church on Sunday saves almost nothing. To complain that tax cuts benefit the rich is roughly equivalent to complaining that most of the benefits of lower fuel prices are enjoyed by the people who drive the most.

WHO ARE THE RICH?

Although **wealth** is obviously passed down from one generation to another, when we look at the **standard of living** of individuals, very little of that standard of living is determined by the financial inheritance they received from their ancestors. Instead, current living standards of people are chiefly determined by the incomes they have earned for themselves. Moreover, these incomes are chiefly the result of what they have produced in the workplace.[1]

---

1. We do inherit plenty of nonfinancial wealth from our parents, of course, including intelligence and work habits, which do play a role in determining how much we produce and hence our standard of living.

Given the great disparities in income across people, this may seem strange, but it is easily seen in professional sports. You may have noticed huge disparities in the income received by different athletes, even when they are playing in the same position on the same team. A closer look reveals that these differences are not randomly determined. Instead, more productive players are paid more than less productive ones—lots more. (Tiger Woods doesn't earn $120 million a year just because he went to Stanford.) And although it is easier to see with sports, the link between **productivity** and pay is just as true across all occupations: More productive people are usually paid more.

How Marginal Tax Rates Change Behavior

Now, what happens if we decide to "soak the rich" in the sports world? That is, suppose we decided to reduce the salaries of the most productive athletes and hand it out to the least productive. Economics predicts that overall performance would suffer. Athletes would spend less time working out in the off-season; they would spend less time practicing year round; they would devote less effort to studying their opponents— the list goes on and on. And the result would be a decline in the quality of the competition and less enjoyment for fans: Output, no matter how we measure it, would fall. To be sure, many players would still be motivated by pride and inherent competitive drive, but the extra edge offered by financial rewards would be gone—and so would the performance edge.

The same sorts of incentives are established when we use taxes to "soak the rich." As long as incomes are determined chiefly by performance (and the evidence is that they are), higher marginal tax rates on high-income earners are equivalent to higher tax rates on the most productive people. As in sports, the result is reduced performance and lower output. And this is not hypothetical, as revealed by the converse: Tax rate *cuts* lead to more work effort and more output—as occurred in the 1960s, the 1980s, and the early 2000s.

Does this mean that highly progressive tax systems are "good" or "bad"? That we cannot answer, for it entails a value judgment on which economics offers no guidance. What we can say is that taxes discourage production, and the higher the tax rate, the greater the discouragement. This is the cost of taxes that concerned John Kennedy. In contrast, when the rich are in the minority, soaking the rich can generate a lot of tax dollars with hissing by relatively few people. And this was exactly the point made by Jean-Baptiste Colbert so long ago.

For Critical Analysis

1. President Obama campaigned on the theme that he was going to reduce taxes for 95 percent of working Americans. Why would such a campaign promise be difficult to put into practice?

2. Some countries, particularly in Europe, have imposed a **wealth tax**. It is typically based on everything a person owns minus everything the person owes (the difference between what is owned and what is owed is called **net worth**). Put yourself in the shoes of an individual in a country that has just decided to impose a wealth tax. How does a wealth tax affect your incentive to accumulate wealth? How does it affect your incentive to work hard?

3. Explain why individuals and businesses respond more to changes in marginal tax rates than to changes in **average tax rates.**

CHAPTER 31

The Myths of Social Security

You have probably heard politicians debate the need to reform Social Security. If you are under the age of thirty, this debate has been going on for your entire lifetime. Why has nothing been done? The reason is that the politicians are debating over "facts" that are not facts: Most of the claims made about Social Security are myths—urban legends, if you like. Sadly, the politicians have been repeating these myths so often for so long that they believe them, and so do their constituents (perhaps including you). As long as these myths persist, nothing meaningful will be done about Social Security, and the problem will simply get worse. So let's see if we can't cut through the fog by examining some of the worst Social Security myths.

MYTH 1: THE ELDERLY ARE POOR

The Social Security Act was passed in 1935 as the United States was emerging from the Great Depression. The **unemployment rate** at the time was the highest in our nation's history. **Bank runs** and the stock market crash of 1929 had wiped out the savings of millions of people. Many elderly people had little or no **resources** to draw on in retirement, and their extended families often had few resources with which to help them. In the midst of these conditions, Social Security was established to make sure that the elderly had access to some *minimum* level of income when they retired. It was never meant to be the sole source of retirement funds for senior citizens.

Given the circumstances of the program's founding, it is not surprising that many people associate Social Security with poverty among the elderly. The fact is that both the Social Security program and the financial condition of older people have changed dramatically over the years. For example, measured in today's dollars, initial Social Security payments were as little as $110 per month and reached a maximum of $450 per month, or about $5,400 per year. Today, however, many recipients are eligible for payments well in excess of $25,000 per year. More important, people over age sixty-five are no longer among the poorest in our society.

Despite the ravages of the recession of 2007–2009, today's elderly have accumulated literally *trillions* of dollars in **assets.** These assets include homes that are fully paid for and substantial portfolios of stocks and **bonds.** In addition, millions of older Americans are drawing *private* pensions, built up over years of employment. Social Security payments, for example, now provide only about 40 percent of the income of the average retired person, with the rest coming about equally from private pensions, employment earnings, and investment income. Far from being the age group with the highest poverty rate, the elderly actually suffer about 25 percent *less* poverty than the average of all U.S. residents. To be sure, Social Security helps make this possible, but just as surely, only about 10 percent of the elderly are living in poverty. In contrast, the poverty rate among children is twice as high as it is among people over age sixty-five.

Myth 2: Social Security Is Fixed Income

Most economic and political commentators and laypersons alike treat Social Security benefits as a source of fixed income for the elderly, one that supposedly falls in **real purchasing power** as the general **price level** rises. This myth, too, has its roots in the early days of Social Security, when payments were indeed fixed in dollar terms and thus were subject to the ravages of **inflation.** But this is no longer true. In 1972, Congress decided to link Social Security payments to a measure of the overall price level in the economy. The avowed reason for this change was to protect Social Security payments from any decline in real value during inflation. In fact, because of the price level measure chosen by Congress, the real value of payments actually rises when there is inflation.

Although there are many potential measures of the average price of goods and services, Congress decided to tie Social Security payments to the **consumer price index (CPI).** The CPI is supposed to measure changes in the dollar cost of consuming a bundle of goods and services that is representative for the typical consumer. Thus a 10 percent rise in the CPI is supposed to mean that the **cost of living** has gone up by 10 percent. Accordingly, the law provides that Social Security benefits are automatically increased by 10 percent.

As it turns out, however, the CPI actually overstates the true inflation rate: It is *biased upward* as a measure of inflation. This bias has several sources. For example, when the price of a good rises relative to other prices, people usually consume less of it, enabling them to avoid some of the added cost of the good. But the CPI does not take this into account. Similarly, although the average quality of goods and services generally rises over time, the CPI does not adequately account for this fact. Overall, it has been estimated that until recently, the upward bias in the CPI amounted to about 1.1 percentage points per year on average. Revisions to the CPI have reduced this bias to about 0.8 percent per year. Thus currently, if the CPI says prices have gone up, say, 1.8 percent, they've really gone up only 1.0 percent. Nevertheless, Social Security payments are automatically increased by the full 1.8 percent.

Now, 0.8 or 1.1 percentage points don't sound like much. And if it happened only once or twice, there wouldn't be much of a problem. But almost every year for nearly forty years, this extra amount has been added to benefits. And over a long time, even the small upward bias begins to amount to a real change in **purchasing power.** Indeed, this provision of the Social Security system has had the cumulative effect of raising real (inflation-adjusted) Social Security benefits by almost 50 percent over this period. So despite the myth that Social Security is fixed income, in reality the benefits grow even faster than inflation.

MYTH 3: THERE IS A SOCIAL SECURITY TRUST FUND

For the first few years of Social Security's existence, taxes were collected but no benefits were paid. The funds collected were used to purchase U.S. Treasury bonds, and that accumulation of bonds was called the Social Security Trust Fund. Even today, tax collections (called **payroll taxes**) exceed benefits paid each year—currently by more than $150 billion per year—so that the trust fund now has well over $2 *trillion* in Treasury bonds on its books. Eventually, after the fund reaches a peak of around $2.6 trillion, retiring baby boomers will drive outgoing benefits above incoming tax collections. The bonds will be sold to finance the difference; by around 2040, all of them will be sold, and thereafter all benefits in excess of payroll taxes will have to be financed explicitly out of current taxes.

The standard story told (by politicians at least) is that the bonds in the trust fund represent net assets, much like the assets owned by private pension plans. This is false. Congress has already spent the past excess of taxes over benefits and has simply given the trust fund IOUs. These IOUs are called U.S. Treasury bonds, and they are nothing more than promises by the U.S. Treasury to levy taxes on someone to pay benefits. When it is time for the trust fund to redeem the IOUs it holds, Congress will have to raise taxes, cut spending on other programs, or borrow more to raise the funds. But this would be true even if there were *no* Treasury bonds in the trust fund: All Social Security benefits must ultimately be paid for out of taxes. So whatever might have been intended for the trust fund, the only asset actually backing that fund is nothing more and nothing less than an obligation of Americans—you—to pay taxes in the future.

MYTH 4: SOCIAL SECURITY WILL BE THERE FOR YOU

Social Security was a great deal for Ida Mae Fuller, who in 1940 became the first person to receive a regular Social Security pension. She had paid a total of $25 in Social Security taxes before she retired. By the time she died in 1975 at the age of one hundred, she had received benefits totaling $23,000. And although Ida Mae did better than most recipients, the *average* annual real rate of return for those early retirees was an astounding 135 percent *per year.* (That is, after adjusting for inflation, every initial $100 in taxes paid yielded $135 *per year* during each and every year of that person's retirement.)

People retiring more recently have not done quite so well, but everyone who retired by about 1970 has received a far better return from Social Security than could likely have been obtained from any other investment. These higher benefits relative to contributions were made possible because *at each point in time, current retirees are paid benefits out of the taxes paid by individuals who are currently working.* Social Security is a **pay-as-you-go system;** it is not like a true retirement plan in which participants pay into a fund and receive benefits according to what they have paid in and how much that fund has cumulatively earned. So as long as Social Security was pulling in enough new people each year, the system could offer benefits that were high relative to taxes paid. But the number of people paying Social Security taxes is no longer growing so fast, and the number of retirees is growing faster. Moreover, today's trickle of new retirees is becoming tomorrow's flood as the baby boom generation exits the workforce. The result is bad news all around.

One way to think about the problem facing us—which is chiefly a problem facing *you*—is to contemplate the number of retirees each worker must support. In 1945, forty-two workers shared the burden of each Social Security recipient. By 1960, nine workers had to pick up the tab for each person collecting Social Security. Today, the burden of a retiree is spread out among slightly more than four workers. By 2030 or so, fewer than three workers will be available to pay the Social Security benefits due each recipient.

The coming tax bill for all of this will be staggering. If we *immediately* raised Social Security (payroll) taxes from 15.3 percent to a bit over 19 percent—more than a 24 percent increase—and kept them there for the next seventy-five years or so, the system's revenues would probably be large enough to meet its obligations. But this would be the largest tax increase in U.S. history, which makes it extremely unlikely that it will occur. Yet every day that Congress delays, the situation gets worse. If Congress waits until 2030 to raise taxes, they will have to be increased by more than 50 percent. Indeed, some commentators are predicting that without fundamental reforms to the system, payroll taxes *alone* will have to be hiked to 25 percent of wages—in addition to regular federal, state, and local income taxes, of course.

And what form are these reforms likely to take? Well, rules will specify that people must be older before they become eligible for Social Security benefits. Existing legislation has already scheduled a hike in the age for full benefits up to sixty-seven from its current sixty-six. Almost certainly, this age threshold will be raised again, perhaps to seventy. Moreover, it is likely that all Social Security benefits (rather than just a portion) will eventually be subject to federal income taxes. It is even possible that some high-income individuals—you, perhaps—will be declared ineligible for benefits because their income from other sources is too high.

So what does all this mean for you? Well, technically, a Social Security system will probably be in existence when you retire, although the retirement age will be higher than today and benefits will have been scaled back significantly. It is also likely that, strictly speaking, the Social Security Trust Fund will still be around when you hit the minimum age for benefits. But whatever else happens to the Social Security system between now and your retirement, you can be secure in your knowledge of one thing: You will be getting a much bigger tax bill from the federal government to pay for it.

For Critical Analysis

1. Where has all of the Social Security money gone?

2. People over the age of sixty-five have been highly successful in protecting and enhancing the real benefits they receive from Social Security. This has come at the expense of other people in society, particularly young people. What do you think explains the ability of older people to win political battles with younger people?

3. Analyze how each of the following hypothetical policy changes would affect people's decision to retire. Would the change induce people to retire sooner or later? Explain your reasoning.

(a) An increase in the age at which one can receive full Social Security benefits (currently age sixty-six to sixty-seven, depending on the year in which a person was born)

(b) A decrease in the fraction (currently 70 percent) of full benefits that one can receive if retirement occurs at age sixty-two

(c) An increase in the Medicare eligibility age from its current level of sixty-five

(d) An increase to 100 percent from its current 85 percent in the maximum fraction of Social Security benefits that is subject to the federal income tax

CHAPTER 32

The Hazards of High Taxes

Politicians always seem to be looking for additional ways to raise tax revenues. And most often, politicians talk (and even act) as though their taxing decisions have no effect on the quantity supplied or the quantity demanded of whatever good or service they wish to tax. Indeed, there is a saying among economists that politicians believe that all demand curves and supply curves are **perfectly inelastic.** In such a world, higher taxes would have no effect on either quantity demanded or quantity supplied. What a wonderful world that would be—at least for politicians. In this chapter, you will see how important **microeconomics** is for understanding what are thought to be macroeconomic issues. Tax policies are often thought of as one of the latter, which they are. But tax policies cannot be understood without putting them in the context of how people respond to them.

THE FAILURE OF LUXURY-GOOD TAXES

In the real world, changes in taxes cause changes in **relative prices,** and individuals in their roles as consumers, savers, investors, and workers do react to these relative price changes. Consider a truly telling example from not so long ago—the luxury tax enacted by Congress in 1991. Members of Congress were looking for additional revenues to reduce the **federal budget deficit.** What better place to find those needed revenues than with new taxes on the purchases of high-priced luxury items, such as big boats, expensive cars, furs, planes, and jewelry? After all, rich people don't really care how much they pay, right? That is why we call them rich. So Congress passed a 10 percent luxury surcharge tax on boats priced over $100,000, cars priced over $30,000, aircraft priced over $250,000, and furs and jewelry priced over $10,000.

The federal government estimated that it would rake in $9 billion in extra tax revenues over the following five-year period. Yet just a few years later, the luxury boat tax was quietly eliminated. The luxury car tax was also dropped, as were those special taxes imposed on furs, aircraft, and jewelry. Why? Because the actual take for the federal government was almost *nothing*.

Rich people, it turns out, react to relative price changes just like everyone else. Instead of buying high-priced new boats, for example, they found alternatives. Some purchased used luxury boats instead of new ones. Others decided not to trade in their older boats for new ones. Still others bought their new boats in other countries and never brought them back to the United States to be taxed. Similar changes in behavior occurred in the markets for other luxury goods. The moral of the story for politicians is that the laws of **supply** and **demand** apply to everyone, rich and poor, young and old.

Static versus Dynamic Analysis

The discrepancy between the fantasyland of many politicians and the reality of human behavior can be traced in part to the fact that politicians routinely engage in what is called **static economic analysis.** They assume that people's behavior is static (unchanging), no matter how the constraints they face—such as higher taxes—might change. If the politicians who had pushed for the luxury tax had used **dynamic economic analysis,** they would have correctly anticipated that consumers (even rich ones) were going to change their buying decisions when faced with the new taxes.

Dynamic analysis takes into account the fact that the impact of the **tax rate** on tax revenues actually collected depends crucially on the **elasticity** of the relevant demand or supply curves. That is, even a high *rate* (measured in tax per item or as a percentage of the value of the item) can yield relatively little *revenue* (total dollars collected) if consumers are highly responsive to the tax-inclusive price of the good. For example, in the case of the luxury tax, the elasticity of demand for new, high-end boats was relatively high: When the tax per boat went up, the quantity demanded fell so far that tax collections were negligible.

Responding to Higher Federal Marginal Income Tax Rates

Now let's shift from the demand side of this taxing issue to the supply side. Does quantity supplied react to changing relative prices? Yes, but you might not know it from listening to members of Congress (and even some presidents). The first modern federal personal income tax was imposed in 1916. The highest rate was 15 percent. Eventually, the top federal personal marginal income tax rate reached an astounding 91 percent, during the years 1951 to 1964. This **marginal tax rate** dropped to 70 percent in 1965. In 1980, it was lowered to 50 percent. For much of the 1980s and since, the highest federal marginal income tax rate has ranged from 31 percent to just under 40 percent.

Often politicians (and even some members of the general public) believe that the income tax rates paid by America's richest individuals do not matter to them because they are so rich that even after paying taxes, they are still very rich. The underlying "theory" behind such a belief is that the supply of labor is completely unresponsive to the net, after-tax price received by the providers of labor. Stated another way, if you were to draw the supply curve of labor, it would be a nearly vertical line for each individual at some fixed number of work hours per year; supposedly, the elasticity of supply of labor is low.

To be sure, you might know somebody who loves work so much that she or he will work with the same intensity and quality and for the same number of hours per year no matter what the income tax rate is. But changes occur at the margin in economics (meaning in the real world). If there are *some* individuals who respond to higher federal marginal tax rates by working less, the overall supply curve of labor is going to be upward-sloping even for the ultra-rich—just like all other supply curves for goods and services.

The data seem to confirm our economic predictions. In 1980, the top marginal income tax rate was 70 percent. The highest 1 percent of income-earning Americans paid 19 percent of all federal personal income taxes in that year. In 2007, when the top tax rate was 35 percent, the richest 1 percent paid roughly double that share. How can this be explained? The answer is relatively straightforward: Lower marginal federal personal income tax rates create an incentive for people to work more and harder, because the rewards of doing so are greater. Also, in their role as risk-taking entrepreneurs, individuals are almost always going to be willing to take bigger risks if they know that success will yield greater net after-tax increases in their incomes.

RESPONDING TO INCENTIVES

Data from Europe suggest that exactly the same incentives are at work across a broad spectrum of income earners. Researchers have found that a tax increase of just over 12 percentage points induces the average adult in Europe to reduce work effort by over 120 hours per year—the equivalent of almost four weeks' work. Such a tax change also causes a sharp reduction in the number of people who work at all and causes many others to join the **underground economy,** where no income is taxed. Overall, then, higher tax rates cause lower output and higher unemployment and also induce marked increases in efforts devoted to **tax evasion.**

It is also true that what we have been talking about applies even among people who are at the very bottom of the income distribution. In many countries today, and in many circumstances in the United States, poorer individuals receive benefits from the government. These benefits can be in the form of food stamps, subsidized housing, subsidized health care or health insurance, and direct cash payments (often referred to as "welfare"). Those who receive such government benefits typically pay no income taxes on these benefits. In the case of the United States, they may even receive an **earned income tax credit,** which is a type of **negative tax** or **tax credit.**

If such individuals accept a job (or a higher-paying job, if already employed), two things will normally occur. The first is that they will lose some or all of their government benefits. The second is that they may have to start paying federal (and perhaps state) personal income taxes. They understand that the loss of a benefit is the equivalent of being taxed more. And when they also have to pay explicit taxes, they know that the result is effectively double taxation.

Just as at the top end of the income ladder, the quantity of labor supplied by people at the lower end is affected by changes in the marginal income tax rates they face. If taking a good job and getting off the welfare rolls means losing benefits plus paying income taxes, the person on welfare has less incentive to accept a job.

IRELAND: FROM BASKET CASE TO SUPERSTAR

A good case in point is Ireland, which for most of the past two decades was the fastest-growing economy in all of Europe. Twenty-five years ago, its economy was a disaster, among the poorest of European countries. One of the problems was that people on welfare faced an effective (implicit) marginal income tax rate of about 120 percent if they got off welfare and went back to work. Obviously, they weren't directly taxed at 120 percent, but with the actual income tax that would apply plus the loss in welfare benefits, the implicit marginal tax rate was indeed 120 percent. Stated differently, their available spendable income would drop by about 20 percent if they went back to work! Needless to say, large numbers of poorer Irish stayed on the welfare roles until the program was completely overhauled.

Interestingly, this overhaul of the incentives facing low-income individuals was accompanied by an overhaul of the **tax rates** (and thus incentives) facing high-income corporations, with much the same results. In the 1990s, the Irish slashed the corporate **profits** tax to 12.5 percent, the lowest in Europe and only about one-third as high as the U.S. rate of 35 percent. Beginning in 2004, the Irish government also began offering a 20 percent tax credit for company spending on research and development, offering high-tech firms an opportunity to cut their taxes by starting up and expanding operations in Ireland. Almost immediately, Ireland became a magnet for new investment and for successful companies that didn't want to hand over a third or more of their profits to the tax collector.

The combination of lower corporate tax rates and tax breaks on research and development induced hundreds of multinational corporations to begin operations in Ireland. They brought with them hundreds of thousands of new jobs (and this to a nation of only 4 million residents), and Ireland quickly became number one among the **European Union's** fifteen original members in being home to companies that conduct research and development. And tax revenues of the Irish government? Well, despite the drastic cut in tax rates, tax revenues actually soared to levels never seen before. Indeed, measured as a share of **gross domestic product,** the Irish collected 50 percent *more* tax *revenues* out of corporate profits than America did, despite Ireland's lower tax *rate.*

THE MORAL OF THE STORY

The lesson of our story is simple. It is surely true that "nothing in life is certain but death and taxes." But it is equally true that higher tax rates don't always mean higher tax revenues. And that is a lesson that politicians can ignore only at their own peril.

FOR CRITICAL ANALYSIS

1. If you found yourself in the 91 percent federal personal income tax bracket in 1951, how great would have been your incentive to find legal **loopholes** to reduce your federal tax **liabilities?** If you found yourself in the lowest federal personal income tax bracket of, say, 15 percent, would your incentive to find loopholes to reduce your tax bill have remained the same? Explain.

2. Let's suppose that federal marginal personal income tax rates rise significantly over the next ten years. Explain the ways in which individuals at all levels of income can react over time, not just immediately after taxes are raised. How will the size of the response differ,

say, a year after the rise in tax rates compared to a week after the increase? Is it possible that some people will actually change their behavior *before* the higher tax rates go into effect? Explain.

3. How does the structure of a country's tax system affect who decides to immigrate into the nation or emigrate out of the nation? Contrast, for example, nations A and B. Assume that nation A applies a 20 percent tax rate on every dollar of income earned by an individual. Nation B applies a 10 percent tax rate on the first $40,000 per year of income and a 40 percent tax rate on all income above $40,000 per year earned by an individual. Start by computing the tax bill in each country that must be paid by a person earning $40,000 a year and the tax bill that must be paid by a person earning $100,000 per year. Then consider the more general issue: If the language, culture, and climate of the two nations are similar, and if a person can choose to live on one side or the other of a river separating the two nations, who is more likely to choose to live in A, and who is more likely to choose to live in B? To what extent does your reasoning apply if an ocean, rather than a river, separates the two countries? Does it apply if the language, culture, or climate in the two nations differs? Explain.

PART SEVEN

Monetary Policy

CHAPTER 33

The Fed and Financial Panics

The Panic of 1907 began after an attempt by Otto Heinze to "corner the market" on **shares of stock** in the United Copper Company. Heinze expected the demand for United's shares to increase in the near term and thought that if he bought up enough shares quickly at low prices, he could turn around and sell them at a handsome **profit.** His judgment proved wrong, and Heinze had to sell out at disastrously low prices. Not only did his stock brokerage firm go out of business as a result; more disastrously, the public's confidence in the financial condition of banks that had large holdings of United Copper shares evaporated. Confidence also plummeted regarding the financial health of several banks with whom Otto's brother Augustus was associated.

All of these banks suffered **bank runs,** in which large numbers of customers simultaneously withdrew their deposits, and some ultimately failed as a result. The banking panic soon spread more widely, threatening the security of the entire financial system. It was eventually halted only when the famed financier J. P. Morgan induced a large number of banks to join a consortium and mutually stand behind each other's financial obligations.

BIRTH OF THE FED

The Panic of 1907 achieved notoriety at the time by causing the recession of 1907–1908, but the panic's longer-term importance lies elsewhere. Hoping to avoid a repeat of 1907's financial meltdown, Congress in 1913 established the **Federal Reserve System,** commonly referred to as **the Fed.** The Fed is now the nation's monetary authority and, among other things, our first line of defense against financial panics.

As it had been in prior financial panics, the crux of many banks' woes in 1907 was their inability to convert their assets into the cash that panicked depositors desperately wanted. So the Fed was created to serve as "lender of last resort" to the nation's **commercial banks.** Congress empowered the Fed to lend funds to banks to meet whatever demands that depositors put on the banks, regardless of how great those demands might be. The intention was that there would never be another financial panic in the United States, an objective that, if achieved, would significantly reduce the number and severity of the nation's economic **recessions.**

OPPORTUNITY AND FAILURE

The Fed's first real chance to perform as lender of last resort—the function for which it was created—came in 1930 when several prominent New York banks got into financial difficulties. Customers of those and other banks started withdrawing funds, fearing that their banks might be weak. This spreading lack of confidence was exactly the scenario the Fed was created to defend against—yet it did nothing. The result was a banking panic and a worsening of the economic downturn already under way.

The next year, the Fed had two more opportunities to act as lender of last resort when confidence in banks sagged, yet in both cases it again failed to act. The results were recurrent bank panics in 1931 and an intensification of what was by then an extremely severe recession. Early in 1933, eroding public confidence in the banking system gave the Fed yet another opportunity to step in as lender of last resort, and *again* it failed to do so. The resulting banking panic was disastrous and ushered in the deepest stages of what has come to be known as the Great Depression. It is little wonder that Herbert Hoover, who was president of the United States at the time, referred to the Fed as "a weak reed for a nation to lean on in time of trouble."

LESSONS LEARNED

Thirty years after the end of the Great Depression, Nobel laureate Milton Friedman and Anna Schwartz published *A Monetary History of the United States.* Among other things, this book laid out in detail the story of the Fed's failings during the 1930s. The book's lessons were absorbed by at least two people who have since served as the head of the Fed—Alan Greenspan, who was chair of the Fed from 1987 to 2006, and Ben Bernanke, who succeeded Greenspan.

Greenspan's opportunity to have the Fed serve as the banking system's lender of last resort came in September 2001, in the wake of the terrorist attacks on the World Trade Center towers. Banks found themselves in need of a quick infusion of funds as panicked depositors made large-scale withdrawals of cash. The Fed quickly stepped in to provide funds to banks, enabling them to meet the demands of depositors without having to sell off **assets** quickly at depressed prices. A terrorist attack had surely never been contemplated by the legislators who created the Fed. Nevertheless, the Fed acted vigorously as a lender of last resort and thus certainly achieved the objectives of its creators: prevention of financial panic.

THE PANIC OF '08

Only two years after he replaced Greenspan as chair of the Fed, Ben Bernanke had an even bigger opportunity to put the Fed to work. Late in 2008, rapidly eroding confidence in America's financial system led to the near or total collapse of several major financial firms. Many commercial banks, investment banks, and even insurance companies were suddenly in dire condition, and potential borrowers across the country found themselves unable to obtain funds from anyone, at any rate of interest. Although circumstances differed from 1907 in that commercial banks were not at the center of the panic, there was no doubt about one point: The Panic of '08 was just as threatening to the U.S. economy as its century-old predecessor had been.

Mindful of the costs of inaction, the Fed moved swiftly to maintain and restore confidence in key components of the financial system. But its actions were considerably broader than ever before. Historically, for example, the Fed has lent funds to commercial banks and to the federal government itself. But in 2008, the Fed also lent hundreds of billions of dollars directly to nonbank corporations around the country, including tens of billions to insurance giant AIG. The Fed also began purchasing obligations of government-sponsored **mortgage** market giants Fannie Mae and Freddie Mac, hoping to encourage more lending for home purchases. And finally, the Fed agreed to the following trade with commercial banks: It would exchange billions of dollars of risk-free federal **bonds** it held for billions of dollars of high-risk private bonds that they held. In effect, the Fed helped the banks remove high-risk assets of questionable value from their **balance sheets,** thus reducing the chances that skittish depositors might suddenly make large-scale withdrawals of funds from commercial banks.

THE SURGE IN EXCESS RESERVES

On many of their deposits, commercial banks are required to keep a minimum amount of **reserves** on hand, either in their vaults or on deposit with the Fed. These are referred to as **required reserves.** Any reserves above these minimum required levels are called **excess reserves.** Over the past seventy years, bank holdings of excess reserves have generally been quite small, amounting to no more than a few billion dollars for the entire banking system. And this is not surprising. In normal times, banks generally keep only enough excess reserves to handle day-to-day transactions with depositors because they can earn interest on any funds they lend out.

By 2009, excess reserves soared to more than $800 billion. Total reserves (required plus excess) were up sharply because the Fed was giving banks reserves in return for other assets. Among the purchases: commercial paper (debts issued by private companies), securities backed by credit-card debt and home mortgages, and even home mortgages themselves. But almost all of these reserves simply sat there—either in bank vaults or on deposit with the Fed—because banks lent almost none of them out.

Banks across the country held on to the excess reserves for three reasons. First, the deteriorating economy meant that borrowers were riskier and hence less profitable at any given interest rate. Second, depositors were growing increasingly concerned about the financial condition of commercial banks. The banks therefore wanted plenty of funds on hand—in the form of excess reserves—in case they had to meet increased withdrawal demands by depositors. Oddly enough, the third reason for the failure of banks to lend out reserves was a new policy implemented by the Fed itself.

PAYING INTEREST ON RESERVES

In 2008, the Fed began paying interest on the reserves held by commercial banks, something it had never done before. And it was paying interest not just on required reserves but on excess reserves as well. This policy encouraged banks to hold excess reserves rather than to lend the funds to customers. Thus the payment of interest on commercial bank reserves made it *more difficult* for companies and individuals to get loans.

On balance, it remains to be seen whether the Fed actions of 2008 lived up to the expectations that the Fed's founders had more than a century ago. By providing funds to banks and other financial institutions, the Fed helped reduce the impact of the financial panic and helped prevent widespread runs on commercial banks. Nevertheless, the Fed decision to pay interest on reserves markedly discouraged banks from lending those reserves to companies and households across the land. Only time and further study will tell whether the Fed's actions prevented the recession of 2007–2009 from becoming one of the worst of the past century.

FOR CRITICAL ANALYSIS

1. How did the Fed's long-standing policy of not paying interest on bank reserves act much like a tax on bank reserves?

2. If the Fed continued to pay interest on required reserves but stopped paying interest on excess reserves, how would bank lending incentives be changed?

3. If the Fed had not injected reserves into the banking system in 2008, what would have been the consequences for the banks and for **aggregate demand?**

CHAPTER 34

Monetary Policy and Interest Rates

"Fed cuts interest rates by half a point." Similar headlines appeared numerous times in the financial press in the first decade of the 2000s. The **Federal Reserve System**—the Fed for short—is America's **central bank.** Interest rates can be affected by the Fed; when they are, that is part of **monetary policy,** defined as the use of changes in the amount of money in circulation to affect interest rates, credit markets, **inflation,** and unemployment.

The theory behind monetary policy is relatively simple. An increase in the **money supply** raises spending on goods and services and thus stimulates the economy, tending to lower unemployment in the short run and raise inflation in the long run. (One important version of the money supply is composed of checking-type account balances and **currency** in the hands of the public.) The flip side is that a decrease in the money supply reduces spending, thereby depressing the economy; the short-run result is higher unemployment, and the long-run effect is a lower inflation rate.

MONETARY POLICY AND THE FED

Congress established the Federal Reserve System in 1913. A board of governors consisting of seven members, including the very powerful chairperson, governs it. All of the governors, including the chair, are nominated by the president and approved by the Senate. Their appointments are for fourteen years (although the chair serves in that role for only four years at a time).

Through the Fed and its Federal Open Market Committee (FOMC), decisions about monetary policy are made eight times a year. The Federal Reserve System is independent; the board even has its own budget, financed with interest earnings on the portfolio of **bonds** it owns. The president can attempt to persuade the board to follow a particular policy, and Congress can threaten to merge the Fed with the Treasury or otherwise restrict its behavior. But unless Congress takes the radical step of passing legislation to the contrary, the Fed's chair and governors can do as they please. Hence talking about "the president's monetary policy" or "Congress's monetary policy" is inaccurate. To be sure, the Fed has, on occasion, yielded to presidential pressure to pursue a particular policy, and the Fed's chair follows a congressional resolution directing him to report on what the Fed is doing on the policy front. But now more than ever before, the Fed remains the single most important and truly independent source of economic power in the federal government. Monetary policy is Fed policy and no one else's.

Federal Reserve monetary policy, in principle, is supposed to be countercyclical. That is, it is supposed to counteract other forces that might be making the economy contract or expand too rapidly. The economy goes through **business cycles,** made up of **recessions** (and sometimes **depressions**) when unemployment is rising and **expansions** when unemployment is falling and businesses are often straining their productive capacity. For the Fed to stabilize the economy, it must implement policies that go counter to business activity. Although Fed policy can be put into place much faster than most federal policies, it still does not operate instantaneously. Indeed, researchers have estimated that it takes almost fourteen months for a change in monetary policy to become effective. Thus by the time monetary policy goes into effect, a different policy might be appropriate.

POLICY IN PRACTICE

Researchers examining the evidence over the period from 1913 to the 1990s have concluded that on average, the Fed's policy has turned out to be procyclical rather than countercyclical. That is, by the time the Fed started pumping money into the economy, it was time to do the opposite, and by the time the Fed started reducing the growth rate of the money supply, it was time to start increasing it. Perhaps the Fed's biggest procyclical blunder occurred during the Great Depression in the 1930s. Many economists believe that what would have been a severe recession turned into the Great Depression because the Fed's actions resulted in an almost one-third decrease in the amount of money in circulation, drastically reducing **aggregate demand.** It has also been argued that the rapid inflation experienced in the 1970s was largely the result of excessive monetary expansion by the Fed.

In the 1990s, few commentators were able to complain about monetary policy. Inflation almost disappeared by the end of the decade, which also saw the **unemployment rate** drop to its lowest level in nearly forty years. Why the Fed was successful in the 1990s remains unclear. It could have been due to the uniquely superior insights of its chair during this period, Alan Greenspan. Or perhaps the Fed had learned from its past experiences. Or it may simply have been a run of good luck. But whatever the reason, it is clear that the Fed remains far from perfect. Late in the decade, it tightened monetary policy sharply, reducing monetary growth and thereby contributing to the recession of 2001.

In 2001 and 2002, the Fed moved to increase the money supply more rapidly, which in turn helped produce economic expansion but also caused the inflation rate to double between 2002 and 2005. The Fed responded to the higher inflation by cutting monetary growth over the period 2004–2006, and by late 2007, we had another recession on our hands. This led the Fed to change gears again, cutting interest rates in 2007 and especially in 2008 as the recession deepened. By the time you read this, our forecast is that the Fed will have altered policy once more.

INFLATION AND INTEREST RATES

Most newspaper discussions of Fed policy focus on its decisions to raise or lower interest rates. Before we can make any sense out of such discussions, we need first to understand the relationship between **nominal interest rates,** which are the rates that you see in the newspaper and pay for loans, and the **expected rate of inflation.**

Let's start in a hypothetical world where there is no inflation, so expected (or anticipated) inflation is zero. In that world, you might be able to borrow—obtain a **mortgage** to buy a home, for example—at a nominal rate of interest of, say, 4 percent. If you borrow the funds and your anticipation of zero inflation turns out to be accurate, neither you nor the lender will have been fooled. The dollars you pay back in the years to come will be just as valuable in terms of **purchasing power** as the dollars that you borrowed. In this situation, we would say that the **real interest rate** (equal to the nominal interest rate minus the expected rate of inflation) was exactly equal to the nominal interest rate.

Contrast this with a situation in which the expected inflation rate is, say, 5 percent. Although you would be delighted to borrow at a 4 percent interest rate, lenders would be reluctant to oblige you, and their reluctance would be based on exactly the same reasoning you would be using: The dollars with which you would be repaying the debt would be declining in purchasing power every year. Lenders would likely insist on (and you would agree to) an **inflationary premium** of 5 percent to make up for the expected inflation. The nominal interest rate would rise to about 9 percent, keeping the real rate at its previous level of 4 percent. There is strong evidence that inflation rates and nominal interest rates move in parallel. During periods of rapid inflation, people come to anticipate that inflation rather quickly, and higher nominal interest rates are the result. In the early 1970s, when the inflation rate was between 4 and 5 percent, nominal interest rates on mortgages were around 8 to 10 percent. At the beginning of the 1980s, when the inflation rate was near 10 percent, nominal interest rates on mortgages had risen to between 14 and 16 percent. By the middle of the 1990s, when the inflation rate was 2 to 3 percent, nominal interest rates had fallen to between 6 and 8 percent.

POLICY AND INTEREST RATES

Now let's go back to Fed policy and the headlines. When the chair of the Fed states that the Fed is dropping "the interest rate" from, say, 1.5 percent to 1 percent, he really means something else. In the first place, the interest rate referred to is the **federal funds rate,** the rate at which banks can borrow **excess reserves** from other banks. Any effects of Fed policy here will show up in other rates only indirectly. More important, when the Fed decides to try to alter the federal funds rate, it can do so only by actively entering the market for federal government securities (usually Treasury bills). So if the Fed wants to lower "the interest rate," it essentially must buy Treasury bills from banks and other private holders of the bills. This action bids up the prices of these bills and simultaneously lowers the interest rates on them. This in turn lowers the interest rates at which banks are willing to lend to each other and to the public. (In terms of our earlier discussion, this policy also has the effect of increasing the money supply and so increases spending throughout the economy.) Conversely, when the Fed wants to increase "the interest rate," it *sells* Treasury bills, driving their prices down and pushing up interest rates. The result is a reduction in the money supply and a reduction in spending throughout the economy. A Fed declaration that interest rates are going to be changed simply serves to alert people that a new policy is on the way.

The other key point to note is that the changes in interest rates we have been talking about are strictly short-term changes, occurring over a period of time so short that the expected inflation rate is constant. Once the effects of the Fed's new policy begin to kick in, however, the expected inflation rate will tend to respond, which can create a whole new set of problems. For example, suppose the Fed decides to "lower interest rates," that is, to increase the money supply by buying Treasury bills. In the early weeks and months, this will indeed lower interest rates and stimulate spending. But for a given level of productive capacity in the economy, this added spending will eventually be translated into a higher inflation rate. This will soon cause nominal interest rates to *rise* as inflationary expectations get added onto the real interest rate.

The fact of the matter is that although the Fed can cause interest rates to move up or down in the short run via its choice of monetary policy, forces beyond its control determine what interest rates will be in the long run. The real rate is determined by the underlying **productivity** of the economy and the **consumption** preferences of individuals, and the expected inflation rate is determined by people's beliefs about future policy. So when you read that the chair of the Fed has lowered "the interest rate," you know that the growth of the money supply has been increased. But you also now know that whether the Fed likes it or not, if this policy persists long enough, the eventual result will be more inflation in the future and higher, not lower, interest rates.

FOR CRITICAL ANALYSIS

1. Why do you suppose the Fed likes to signal its intentions about monetary policy ahead of time?

2. Some economists have argued that the Fed should stick to a simple monetary rule, such as a stable growth rate of the money supply, regardless of what is going on in the economy. In light of the Fed's performance history, can you suggest why we might benefit from such a rule? Why do you think the Fed has steadfastly refused to implement such a rule?

3. In response to the Panic of '08, the Fed took unprecedented steps to increase the money supply. For example, for the first time ever, it made large-scale acquisitions of commercial paper (indebtedness of private companies), in addition to buying Treasury bonds. At the time, the stock market was falling and unemployment was rising. What do you predict would have happened to both, and to interest rates, if the Fed had not undertaken expansionary monetary policy at this time?

CHAPTER 35

Credit Chaos

The **recession** of 2007–2009 had its origins as far back as 2006. That's when housing prices across the country first began to turn down, leading to widespread **foreclosures** on home **mortgages** and **defaults** on the securities backed by those mortgages. These defaults brought on the collapse of some of the world's largest financial companies and effectively shut down credit markets around the world. The credit collapse caused a massive reduction in business spending, at the same time that falling house prices forced frightened consumers to slash their own spending. By 2008, this one-two punch of lower **investment** and reduced **consumption** had pushed the economy into full-scale recession. But we are getting ahead of ourselves, so let's go back in time just a bit.

HOUSING MARKET ROLLER COASTER

Between 1995 and 2009, the U.S. housing market went on the wildest ride in its history. Over the years 1995 to 2005, median real (inflation-adjusted) house prices soared 60 percent nationwide and then promptly crashed, falling 40 percent in just four years. Over the same period, the proportion of Americans who owned homes, normally a variable that changes quite slowly, leapt from 64 percent to 69 percent and then quickly dropped back to 66 percent. Meanwhile, the number of new houses built each year soared from 1.4 million to 2 million and then plunged to 500,000 per year.

But what really got people's attention—and created huge pressures on financial markets here and abroad—was the fact that just as quickly as people had snapped up houses during the boom years of 1995–2005, they simply *abandoned* their houses beginning in 2006, refusing to make any more payments on their mortgages. In a typical year, about 0.3 per-cent of homeowners (fewer than one out of three hundred) stop making mortgage payments and thus have their houses go into foreclosure, a process in which the borrower must give up any **equity** (ownership) in a home because of a failure to meet payment obligations. The foreclosure rate doubled to 0.6 percent in 2006, doubled again in 2007, and rose yet again in 2008 and 2009. In some hard-hit states, such as Nevada, foreclo-sures exploded to more than *ten times* the normal nationwide rate, with one home out of thirty going into foreclosure each year.

Across the country, people were literally walking away from their homes, leaving them in the hands of banks and other lenders. These lenders then took huge financial losses when forced to sell the abandoned properties in a market in which house prices were already falling. The result was further downward pressure on prices, which gave more own-ers the incentive to walk away from their homes, which raised foreclo-sures, and so forth. Within just a few years, the housing market was more depressed than it had been at any time since the Great Depression of the 1930s.

What happened? Specifically, we want to know why over this fif-teen-year period, the housing market first exploded and then imploded, creating financial chaos on a worldwide scale. Although numerous fac-tors no doubt played a role, there is just as little doubt that the principal culprit was none other than our own Congress. Operating under a banner promoting "affordable housing," Congress first amended key mortgage-lending legislation and then put considerable implicit and explicit pres-sure on two crucial government-sponsored mortgage agencies. Together, these actions caused mortgage lenders to dramatically reduce the finan-cial standards expected of home-buyers who wished to obtain a mort-gage. These lower standards enabled many more people to qualify for mortgages, increasing the demand for housing and leading to the hous-ing boom of 1995–2005. But these same lower standards meant that peo-ple in weaker financial condition were heavily represented among new home buyers, which in turn played a central role in creating the housing crash and mortgage meltdown of 2006–2009. To see how this evolved, we are going to have to do some digging in the history books.

SOME HOUSING HISTORY

Prior to World War II, most home mortgages were of short duration, such as a year or two (as opposed to fifteen to thirty years, which is common now). During the Great Depression, many risk-weary lenders refused to renew mortgages when they came due. The state of the economy was such that most borrowers were unable to repay immediately, and so their homes were foreclosed. In response, the U.S. government in 1934 created the Federal Housing Administration (FHA), to guarantee some home mortgages from default, and in 1938 created the Federal National Mortgage Association (FNMA, known as Fannie Mae), to purchase mortgages from the FHA, enabling the latter to guarantee still more mortgages. In 1968, Congress authorized Fannie Mae to buy mortgages from virtually all lenders, and in 1970, Congress created Freddie Mac (the Federal Home Mortgage Loan Corporation) to offer competition to Fannie Mae. Both Fannie Mae and Freddie Mac are referred to as **government-sponsored enterprises (GSEs)**; both are technically independent of the federal government, but both are subject to congressional oversight and, it turns out, to political pressure to do what Congress wants them to do.

The next key congressional action came in 1977 when the Community Reinvestment Act (CRA) was passed, a law that required banks to lend in all neighborhoods of the geographic areas where they operated, even where risks were likely to be much higher than the banks would normally undertake. In 1995, the CRA was amended so that banks were, in effect, compelled to ignore their lending standards when making loans in low-income and minority neighborhoods or else face the wrath of government regulators. Not long thereafter, Congress began putting considerable pressure on Fannie Mae and Freddie Mac to buy up the low-quality mortgages being made under the CRA in the hopes that this would encourage lenders to make still more high-risk loans. And indeed it did: The banks soon recognized that with the two GSEs standing ready to take the worst of their mortgages off their hands, they could earn hefty fees for originating the mortgages and then dump the risks of default off onto Fannie Mae and Freddie Mac. At this point, many potential lenders, including banks, savings and loans, and mortgage brokers, concluded that if Fannie Mae and Freddie Mac were happy to buy up risky mortgages at the drop of a hat, so to speak, then it was OK to hold on to some of the risky mortgages they were making. After all, these mortgages (called **subprime mortgages**) fattened **profits** with their above-average interest rates, and if the market turned sour, the GSEs would presumably stand ready to take them off lenders' hands.

Standards? What Standards?

Thus it was regulatory and legislative pressure from the federal government (spearheaded by Congress) that pushed mortgage lenders to cut their lending standards in truly remarkable ways. For example, lenders historically insisted on down payments ranging from 5 to 20 percent on home loans. This gives borrowers an incentive to keep making monthly payments (lest they lose their down payment upon foreclosure), and it provides a cushion for the lender (to ensure that it gets all its money back upon foreclosure). Under pressure from federal regulators, however, lenders were induced to cut required down payments and even to make so-called piggyback loans, giving borrowers a second mortgage on top of the first to provide the cash for the down payment. In effect, down payments were driven to zero or close thereto.

But there was more. Federal regulators pushed banks to largely ignore mortgage applicants' credit histories if they were less than stellar, to forgo confirmation of applicants' current or past employment or income levels, to permit applicants to have lower income-to-loan ratios, and to count as part of income such sources as unemployment insurance and welfare payments, despite the temporary nature of such payments. Banks that had never before offered loans under such conditions soon made them routinely, pushed by the requirements of the CRA and pulled by the willingness of Fannie Mae and Freddie Mac to acquire the loans as soon as the ink was dry. And because the GSEs were so active in making the market for loans, many lenders felt comfortable making and holding on to such loans, even buying more loans from other lenders.

Congress's avowed intention in this process was to "help promote affordable housing," especially for low-income and minority individuals. Congress claimed to be particularly interested in making home ownership possible for people who had been renters all their lives. And indeed, a great many low-income and minority individuals were for the first time able to own their homes—at least for a while. But once the banks became comfortable making and disposing of high-risk loans, they quickly became amenable to making such loans to anyone who showed up, first-time buyer or not. And if the loan was to buy a house in a low-income or minority neighborhood, so much the better because of the possibility that it would keep the bean-counting regulators happy. Thus beginning in the late 1990s and accelerating rapidly in 2002 (when the house price trajectory turned up), speculators—people buying a second or third house in the hopes of selling quickly for a profit—became an increasingly important part of the market. Indeed, it is now estimated that one-quarter of all borrowers over this period were making speculative purchases of this sort.

Not surprisingly, speculators wanted to make low down payments and to obtain **adjustable-rate mortgages (ARMs)**. Not only did ARMs offer slighter lower initial interest rates and payments (because borrowers absorbed the risk of higher rates in the future), but ARMs also gave lenders the flexibility to offer low "teaser" interest rates (and thus ultra-low payments) during the first few years of the mortgage. Such mortgages were considerably riskier for borrowers because of the prospect of higher payments later, when the mortgages "popped" (automatically adjusted their interest rates to full long-run levels). But by then, of course, speculators hoped to have sold for a profit and paid off the mortgage. The spread of ARMs, especially those with low teaser rates, was accelerated by people who bought homes hoping to refinance at a low fixed rate later, after rising home prices created equity for them in their houses.

MARKET COLLAPSE

All went well until 2005, when many of the early ARMs began to pop (with payments adjusting upward sharply). Some borrowers found they were unable to make the higher payments and were thus forced to sell their homes. This slowed the rise in house prices, making housing less attractive as an investment, which in turn reduced the speculative **demand** and put further downward pressure on prices. In markets such as Arizona, California, Florida, and Nevada, where speculative activity had been the greatest, house prices started to *fall,* and growing numbers of individuals (especially those with low or no down payments) found themselves "upside down," that is, owing more on their mortgages than their houses were worth. By the middle of 2006, the prudent financial course for such people was to stop making payments (especially on ARMs that had popped) and to simply walk away when the lender began foreclosure proceedings.

Many accounts of this process in the popular press have claimed that it is exclusively high-risk, subprime mortgages that were at the root of the crisis. This sounds sensible enough, because subprime mortgages have always had relatively high foreclosure rates; indeed, historically, the subprime foreclosure rate has been about eight times as high as the rate on prime mortgages (1.6 percent per year versus 0.2 percent per year). Hence subprime mortgages now, as in normal times, are disproportionately represented among foreclosures. But a closer look at the data also reveals that foreclosures on *both* types of mortgages shot upward in the middle of 2006, with foreclosures on subprime mortgages soon reaching 4 percent and those on prime mortgages hitting 0.5 percent. Thus it appears that both types of borrowers began to get in trouble at the same time; subprime mortgages were not uniquely affected.

A close look at the data also reveals another key fact: It is chiefly the borrowers who obtained adjustable-rate mortgages who caused the current mess. Prior to 2006, foreclosure rates on ARMs and on fixed-rate mortgages were very close to the same. But beginning in early 2006, even as the foreclosure rate on fixed-rate mortgages hardly budged, the rate on ARMs exploded: On prime ARMs, the rate leapt by a factor of five, while the foreclosure rate on subprime ARMs tripled. Moreover, it was the ARMs where foreclosures leapt initially first (at the very beginning of 2006). Thus it was forced sales on these homes that started the downward pressure on house prices, which gave more owners the incentive to walk away from their homes, which raised foreclosures, and so forth. Soon enough, the entire market had begun its meltdown.

By the time you read this, we expect (and hope!) that the housing market will have shown signs of recovery. But we also hope that the lesson of this episode will not be forgotten. The mortgage meltdown of 2006–2009 had its foundation laid by our very own Congress, which sought to subvert the housing market to achieve political goals. The methods used are perhaps little different than Congress usually employs when it desires to achieve politically popular social objectives. But the very real difference of this episode is the enormous social cost that it imposed on Americans of all races and all income levels. Millions of Americans had their hopes of home ownership first artificially raised and then cruelly dashed. The financial losses and emotional stresses inflicted on individuals, the blighted neighborhoods littered with abandoned houses, and the turmoil felt throughout the states most affected are all costs that will imprint the American scene for years to come.

FOR CRITICAL ANALYSIS

1. It seems likely that members of Congress, even the strongest supporters of the CRA and those who put the most pressure on the GSEs to buy high-risk mortgages, will likely escape being held responsible for any part of the mortgage meltdown. Can you suggest why?

2. In light of the fact that foreclosure rates have been much higher on ARMs than on fixed-rate mortgages, what do you predict will happen in the future to the proportion of mortgages that are of each type? Explain.

3. In effect, the CRA and the actions of Fannie Mae and Freddie Mac acted to subsidize home purchases by people who would otherwise not have purchased houses. All subsidies must be financed by taxes, implicit or explicit, on someone. Who is paying the "taxes" in this case? Explain.

CHAPTER 36

Deposit Insurance and Financial Markets

During the Panic of '08, the federal government announced a key new policy: It was insuring against loss all bank deposits up to $250,000 per account. So if your depository institution happened to be holding some toxic (possibly even worthless) **mortgage**-backed securities, you were home free. The bank could suffer terrible losses, even go out of business, and yet your accounts, up to $250,000 each, would be guaranteed by the full faith and of the United States government—which is to say, the U.S. taxpayer.

If you happened to notice the announcement of this policy, you may have wondered to yourself, why would the government do this? For example, although the federal government bought **shares of stock** in numerous banks at the same time, it most assuredly does not guarantee the value of those shares. Why treat deposits differently? A more subtle question is this: How do banks and other **depository institutions** behave differently because of this special deposit insurance? And you might even have wondered whether *your* behavior is likely to be any different because of this insurance. To get a handle on these and other questions, we must look back to the 1930s, before the notion of deposit insurance had even been conceived.

RUNS ON BANKS

Bank runs are defined as the simultaneous rush of depositors to convert their deposits into **currency.** Until the federal government set up deposit insurance in 1933, runs on banks were an infrequent but seemingly unavoidable occurrence, sometimes becoming widespread during economic **recessions.** The largest number of bank runs in modern history occurred during the Great Depression; as a result, more than *nine thousand* banks failed during the 1930s.

Just put yourself in the shoes of the depositor in a typical bank in 1930 and remember that you are a **creditor** of the bank. That is to say, your deposits in the bank are its **liabilities.** Suppose a rumor develops that the **assets** of the bank are not sufficient to cover its liabilities. In other words, the bank is, or will soon be, **insolvent.** Presumably, you are worried that you won't get your deposits back in the form of currency. Knowing this, you are likely to rush to the bank. All other depositors who hear about the bank's supposedly weak financial condition are likely to do the same thing.

This is the essence of a bank run: Regardless of the true state of the bank's financial condition, rumors or fears that a bank is in trouble can cause depositors to suddenly attempt to withdraw all of their funds. But many assets of a bank are in the form of loans that cannot immediately be converted into cash. Even if solvent, the bank is said to be **illiquid** because it doesn't have enough cash on hand to meet the demands of fearful depositors. And when it attempts to get that cash by selling some assets, any resulting decline in the market value of those assets can quickly turn a **solvent** bank into an insolvent one.

Bank runs can be disastrous for the economy because when they occur, the nation's **money supply** shrinks as people pull cash out of banks and stuff it under their mattresses (or wherever they think it might be safe). This is turn causes **aggregate demand** to fall, leading to higher unemployment, business failures, and yet more concerns for the solvency of banks. Quickly enough, the result can be an economic recession and widespread hardship.

DEPOSIT INSURANCE

When bank failures hit four thousand in 1933, the federal government decided to act to prevent further bank runs. That year, Congress passed, and the president signed into law, legislation creating the Federal Deposit Insurance Corporation (FDIC) and the next year created the Federal Savings and Loan Insurance Corporation (FSLIC). Many years later, in 1971, the National Credit Union Share Insurance Fund (NCUSIF) was created to insure credit union deposits, and in 1989, the FSLIC was replaced by the Savings Association Insurance Fund (SAIF). To make our discussion simple, we will focus only on the FDIC, but the general principles apply to all of these agencies.

When the FDIC was formed, it insured each account in a commercial bank against a loss of up to $2,500. That figure has been increased on seven different occasions, reaching $250,000 in 2008. The result of federal deposit insurance is that there has not been a widespread bank run in the United States since the Great Depression, despite numerous bank failures in the interim. Even during the Panic of 2008, when confidence in many financial institutions collapsed, federally insured depository institutions continued to operate; indeed, total deposits in them actually rose. The good news about federal deposit insurance is that it has prevented bank runs. But this has come at a significant cost, arising largely due to the unintended consequences of deposit insurance.

ADVERSE SELECTION

Suppose someone offers you what he or she claims is a great **investment** opportunity. That person tells you that if you invest $50,000, you will make a very high rate of return, say, 20 percent per year, much higher than the 3 percent your funds are currently earning elsewhere. No matter how much you trusted the person offering you this deal, you would probably do some serious investigation of the proposed investment before you handed over fifty thousand hard-earned dollars. You, like other people, would carefully evaluate the risk factors involved in this potential opportunity.

For example, if you use part of your **savings** to buy a house, you will undoubtedly have the structural aspects of the house checked out by an inspector before you sign on the dotted line. Similarly, if you planned to purchase an expensive piece of art, you surely would have an independent expert verify that the artwork is authentic. Typically, the same is true every time you place your accumulated savings into any potential investment: You look before you leap. In circumstances such as these, there is initially **asymmetric information**—in this case, the seller knows much more than the potential buyer. But with diligence, the buyer can eliminate much of this gap in knowledge and make a wise decision.

Now ask yourself, when is the last time you examined the financial condition or lending activities of the depository institution at which you have your checking or savings account? We predict that the answer is never. Indeed, why should you investigate? Because of federal deposit insurance, you know that even if the depository institution that has your funds is taking big risks, you are personally risking nothing. If that depository institution fails, the federal government will—with 100 percent certainty—make sure that you get 100 percent of your deposits back, up to the insurance limit.

So here we have it, the first unintended consequence of depository insurance. Depositors like you no longer have any substantial incentive to investigate the track record of the owners or managers of banks. You care little about whether they have a history of risky or imprudent behavior because at worst you may suffer some minor inconvenience if your bank fails. So unlike in the days before deposit insurance, the marketplace today does little to monitor or punish past performance of owners or managers of depository institutions. As a result, we tend to get **adverse selection**—instead of banks owned and operated by individuals who are prudent at making careful decisions on behalf of depositors, many of them end up run by people who have a high tolerance for taking big risks with other people's money.

MORAL HAZARD

Now let's look at bank managers' incentives to act cautiously when making loans. You must first note that the riskier the loan, the higher the interest rate that a bank can charge. For example, if a developing country with a blemished track record in paying its debts wishes to borrow from a U.S. depository institution, that country will have to pay a much higher interest rate than a less risky debtor. The same is true when a risky company comes looking for a loan: If it gets one at all, it will be at a higher-than-average interest rate.

When trying to decide which loan applicants should receive funds, bank managers must weigh the trade-off between risk and return. Poor credit risks offer high **profits** if they actually pay off their debts, but good credit risks are more likely to pay off their debts. The right choice means higher profits for the bank and likely higher salaries and promotions for the managers. The wrong choice means losses and perhaps insolvency for the bank and new, less desirable careers for the managers.

To understand how bank mangers' incentives are changed by deposit insurance—even for managers who otherwise would be prudent and conservative—consider two separate scenarios. In the first scenario, the bank manager is told to take $50,000 of depositors' funds to Las Vegas. The rules of the game are that she can bet however she wants, and the bank will *share* the winnings *and losses* equally with the deposit holders whose funds she has in trust. In the second scenario, the same bank manager with the same funds is given a different set of rules. In this case, the bank doesn't have to share in any of the losses, but it will share in any of the gains when betting in Las Vegas.

Under which set of rules do you think the bank officer will take the higher risks while betting in Las Vegas? Clearly, she will take higher risks in the second scenario, because her bank will not suffer at all if she loses the entire $50,000. Yet if she hits it big, say, by placing a successful bet on double-zero in roulette, her bank will share the profits, and she is likely to get a raise and a promotion.

Well, the second scenario is exactly the one facing the managers of federally insured depository institutions, especially since the fall of 2008. If they make risky loans, thereby earning, at least in the short run, higher profits, they share in the "winnings." The result for them is higher salaries. If, by contrast, some of these risky loans are not repaid, what is the likely outcome? The bank's losses are limited because the federal government (which is to say you, the taxpayer) will cover any shortfall between the bank's assets and its liabilities. Thus federal deposit insurance means that banks get to enjoy all of the profits of risk without bearing all of the consequences of that risk.

So the second unintended consequence of deposit insurance is to encourage **moral hazard**. Specifically, bank managers of all types (risk lovers or not) have an incentive to take higher risks in their lending policies than they otherwise would. Indeed, when the economy turned down in the early 1980s, we got to see the consequences of exactly this change in incentives. From 1985 until the beginning of 1993, 1,065 depository institutions failed, at an average rate of more than ten times that for the preceding forty years. The losses from these failures totaled billions of dollars—paid for in large part by you, the taxpayer.

What, then, might be expected from the 2008 insurance hike to $250,000? Well, in the short run, confidence in banks was renewed and depositors were encouraged to keep more funds in banks. This was good news, for it helped the economy adjust to the financial shocks of 2008–2009. But the bad news will be forthcoming in the long run: The higher deposit insurance limits will encourage both adverse selection (more risk-loving bank managers) and moral hazard (more risk-taking by bank managers of all stripes). Eventually, the lending standards of banks will deteriorate to the point that losses mount once again—paid for in part by you, the taxpayer.

PAYING FOR DEPOSIT INSURANCE

For the first sixty years or so of federal deposit insurance, all depository institutions were charged modest fees for their insurance coverage. Unfortunately, the fee that these depository institutions paid was completely unrelated to the riskiness of the loans they made. A bank that made loans to Microsoft was charged the same rate for deposit insurance as a bank that made loans to a startup company with no track record whatsoever. Hence not even the fees paid by banks for their insurance gave them any incentive to be prudent. This is completely unlike the case in private insurance markets, in which high-risk customers are charged higher premiums, giving them at least some incentive to become lower-risk customers.

In the early 1990s, the federal government made a feeble attempt to adjust fees for depository insurance to reflect the riskiness of their lending activities. But the political strength of the depository institutions prevented any fundamental change in the system. In 2008, the insurance fees paid by depository institutions were doubled, but even this was not enough to keep up with the added risks of the higher insurance limits. Just as important, more than 90 percent of all depository institutions pay the same insurance rate. Only the 9 percent who are the highest-risk pay a higher premium, and that amount is only 20 percent above the base rate—not nearly enough to cover the likely losses of those banks or enough to get them to change their risky behavior.

So while your banker is headed to Vegas, you'd better plan on staying at home to work. Sooner or later, as a U.S. taxpayer, your bill for deposit insurance will come due.

FOR CRITICAL ANALYSIS

1. If federal deposit insurance costs nothing, who pays when an insured depository institution fails and its depositors are nonetheless reimbursed for the full amount of their deposits?

2. In a world without deposit insurance, what are some of the mechanisms that would arise to "punish" bank managers who acted irresponsibly? (*Hint:* There are similar types of mechanisms for consumer goods and in the stock market.)

3. Explain how "experience rating" of insurance—charging higher premiums to higher-risk customers—affects the incidence of both adverse selection and moral hazard.

CHAPTER 37

How (Not) to Beat
the Market

Within a few weeks in October 2008, the stock market lost more than 25 percent of its value. Virtually all commentators proclaimed it the most disastrous performance by the market since 1931, in the throes of the Great Depression. By the end of October, many observers were predicting that the market would surely decline by *another* 25 percent before any recovery could be expected. Yet within six weeks, the market had *risen* 15 percent. And in the months since, day-to-day and month-to-month movements in the stock market have been almost as volatile, sharing only one common feature: They have all been unpredictable.

Now, there is no doubt that a knowledge of macroeconomics can help you understand many important economic factors, including the determinants of the **unemployment rate** and the **inflation** rate and what causes changes in interest rates and the prices of the stocks issued by corporations. But sometimes people think that this level of understanding can take them a step further and enable them to *predict* the behavior of key macroeconomic variables in the future. It is true that when it comes to forecasting the unemployment rate, the inflation rate, or even the level of **real GDP,** the principles of macroeconomics can help. But when it comes to the stock market or interest rates, we want to emphatically (albeit sadly) inform you of this: Nothing you learn from this book (or any other) will enable you to "beat the market" by figuring out ahead of everyone else where stock prices, **bond** prices, or interest rates are going to be tomorrow or next year.

STOCKS, BONDS, AND BROKERS

Let's begin with the financial pages (sometimes called the business section) of the daily newspaper. There you will find column after column of information about the stocks and bonds of U.S. corporations. A **share of stock** in a corporation is simply a legal claim to a share of the corporation's future **profits;** owners of stocks are called **shareholders.** If there are 100,000 shares of stock in a company and you, as a shareholder, own 1,000 of them, then you own the right to 1 percent of that company's future profits.

A bond is a legal claim against a firm, entitling the bond owner to receive a fixed annual "coupon" payment, plus a lump-sum payment at the bond's maturity date. (Coupon payments on bonds get their name from the fact that bonds once had coupons attached to them when issued. Each year, the owner would clip a coupon off the bond and send it to the issuing firm in return for that year's interest payment.) Bonds are issued in return for funds lent to the firm. The coupon payments represent interest on the amount borrowed by the firm, and the lump-sum payment at maturity generally equals the amount originally borrowed. Bonds are *not* claims to the future profits of the firm; legally, the owners of the bonds, called **bondholders,** are to be paid whether the firm prospers or not. (To ensure this, bondholders generally must receive their coupon payments each year, plus any principal due, before *any* shareholders can receive their share of the firm's profits, called **dividends.**)

Now, suppose that in your quest for riches, you decide to buy some shares of stock in a corporation. How should you choose which corporation's stock to buy? One way is to consult a specialist in stocks, called a **stockbroker.** Such brokers have access to an enormous amount of information. They can tell you what lines of business specific corporations are in, who the firms' major competitors are, how profitable the firms have been in the past, and whether their stocks' prices have risen or fallen. If pressed, they will probably be willing to recommend which stocks to buy. Throughout your discussion, the broker's opinion will sound highly informed and authoritative.

Strange as it may seem, though, a broker's investment advice is not likely to be any better than anyone else's. In fact, *the chances of the broker's being right are no greater than the chances of your being right!* Indeed, you are just as likely to get rich (or avoid going broke) by throwing darts at the financial pages of your newspaper. Let's see why.

THE MAGIC OF THE DARTS

Some years ago, the editors of *Forbes,* a respected business magazine, taped the financial pages of a major newspaper to a wall and threw darts at the portion listing stock prices. They hit the stocks of twenty-eight different companies and invested a hypothetical $1,000 in each. When the editors halted their experiment, the original $28,000 had grown to $132,000—a gain of 370 percent. Over the same period, the Dow Jones Industrial Average (a leading measure of the stock market's overall performance) grew less than 40 percent in value. Perhaps even more impressive, *Forbes*'s random selection of stocks outperformed the recommended stock portfolios of most of the stock market–forecasting "gurus."

More recently, the editors of the *Wall Street Journal,* a major financial newspaper, tried a similar experiment. Each month, they invited four stockbrokers to recommend a stock to buy; the four stocks became the "experts' portfolio" for the month. Then the editors threw four darts at the financial pages of their newspaper to select four stocks that became the "darts' portfolio" for the month. Over time, the particular expert brokers changed, depending on how well their picks performed relative to the darts' portfolio. Any broker whose stock beat the darts got to pick again the next month. Any expert beaten by the darts was replaced the next month by a new broker. At six-month intervals, the newspaper tallied up the performances of the experts versus the darts. After several years of running the experiment, the general result was this: Although the experts beat the darts over the long haul, the winning margin was tiny. Moreover, there were several six-month periods in which the darts actually *outperformed* the experts. How did the darts do it?

BUY LOW, SELL HIGH

Suppose that you, and you alone, noticed that the price of a particular stock moved in a predictable manner. Specifically, assume that the price *rose* 5 percent on even-numbered days and *fell* 5 percent on odd-numbered days, resulting in (approximately) no average change over time. Knowing this fact, how do you make money? You simply buy shares of the stock just before their price is due to rise and sell those shares just before it is due to fall. If you start the year with $1,000 and reinvest your profits, following this strategy would yield profits in excess of $500,000 by the end of the year. If you successfully continue this strategy for a second year, your **wealth** would exceed $250 million!

Of course, as your wealth accumulates—"buying low and selling high"—your purchases and sales would start to affect the price of the stock. Your purchases would drive up the low prices, and your sales would drive down the high prices. Ultimately, your buying and selling in response to predictable patterns would *eliminate* those patterns, and there would be no profit potential left to exploit. This is *exactly* what happens in the stock market—except it happens far faster than a single person could accomplish alone.

A RANDOM WALK DOWN WALL STREET

At any point in time, there are tens of thousands, perhaps millions, of people looking for any bit of information that will help them forecast the future prices of stocks. Responding to any information that seems useful, these people try to "buy low and sell high," just as you would like to do. As a result, all publicly available information that might be used to forecast stock prices gets taken into account, leaving no predictable profits. Furthermore, because there are so many people involved in this process, it occurs quite swiftly. Indeed, there is evidence that all information entering the market is fully incorporated into stock prices within *less than a minute* of its arrival.

The result is that stock prices tend to follow a **random walk**—which is to say that the best forecast of tomorrow's price is today's price plus a random component. Although large values of the random component are less likely than small values, nothing else about its magnitude or sign (positive or negative) can be predicted. Indeed, the random component of stock prices exhibits behavior much like what would occur if you rolled a pair of dice and subtracted 7 from the resulting score. *On average,* the dice will total 7, so after you subtract 7, the average result will be zero. It is true that rolling a 12 or a 2 (yielding a net score of + 5 or –5) is less likely than rolling an 8 or a 6 (producing a net score of +1 or –1). Nevertheless, positive and negative net scores are equally likely, and the expected net score is zero.[1]

It is worth emphasizing that the bond market operates every bit as efficiently as the stock market. That is, investors in bonds study the available information and use whatever might help them forecast future bond prices. Because they exploit this information up to the point that the added benefits of doing so are just matched by the added costs, there remains no publicly available information that can be used profitably to improve bond price forecasts. As a result, bond prices, like stock prices, follow a random walk. Moreover, because interest rates are inextricably linked to the prices of bonds, interest rates also follow a random walk.

WHAT ARE THOSE PEOPLE DOING?

In light of this discussion, two questions arise. First, are all the efforts put into forecasting stock and bond prices simply a waste? The answer is no. From a social viewpoint, this effort is productive because it helps ensure

---

1. Strictly speaking, stock prices follow a random walk with **drift;** that is, on average, they rise at a real (inflation-adjusted) rate of about 3 percent per year over long periods of time. This drift, which is the average compensation investors receive for deferring **consumption,** can be thought of as the 7 that comes up on average when two dice are rolled.

that **asset** prices correctly reflect all available information and thus that **resources** are allocated efficiently. From a private standpoint, the effort is also rewarding, just as any other productive activity is rewarding. At the margin, the added gains from trying to forecast future stock and bond prices are exactly equal to the added costs; there are no unexploited profit opportunities. Unless you happen to have some unique ability that makes you better than others, you will earn only enough to cover your costs—but, of course, the same is true of growing wheat or selling women's shoes. So absent some special ability, you are just as well-off investing in the market based on the roll of the dice or the throw of a dart.

The second question is a bit trickier: Isn't there any way to "beat the market"? The answer is yes—but only if you have **inside information,** knowledge that is unavailable to the public. Suppose, for example, that your best friend is in charge of new product development for Mousetrap, Inc., a firm that just last night invented a mousetrap superior to all others on the market. No one but your friend—and now you—are aware of this. You could indeed make a killing with this information by purchasing shares of Mousetrap, Inc., and then selling them (at a higher price) as soon as the invention is publicly announced. There is one problem: Stock trading based on such inside information is illegal, punishable by substantial fines and even imprisonment. Unless you happen to have a stronger-than-average desire for a long vacation in a federal prison, our money-making advice to you is simple: Invest in the mousetrap after it hits the market—and throw darts in the meantime.

FOR CRITICAL ANALYSIS

1. Why do you think the government prohibits insider trading?

2. When the prices of stocks fall, newspapers often report that the decline in prices was caused by a "wave of selling." By the definition of exchange, every sale must be accompanied by a purchase. Why, then, do the newspapers not report that the decline in stock prices was caused by a "wave of purchasing"?

3. If stockbrokers cannot "beat the market," why do people use their services?

CHAPTER 38

Credit-Card Crunch

By the time you read this, you may already have had a credit-card application denied or an existing card canceled. No, we are not talking about the credit-card cutbacks that resulted from the recession of 2007–2009. We are referring to the effects of new **Federal Reserve** regulations (expanded by Congress) that are said to benefit you but have in many cases had exactly the opposite effect.

We speak of federal restrictions on the interest rates and fees that credit-card firms may charge their customers. Effective in 2010, such companies are sharply limited in their ability to raise interest rates on existing credit balances, even if interest rates soar elsewhere in the economy. Moreover, the companies are limited in the fees they may charge customers who have little or no credit background or customers who have a troubled credit history. The result is a reduction in the credit available and credit that is more, not less, expensive to obtain.

CREDIT-CARD COMPLAINTS

If you have had a credit card for several years or know people who have, you have likely heard one or more "horror stories" about outrageous late fees or sky-high interest rates or other charges imposed by credit-card companies. Some of these incidents are no doubt the result of unscrupulous practices by companies that prey on naïve consumers. Some companies have actually been able to commit fraud under the guise of being a credit-card issuer.

But the vast majority of all credit cards are issued by companies that are in the business for the long haul. The interest rates and fees they charge are competitively determined and dependent on the (often substantial) risks of dealing with their cardholders. The practices of companies such as these are generally beyond reproach. Nevertheless, in 2008, the Fed and the other federal agencies that regulate credit-card firms decided that the fly-by-night operators needed to be reined in. Congress got involved in 2009, passing legislation that buttressed the Fed's rules. Hence a sweeping new series of regulations have been instituted, taking full effect in 2010. A positive result of the regulations is that some customers will be protected from fraudulent activities; those elements of the new rules have proved beneficial to a limited set of consumers. But the new rules also severely hamper the way the *reputable* companies do business. The result of this has been less credit and more expensive credit— a lesson you may already have learned the hard way.

PRICE CONTROLS ON CREDIT CARDS

Among the myriad details of the new credit-card regulations, the key provisions are those that limit the interest rates and fees that companies can charge. For example, firms are limited in the circumstances under which they can raise the interest rates they charge. Moreover, higher rates can only be applied to new charges, not to past balances—even if market interest rates in general have increased or the borrower has become a worse credit risk since the card was issued. Credit-card firms are also limited in the fees they may charge when customers exceed their preset credit limits and the fees that they may charge for the subprime credit cards they issue to people with bad credit ratings.

As a practical matter, these provisions effectively act as **price controls**—legal limits on the prices that may be charged for goods or services. Here the controls are upper limits on prices, which means that interest rates and fees on credit cards are kept below their competitive levels. This causes firms' revenues to fall relative to their costs, which in turn reduces **profits** and discourages the firms from supplying the good in question, in this case consumer credit. On the other side of the market, because the legal maximum price is below the equilibrium price, people respond according to the law of **demand:** They try to obtain more of the good. In this case, consumers try to borrow more via credit cards. Because the quantity demanded rises and the quantity supplied falls, an excess quantity demanded is the result: People want to acquire far more than firms are willing to provide. In this case, desired borrowing goes up while desired lending goes down. Ultimately, the excess quantity demanded must be rationed somehow. The result is a series of readily predicted—and generally wasteful—consequences in the market. Let's see what those are.

LESS CREDIT

The first and foremost effect of the price controls is to reduce the amount of credit available to consumers. Firms have reduced the number of credit-card offers they make, for example, because the expected profit from those cards is reduced by the limits on interest rates and fees. Many thousands of customers have had existing cards canceled because the new regulations made those cards unprofitable for the issuing companies. Credit-card companies are also denying more consumer applications for credit cards because the firms are no longer able to cover the expected costs of issuing and servicing the cards of high-risk customers. And finally, when the companies do issue credit cards, they are generally imposing lower credit limits (maximum balances that consumers may have). This is because, for a customer with any given credit rating, the higher the credit balances, the higher the expected costs for the supplier of credit. Quite simply, as credit balances rise relative to a person's ability to pay, the chances rise that there will be late payments or no payments at all. Under the new rules, firms are less able to recoup those higher losses, so they have cut credit limits.

MORE EXPENSIVE CREDIT

Paradoxically, the net effect of limits on interest rates and fees has been to *raise* effective costs for many, perhaps most, customers. This is because the limits on interest rates and fees have reduced the amount of credit supplied and thus produced an excess quantity demanded, which, as we have noted, must be rationed somehow. To achieve this rationing, the cost to consumers of that credit must rise. There is simply no way to avoid this in a world of **scarcity.**

Some of these higher costs have come in the form of more onerous application procedures, which now require more documentation and verification. But there is another and even more important way that the cost of credit is driven up by the price controls on credit cards. Many people have been forced to turn to consumer finance companies, which typically charge interest rates of 30 to 40 percent per year, rather than the 15 to 30 percent routinely charged on credit-card balances. In other instances, the new regulations have made life even worse than this for people with bad credit histories. Many of these individuals are now forced to obtain so-called payday loans.[1] These loans, usually made for one week to one

---

1. One variant of these loans is sometimes called a "check into cash" transaction. Here is a simple example: The borrower receives $100 in cash today in return for writing the lender a personal check for $120, which the lender agrees not to cash until two weeks have passed. This deal translates into an implicit interest rate of about 10 percent *per week.*

month at a time, often carry interest rates as high as 500 percent per year! Thus some of the people supposedly helped by the new regulations actually end up paying far more for their credit than they did before—as much as twenty times more.

THE POOR GET POORER

Of course, the developments of which we have spoken so far—reduced credit opportunities and higher credit costs—are not borne equally by all potential customers. In particular, affluent customers with top credit ratings have been essentially untouched. The fees and interest charges most affected by the new regulations are those that apply to people with poor credit ratings—generally, low-income individuals. As a result, it is these people, the ones supposedly helped, who are actually hurt the most. It is their applications that are being denied, and they are the ones turning to consumer finance companies and payday loan operations. For the well-to-do, it is business as usual. For the disadvantaged, it is one more example of a government regulation for which the principal consequences are "unintended," which is to say, directly contrary to the avowed purpose of the regulations.

WASTED RESOURCES

Not surprisingly, the new limits on interest rates and fees must be enforced, so the regulations have spurred growth in the bureaucracies of the Fed, the Office of Thrift Supervision, and the Federal Deposit Insurance Corporation. The credit-card firms also face higher costs due to these regulations because they must demonstrate compliance with them and keep additional records. And because caps on rates and fees have forced the firms to conduct more credit checks and require more documentation, additional resources are being expended here. These are all resources that could have been put to good use elsewhere but are instead being used to implement and enforce the new price controls.

SAVERS LOSE TOO

Clearly, the new rules on interest rates and fees reduce the amount of credit extended to consumers. This means that the people who ultimately provide the funds for that credit lose too, because there is less demand for their savings. You might think that it is the credit-card companies that are the ultimate source of those funds, but you would be wrong. In fact, it is ordinary savers who provide the funds that are lent to consumers by means of credit cards. The credit-card companies merely act as intermediaries, moving the funds from savers to borrowers. Thus people who have savings accounts or money market funds or small certificates of deposit are all now earning lower interest rates on their deposits because the interest rates paid by borrowers are controlled by the government.

THE BOTTOM LINE

The new price controls for credit cards have made the market less effective in allocating funds from savers to borrowers. As a result, our **wealth** as a society has been reduced. But at least the new rules enable us to see some key public policy principles in action.

There is no free lunch. It is nice to think that with the stroke of the regulatory pen, we might "make it so." But in a world of scarcity, that simply doesn't happen. Price controls distort incentives, raise costs, and reduce opportunities. Moreover, they are costly to implement and enforce, and they generally do not accomplish their avowed purpose, which is to help the disadvantaged.

People respond to incentives. When there is a reduction in the profits of making loans via credit cards, fewer of those loans are made. And when that happens, people have an incentive to turn elsewhere for funds. Even though those alternative sources are far more costly, they are not as costly for the borrowers as the option of doing without. And so people do what they must because they can no longer do what they wish.

Things aren't always what they seem. A superficial look at the credit market seems to suggest that people are better off because many of the people who do still have credit cards are paying lower interest and lower fees. But such a look misses the higher costs people are paying elsewhere and the losses that result because some people are unable to obtain any credit at all due to the new controls.

Policies always have unintended consequences, and so their net benefits are almost always lower than anticipated. Surely Congress and policymakers at the Fed didn't go into the regulatory process intending to reduce credit opportunities for low-income individuals. Nor did they hope to increase the credit costs that such individuals must actually bear to obtain credit under the new rules. But this is exactly what has happened, meaning that the rules produced fewer net benefits than the authors of the new rules intended.

So if you are one of the people who was turned down for a credit card or had one canceled or was forced to turn to a higher-cost source of credit, there should be one consolation in all this: At least you have received an education in how the public policy process works in practice.

FOR CRITICAL ANALYSIS

1. Why do you suppose the government regulates interest rates on consumer credit (as with credit cards) but generally does not do so with commercial credit (as with loans to businesses)?

2. What do controls on interest rates do to the incentive of consumers to lie on their credit applications in an effort to qualify for a credit card?

3. More than sixty-five thousand individuals and businesses submitted comments on the Fed's regulations when they were first proposed. How might a look at these comments (which are a matter of public record) help you identify individuals and businesses who are likely to gain or lose as a result of the regulations?

4. Why would a limit on interest rates on *old* credit-card balances reduce the incentive of firms to issue *new* cards?

GLOSSARY

abject poverty: surviving on the equivalent of $1 or less of income per person per day

adjustable-rate mortgage (ARM): debt used to finance house purchases, the interest rate on which changes depending on current market conditions

adverse selection: a process in which "undesirable" (high-cost or high-risk) participants tend to dominate one side of a market, causing adverse effects for the other side; often results from *asymmetric information*

aggregate demand: the total value of all planned spending on goods and services by all economic entities in the economy

appropriations bills: legislation that determines the size of government discretionary spending

asset: any valuable good capable of yielding flows of income or services over time

asset-backed security (ABS): a bond that has other assets (such as home mortgages) as collateral

asymmetric information: a circumstance in which participants on one side of a market have more information than participants on the other side of the market; often results in adverse selection

average tax rate: total taxes divided by income

balance sheet: a written record of assets and liabilities

bank run: an attempt by many of a bank's depositors to convert checkable and savings deposits into currency because of a perceived fear for the bank's solvency

bankruptcy: a state of being legally declared unable to pay one's debts so that some or all of the indebtedness is legally wiped out by the courts

bond: a debt conferring the right to receive a specific series of money payments in the future

bondholders: the owners of government or corporate bonds

book value: asset valuations that are based on the original purchase price of the assets rather than current market values

bubble: an episode in which asset prices exceed their values based on economic fundamentals, as determined by real future profits or service flows

budget constraint: all of the possible combinations of goods that can be purchased at given prices and given income

budget deficit: the excess of government spending over government revenues during a given time period

business cycles: the ups and downs in overall business activity, evidenced by changes in GDP, employment, and the price level

capital account surplus: a net inflow of capital funds (loans and investments) into a nation

capital ratio: the value of assets divided by the value of debt

capital stock: the collection of productive assets that can be combined with other inputs, such as labor, to produce goods and services

cash flow: cash receipts minus cash payments

central bank: a banker's bank, usually a government institution that also serves as the country's treasury's bank; central banks normally regulate commercial banks

checkable deposits: accounts at depository institutions that are payable on demand, either by means of a check or by direct withdrawal, as through an automated teller machine (ATM)

civil law system: a legal system in which statutes passed by legislatures and executive decrees, rather than judicial decisions based on precedent, form the basis for most legal rules

collateral: assets that are forfeited in the event of default on a obligation

collateralized debt obligation (CDO): an obligation to pay that is guaranteed by the pledge of another asset

commercial bank: a financial institution that accepts demand deposits and makes loans and provides other financial services to the public

common law system: a legal system in which judicial decisions based on precedent, rather than executive decrees or statutes passed by legislatures, form the basis for most legal rules

comparative advantage: the ability to produce a good or service at a lower opportunity cost compared to other producers

constant-quality price: price adjusted for any change in the quality of the good or service

consumer price index (CPI): a measure of the dollar cost of purchasing a bundle of goods and services assumed to be representative of the consumption pattern of a typical consumer; one measure of the price level

consumption: spending by consumers on new goods and services

core inflation: a measure of the overall rate of change in prices of goods, excluding energy and food

cost of living: the dollar cost (relative to a base year) of achieving a given level of satisfaction

credit-default swap: a financial contract in which the buyer of the swap makes a series of payments to the seller, who agrees to makes a payoff to the buyer if an underlying financial instrument (such as a bond) goes into default

creditor: an institution or individual that is owed money by another institution or individual

currency: paper money and coins issued by the government to serve as a medium of exchange

default: failure to meet obligations, for example, the failure to make debt payments

default risk: an estimation combining the probability that a contract will not be adhered to and the magnitude of the loss that will occur if it is not

deflation: a decline in the average level of the prices of goods and services

demand: the willingness and ability to purchase goods

depository institutions: financial institutions that accept deposits from savers and lend those deposits out to borrowers

depression: a severe recession

direct foreign investment: resources provided to individuals and firms in a nation by individuals or firms located in other countries, often taking the form of foreign subsidiary or branch operations of a parent company

disability payments: cash payments made to persons whose physical or mental disabilities prevent them from working

discouraged workers: persons who have dropped out of the labor force because they are unable to find suitable work

discretionary spending: government spending that is decided on anew each year, rather than being determined by a formula or set of rules

disposable income: income remaining after all taxes, retirement contributions, and the like are deducted

dividends: payments made by a corporation to owners of shares of its stock, generally based on the corporation's profits

drift: the average annual rate at which stock prices change over a long period of time

dumping: the sale of goods in a foreign country at a price below the market price charged for the same goods in the domestic market or at a price below the cost of production

dynamic economic analysis: a mode of analysis that recognizes that people respond to changes in incentives and that takes these responses into account when evaluating the effects of policies

earned income tax credit: a federal tax program that permits negative taxes, that is, that provides for payments to people (instead of collecting taxes from them) if their incomes go below a predetermined level

economic growth: sustained increases in real per capita income

elasticity: a measure of the responsiveness of one variable to a change in another variable

entitlement programs: government programs for which spending is determined chiefly by formulas or rules that specify who is eligible for funds and how much they may receive

equity: assets minus liabilities; net asset value

European Union (EU): a supranational entity resulting from an agreement among European nations to closely integrate the economic, political, and legal systems of the twenty-seven individual member nations

excess reserves: funds kept on hand by commercial banks to meet the transactions demands of customers and to serve as precautionary sources of funds in the event of a bank run; may be held as vault cash or as deposits at the Fed

exchange rate: the price of a currency expressed in terms of another currency

expansion: a period in which economic activity, measured by industrial production, employment, real income, and wholesale and retail sales, is growing on a sustained basis

expansive monetary policy: actions that tend to increase the level or rate of growth of the money supply

expected rate of inflation: the rate at which the average level of prices of goods and services is expected to rise

fair-value accounting: an accounting method in which the reported values of assets are adjusted to reflect (estimates of) the current market values of those assets rather than their purchase prices or their stated maturity value

federal budget deficit: the excess of the national government's spending over its receipts

federal funds rate: the nominal interest rate at which banks can borrow reserves from one another

Federal Reserve System (the Fed): the central bank of the United States

fiscal policy: discretionary changes in government spending or taxes that alter the overall state of the economy, including employment, investment, and output

fiscal year: the accounting year used by a government or business; for the federal government, the fiscal year runs from October 1 to September 30

flexible exchange rates: exchange rates that are free to move in response to market forces

foreclosure: the legal process by which a borrower in default under a mortgage is deprived of his or her interest in the mortgaged property

gains from trade: the extent to which individuals, firms, or nations benefit from engaging in voluntary exchange

globalization: the integration of national economies into an international economy

government-sponsored enterprise (GSE): a federally chartered corporation that is privately owned, designed to provide a source of credit nationwide, and limited to servicing one economic sector

gross domestic product (GDP): the dollar value of all new, domestically produced final goods and services in an economy

gross public debt: all public debt, including that owned by agencies of the government issuing it

hedge funds: investment companies that require large initial deposits by investors and pursue high-risk investments in the hope of achieving high returns

human capital: the productive capacity of human beings

illiquid: when used in reference to a company or person: having insufficient cash on hand to meet current liabilities; when used in reference to an asset: that which cannot be easily and cheaply converted into cash.

in-kind transfer: the provision of goods and services rather than cash, as in the case of Medicare, Medicaid, or subsidized housing

income mobility: the tendency of people to move around in the income distribution over time

Industrial Revolution: the widespread radical socioeconomic changes that took place in England and many other nations beginning in the late eighteenth century, brought about when extensive mechanization of production systems resulted in a shift from home-based hand manufacturing to large-scale factory production

inflation: a rise in the average level of the prices of goods and services

inflationary premium: the additional premium, in percent per year, that people are willing to pay to have dollars sooner rather than later simply because inflation is expected in the future

inflation tax: the decline in the real value or purchasing power of money balances due to inflation

inside information: valuable information about future economic performance that is not generally available to the public

insolvent: describing a financial condition in which the value of one's assets is less than the value of one's liabilities

insourcing: the use of domestic workers to perform a service traditionally done by foreign workers

institutions: the basic rules, customs, and practices of society

interagency borrowings: loans from one part of the federal government to another

interest group: a collection of individuals with common aims

intermediate goods: goods that contribute to present or future consumer welfare but are not direct sources of utility themselves; typically, they are used up in the production of final goods and services

investment: the creation of new machines, factories, and other assets that enable the production of more goods and services in the future

investment bank: a financial institution that helps companies or municipalities obtain financing by selling stocks or bonds on their behalf

investment security: a debt obligation for which the default risk is low

labor force: individuals aged sixteen and over who either have jobs or are looking and available for work

labor supply curve: a schedule showing the quantity of labor supplied at each wage rate

liabilities: amounts owed; the legal claims against an individual or against an institution by those who are not owners of that institution

loophole: a provision of the tax code that enables a narrow group of beneficiaries to achieve a lower effective tax rate

Luddites: followers of General Ned Ludd who early in the nineteenth century led destructive protests against mechanization in English textile mills; a term used today to refer to people who object to technological change

mandates: in the context of governments, regulations or laws that require other governments, private individuals, or firms to spend money to achieve goals specified by the government

marginal tax rate: the percentage of the last dollar earned that is paid in taxes

mark to market: an accounting practice in which the reported values of assets are adjusted to reflect (estimates of) the current market values of those assets rather than their purchase prices or their stated maturity value

median age: the age that separates the older half of the population from the younger half

median income: the income that separates the higher-income half of the population from the lower-income half

medium of exchange: any asset that sellers will generally accept as payment

mercantilists: believers in the doctrine of mercantilism, which asserted (among other things) that exports were the principal objective of international trade because they permitted the accumulation of gold

microeconomics: the study of decision making by consumers and by firms and of the market equilibria that result

monetary policy: the use of changes in the amount of money in circulation to affect interest rates, credit markets, inflation (or deflation), and unemployment

money supply: the sum of checkable deposits and currency in the hands of the public

moral hazard: the tendency of an entity insulated from risk to behave differently than it would behave if it were fully exposed to the risk

mortgage-backed security (MBS): a debt obligation that pledges home mortgages as collateral

mortgages: debts that are incurred to buy a house and provide that if the debt is not paid, the house can be sold by the creditor and the proceeds used to pay that debt

mutual funds: a pool of money that is invested in assets, often shares of stock in corporations

natural-resource endowments: the collection of naturally occurring minerals (such as oil and iron ore) and living things (such as forests and fish stocks) that can be used to produce goods and services

negative tax: a payment from the government to an individual that is based on the individual's income

net public debt: the portion of the public debt that is owned outside of the government issuing it

net worth: the excess of assets over liabilities

nominal income: income expressed in terms of a monetary unit, such as the dollar

nominal interest rate: the premium, in percent per year, that people are willing to pay to have dollars sooner rather than later

nominal prices: the exchange value of goods, expressed in terms of a unit of account, such as the dollar or the euro

normal good: a good for which the demand increases as people's income or wealth grows

opportunity cost: the highest-valued, next-best alternative that must be sacrificed to obtain something

outsourcing: the use of labor in another country to perform service work traditionally done by domestic workers

pay-as-you-go system: a scheme in which current cash outflows are funded (paid for) with current cash inflows

payroll taxes: taxes that are levied on income specifically generated by workforce participation and that are generally earmarked for spending on specific programs, such as Social Security

per capita income: gross domestic product (GDP) divided by population

per capita real net public debt: net public debt, deflated by the price level and divided by the population

perfectly inelastic: having an elasticity (or responsiveness) of zero

permanent income: the sustained or average level of income that one expects will be observed over a long period of time

physical capital: the productive capacity of physical assets, such as buildings

price controls: government rules that limit the prices firms may charge for the goods or services they sell

price level: the average current-year cost, measured relative to the average base-year cost, of a typical basket of goods and services

productivity: output per unit of input

profits: the difference between revenue and cost

progressive tax system: a set of rules that result in the collection of a larger share of income as taxes when income rises

property and contract rights: legal rules governing the use and exchange of property and the enforceable agreements between people or businesses

proportional tax system: a set of rules that result in the collection of an unchanging share of income as income changes

protectionism: economic policy of promoting favored domestic industries through the use of high tariffs and quotas and other trade restrictions to reduce imports

protectionist: any attitude or policy that seeks to prevent foreigners from competing with domestic firms or individuals

public debt: the amount of money owed by a government to its creditors

purchasing power: a measure of the amount of goods and services that can be purchased with a given amount of money

purchasing power parity (PPP): the principle that the relative values of different currencies must reflect their purchasing power in their home countries

quota: a limit on the amount of a good that may be imported; generally used to reduce imports so as to protect the economic interests of domestic industries that compete with the imports

random walk: a pattern of price (or other) movements in which the best expectation of a future value is today's value and in which the variability of price (or other entity) is constant over time

real gross domestic product (real GDP): the inflation-adjusted level of new, domestically produced final goods and services

real income: income adjusted for inflation; equivalently, income expressed in terms of goods and services

real interest rate: the premium, in percent per year, that people are willing to pay to have goods sooner rather than later

real per capita income: GDP corrected for inflation and divided by the population—a measure of the amount of new domestic production of final goods and services per person

real price: price of a good or service adjusted for inflation; equivalently, the price of a good or service expressed in terms of other goods and services; see *relative prices*

real purchasing power: the amount of goods and services that can be acquired with an asset whose value is expressed in terms of the monetary unit of account (such as the dollar)

real tax rate: share of GDP controlled by the government

real wages: wages adjusted for changes in the price level

recession: a decline in the level of overall business activity

regressive tax system: a set of rules that result in the collection of a smaller share of income as taxes when income rises

relative prices: prices of goods and services compared to the prices of other goods and services; costs of goods and services measured in terms of other commodities

required reserves: funds that a commercial bank must lawfully maintain; they may be held in the form of vault cash or deposits at the Fed

reserves: assets held by depository institutions, typically in the form of currency held at the institution or as non-interest-bearing deposits held at the central bank, to meet customers' transaction needs and Fed legal requirements

resources: any items capable of satisfying individuals' desires or preferences or suitable for transformation into such goods

revealed preferences: consumers' tastes as demonstrated by the choices they make

rule of law: the principle that relations between individuals, businesses, and the government are governed by explicit rules that apply to everyone in society

saving: an addition to wealth, conventionally measured as disposable personal income minus consumption

savings: one's stock of wealth at a given moment in time

scarcity: a state of the world in which there are limited resources but unlimited demands, implying that we must make choices among alternatives

securitized: describing cash flow–producing assets pooled and repackaged into securities that are then sold to investors

shareholders: owners of shares of stock in a corporation

share of stock: claim to a specified portion of future net cash flows (or profits) of a corporation

solvent: describing a financial condition in which the value of one's assets is greater than the value of one's liabilities

standard of living: a summary measure of the level of per capita material welfare, often measured by per capita real GDP

static economic analysis: a mode of analysis that assumes for simplicity that people do not change their behavior when incentives change

stock: as applied to measurement, an amount measured at a particular moment in time

stockbroker: a middleman who sells shares of stock to individuals

subprime mortages: *mortgages* that entail the higher risk of loss for the lender

subsidies: government payments for the production of specific goods, generally intended to raise the profits of the firms producing those goods

supply: the willingness and ability to sell goods

tariff: a tax levied only on imports; generally used to reduce imports so as to protect the economic interests of domestic industries that compete with the imports

tax bracket: a range of income over which a specific marginal tax rate applies

tax credit: a direct reduction in tax liability, occasioned by a specific set of circumstances and not dependent on the taxpayer's tax bracket

tax evasion: the deliberate failure to pay taxes, usually by making a false report

tax rate: the percentage of a dollar of income that must be paid in taxes

tax rebate: a return of some previously paid taxes

trade barrier: a legal rule imposed by a nation that raises the costs of foreign firms seeking to sell goods in that nation; they include tariffs and quotas

trade deficit: an excess of the value of imports of goods and services over the value of the exports of goods and services

trade surplus: an excess of the value of exports of goods and services over the value of the imports of goods and services

underground economy: commercial transactions on which taxes and regulations are being avoided

unemployment rate: the number of persons looking and available for work, divided by the labor force

unfunded taxpayer liabilities: obligations of taxpayers for which no specific debt instruments have been issued

voucher: a written authorization, exchangeable for cash or services

wealth: the present value of all current and future income

wealth tax: a tax based on a person's net worth

World Trade Organization (WTO): an association of more than 150 nations that helps reduce trade barriers among its members and handles international trade disputes among them

write off: declare to be worthless